OTHER BOOKS IN THE SKYLIGHT LIVES SERIES

Simone Weil: A Modern Pilgrimage
by Robert Coles, M.D.

Zen Effects: The Life of Alan Watts
by Monica Furlong

The Life of Evelyn Underhill:
An Intimate Portrait of the Groundbreaking Author of Mysticism
by Margaret Cropper
with a new foreword by Dana Greene

Mahatma Gandhi circa 1930

MAHATMA GANDHI
HIS LIFE AND IDEAS

Charles F. Andrews

With a new foreword by
Dr. Arun Gandhi

Walking Together, Finding the Way
SKYLIGHT PATHS Publishing
Woodstock, Vermont

Mahatma Gandhi: His Life and Ideas

2003 First SkyLight Paths Publishing Edition
Foreword © 2003 by Arun Gandhi
Photographs © Vithalbhai Jhaveri/GandhiServe

For information regarding permission to reprint material from this book, please mail or fax your request in writing to SkyLight Paths Publishing, Permissions Department, at the address / fax number listed below; or e-mail your request to permissions@skylightpaths.com.

08/06

Library of Congress Cataloging-in-Publication Data
Andrews, C. F. (Charles Freer), 1871–1940.
[Mahatma Gandhi's ideas]
Mahatma Gandhi : his life and ideas / Charles F. Andrews ; with a new foreword by Arun Gandhi.
xxxi, 301 p. cm. — (SkyLight lives)
Originally published: Mahatma Gandhi's ideas. New York : Macmillan, 1930. With new foreword.
Includes index.
ISBN 1-893361-89-6 (pbk.)
1. Gandhi, Mahatma, 1869–1948. 2. Gandhi, Mahatma, 1869–1948—Philosophy. 3. Statesmen—India—Biography. 4. Nationalists—India—Biography. I. Title. II. Series.
DS481.G3A6 2003
954.03'5'092—dc21
2003007502

Manufactured in the United States of America

SkyLight Paths Publishing is creating a place where people of different spiritual traditions come together for challenge and inspiration, a place where we can help each other understand the mystery that lies at the heart of our existence.

SkyLight Paths sees both believers and seekers as a community that increasingly transcends traditional boundaries of religion and denomination—people wanting to learn from each other, *walking together, finding the way.*

Walking Together, Finding the Way
Published by SkyLight Paths Publishing
A Division of LongHill Partners, Inc.
Sunset Farm Offices, Route 4, P.O. Box 237
Woodstock, VT 05091
Tel: (802) 457-4000   Fax: (802) 457-4004
www.skylightpaths.com

CONTENTS

Photographs

FOREWORD

Establishing a Culture of Nonviolence

While this resurrected book by Reverend Charles Freer Andrews adds immensely to the understanding of Mohandas K. Gandhi and his philosophy of nonviolence, a word of caution is necessary. When reading Gandhi we must remember what he said when he was accused of being inconsistent. "Truth," Gandhi said, "is always changing and if I hold on to what I said earlier it would be wrong. My perception or understanding of a situation must be based on Truth as it appears to me today." Gandhi advised his readers to take the last statement on any subject to be his stand on that particular issue. This was good advice to follow while he was alive, but how do we now arrive at what he would have thought about a particular subject or situation more than fifty years after his death? The danger in such a situation is that we either accept dogmatically what he said at a different time and under different circumstances or we reject Gandhi and his philosophy as being irrelevant today. Since Gandhi's philosophy is based on love, respect, understanding, acceptance, and compassion, can we say that these positive attributes are irrelevant?

Gandhi always maintained that his life and his work should be described as "The Story of My Experiments with Truth," which eventually became the title of his autobiography. The key word here is "experiment." It required a great deal of humility for him to acknowledge that throughout his life he was "pursuing Truth," which is in stark contrast to the present position when most of us, in our arrogance, feel we already "possess the Truth." Whether we "pursue" or "possess" makes a very big difference in our outlook on life. Pursuit of truth requires us to be honest, humble, open in mind and spirit, and willing to listen and evaluate a situation impartially. And, when we make errors of judgment we should have the magnanimity to acknowledge them and rededicate our search for Truth with greater diligence. It is this form of positiveness that leads to the creation of a culture of nonviolence.

Possession of the Truth is an attitude that has its roots in arrogance and leads to a closed mind and spirit. It also leads to a rejection of all thoughts and influences that are contrary to our own. This form of outright rejection of differences evokes negative attributes in human beings like suspicion, prejudice, hate, division, and so on, leading to a culture of violence.

The word "nonviolence" in Gandhi's lexicon is a literal translation of the Sanskrit word *ahimsa,* which comes from the Hindu scripture known as the Bhagavad-Gita. At the heart of the scriptural message contained in the Gita is the acceptance of *ahimsa parmo dharma,* meaning *ahimsa* as the prime duty of every individual. It is the literal translation of the word *ahimsa,* according to Gandhi, that has done the greatest harm to its universal acceptance. A majority of the Hindus and all of the Jain community have translated *ahimsa* to mean nonviolence, as in not doing any harm to anyone under any circumstances. The consequence of such absolutism is hypocrisy. The absolutists, therefore, will not commit any violence themselves but will get someone else to do it for them. This also leads others to believe that nonviolence is impractical and unattainable.

Gandhi once made a statement that there is much violence in nonviolence and nonviolence in violence. It sounds confusing to the layperson but it comes from the acceptance that as long as there is the will to live among human beings, some violence is an inevitable part of life. This is why Gandhi said *ahimsa* cannot be translated to mean "nonviolence"; it should really mean "love." Explaining this concept Gandhi said, "Sometimes out of Love we are required to commit some violence." For example, a surgeon who cuts through a human body to relieve the patient of suffering is committing selfless violence. When some misguided thugs in South Africa attacked Gandhi, his eldest son asked how he should have protected his father nonviolently if he had been there at the time of the attack. To protect someone nonviolently, Gandhi said, one must be willing to offer his or her life by placing himself or herself in the line of fire without attacking the assailant. However, if one did not have the courage to sacrifice one's life then one would be justified in resorting to violence.

Gandhi's unorthodox translation of *ahimsa* and his controversial support of the war effort are issues that Reverend Andrews attempts to discuss in detail in this book. Since we have to take this book as the final version of Reverend Andrews' thoughts on the subject, we must conclude that he was not quite convinced by Gandhi's interpretation. Also, to be fair, we must acknowledge that Gandhi did change his mind about supporting the war effort when World War II engulfed the world.

Earlier, as a faithful and patriotic citizen of the British Empire, Gandhi's feelings about the war can best be explained with the analogy of a family unit. In a hypothetical situation, if a thief were to break into a family home with the intention to steal, destroy, and even usurp the house by killing all the inhabitants, it would be wrong for some members to claim they are nonviolent and would therefore not do anything to protect the house or the family. Everyone must shoulder the responsibility toward the family and its welfare. However, this argument would be justified only insofar as an outside threat endangers the family. In the event the family becomes aggressive and decides to acquire by force the adjoining property because they want to expand, it is not incumbent on the nonviolent members of the family to participate in the violence.

As already stated, consistent with his changing perception of Truth Gandhi changed his views about supporting the war effort during World War II. Once again, he did not reject the war effort altogether but only to the extent that he refused to endorse the war, to recruit soldiers for the effort, and to participate in any indirect activity relating to war. However, he said, he would not dissuade individuals or even the nation of India if they decided to get involved.

Gandhi strongly believed that wars at the national level and violence at the personal level have their origins in the culture of violence and unless we work to replace that culture we will be unable to reduce the violence that dominates our lives. Thus, instead of supporting or protesting the war effort Gandhi bent his energies to creating a culture of nonviolence.

Ahimsa is as much about positively doing some good as about negatively not doing any harm. The positive and negative aspects of *ahimsa* are as inseparable as the head and tail of a coin. Just as we cannot accept one side of the coin as legal tender, we cannot practice *ahimsa* effectively by ignoring the positive and focusing only on the negative. If we try to put this theory in the context of the Iraqi war in which the United States and Britain were involved, Gandhi would say protest against the war should be accompanied by action for better understanding and relations between people in the country and outside. When we indulge only in the negative without the positive then we have disasters like the hippie movement of the sixties. Millions came out *against* "the establishment" but there was not much thought given to the positive aspect of an acceptable replacement. Being against something is understandable, but the action becomes laudable if there is a clear definition of what we are *for.* To most people all over the world peace has come to mean the absence of war or the absence of violence. Gandhi said peace can only be achieved if we are able to eliminate all forms of exploitation.

There is a story from the Hindu scriptures that my grandfather was very fond of repeating. It is the story of six blind men who were placed at different strategic places around an elephant and asked to describe the animal by feeling it. Each had a different perspective. The one who was feeling the trunk of the elephant said the elephant looked like a huge pipe. The one who had the tail said it was like a snake, and so on. None of them was entirely wrong because they had only an iota of the Truth. It is only through openness, dialogue, and a willingness to know that they would reach somewhere close to the whole Truth. In many ways we human beings are like the six blind men. We have just a small segment of the Truth and yet we do not wish to know more.

This partial understanding of the word *ahimsa* has led to partial understanding of the Truth. *Ahimsa* has come to mean nonviolence and nonviolence is the non-use of physical violence or the absence of war. All other aspects of violence are ignored. When I was living with my grandfather between the ages of twelve and fourteen, part of my education was about conquering violence by understanding the self. I was encouraged to build a family tree of violence on the same principles as a genealogical tree. Violence served as the grandparent with "physical" and "passive" as the two offspring. On a large paper on a wall in my room this tree began to grow as I examined all my experiences every day and put them in their appropriate places on the tree.

Physical violence is the type of violence where physical force is used—war, murder, beating, killing, spanking, and so on—while passive violence is the type of violence where no physical force is used—hate, prejudice, discrimination, waste of resources, uncaring attitude, etcetera. Each of them have several subaspects. For instance, prejudice could involve gender, race, color, and so on. Doing this exercise diligently with the help of my parents or grandfather, I quickly became aware of the extent of violence I was practicing consciously and unconsciously. I had no idea that many of the routine actions that I thoughtlessly indulged in every day were acts of violence because they indirectly had repercussions on someone somewhere in the world. It was only when I began to understand all the different nuances of violence that Grandfather explained the connection between passive and physical violence.

Then it became obvious. All of us practice passive violence all the time in many different ways, causing hurt or deprivation to someone somewhere. For instance, our over-consumption of natural resources in the world leads to inequitable distribution and poverty. The poor become angry at the rich and the poor attempt to get illegally the essentials of life that they are denied legitimately. This begins the cycle of violence since the perpetrators of crime, we are told, must be punished. Anger, it is said, generates more than 80 percent of the violence that we experience in our lives. Yet, as a society, we have consistently ignored this powerful emotion so that all of us have learned to abuse anger rather than use the energy positively. We either lash out verbally or physically in anger and in both cases we create a situation with a potential for violence. It is, therefore, passive violence that fuels the fire of physical violence, which means if it is our intention to put out the fire of physical violence and create peace we need to cut off the supply of fuel that ignites the fire. This is why Gandhi said "we must become the change we wish to see in the world."

Gandhi's work in nonviolence was comprehensive and not simply confined to politics or human rights. It was about building positive relationships based on respect, understanding, acceptance, and appreciation; it was about eliminating exploitation of all kinds and creating harmony among people where compassion and commitment to principles would be the ideal by which people live. To explain every aspect of his philosophy in detail would require a book in itself but suffice it to say there are two little known concepts of his philosophy that need some attention.

Most scholars have been so understandably enamored by Gandhi's political work that they virtually ignored other aspects of his philosophy of nonviolence, such as trusteeship and constructive action. In keeping with his understanding of *ahimsa,* Gandhi felt that his philosophy must be comprehensive enough to enable the practitioner to use it under most circumstances and bring to the oppressed salvation in different ways. His colleagues during the freedom struggle in India were often frustrated with Gandhi because he paid equal attention to social, educational, and other projects even when politics demanded his full attention. There were times when out of frustration the leaders would question him: Why do you dissipate our resources by focusing on all these issues when they can be better dealt with after independence? Gandhi's reply to the question always was: Political freedom will be meaningless as long as people suffer from social, cultural, and educational oppression.

It is this holistic aspect of the philosophy of nonviolence that appealed to Gandhi. The culture of violence, he would say, is used only to restrict and destroy in the process of resolving a conflict, while the culture of nonviolence can be used to transform and transcend all conflicts. Also, we must not forget Gandhi's understanding of *ahimsa* included both the negative and the positive aspects. Thus, the concept of trusteeship and constructive action empowers the giver and the receiver and enables an individual or a collective to do what he or she can to transform society.

Gandhi was also very fond of using analogies to make his point. He would say to all those committed to work with him that for a nonviolent transformation of India they must look at themselves as farmers of peace. A conventional farmer prepares his field, plants the seeds, and then hopes and prays that the seeds will all germinate and he will be blessed with a good crop. If the crop fails he starts over again. Peace workers must likewise go out and prepare society, plant the seeds of peace, and hope and pray that they will germinate and yield a good crop of peace activists. If not, we have to start over again to prepare the soil more carefully. He encouraged people to be creative in identifying conflicts and implementing programs. In the Indian milieu of the thirties and forties of the past century poverty and ignorance were the two most widespread problems. They still are. Expecting the poor and the hungry to participate in a struggle for freedom would be unrealistic. Thus, the two positive concepts of the philosophy enabled workers to diversify their activities. Let me explain the two concepts.

Trusteeship is a fairly simple objective that emphasizes sharing and compassion with differences. Each one of us has a talent that we use personally to achieve our goals and ambitions. As children we are taught that our objectives in life must be high and that the yardstick to measure success is materialistic. Consequently, we have created a world that is steeped to its gills in capitalism and materialism, both of which have a tendency to make us selfish and self-centered. Materialism and morality, Gandhi said, have an inverse relationship, so that when one increases the other decreases. To bring a balance between materialism and morality, Gandhi said, society must change its ancient perception from being owners of the talent to being trustees of the talent. This means giving of ourselves and our talent to help others. We tend to call this charity and we give out of pity rather than compassion. The difference between pity and compassion is that when we are moved by pity we give money and absolve ourselves of all further responsibilities, while compassion moves us to really get involved in trying to find a solution to whatever the conflict may be.

Our distorted priorities manifest themselves in various ways. For instance, corporations today are run more for profit than for people, especially their employees. Commerce without morality, Gandhi said, is one of the seven sins that cause violence, and we see more and more unscrupulous business practices than ever before. The bottom line is to make money by any means possible. Typically, this kind of mindset is generated by the culture of violence.

If we were to promote the culture of nonviolence, then people and profits would assume an equal role; the interest of the people, on occasions, would supersede the need to make profits. An example is the incident that happened a few years ago in Massachusetts when a textile factory caught fire and everything was lost. The owner of the factory would have been within his legal rights to claim his compensation and insurance money and not care about the futures of his employees. But he was obviously aware that all the money in the world would not buy him happiness if his employees were left in distress. He paid every one of them their full salaries for more than a year until the factory was rebuilt.

Trusteeship at the individual level means using one's individual talent to help the less fortunate people in society attain a better standard of living or in other ways enhance their quality of life. The world as a whole and the societies that make up the world are divided between the rich and the poor. The rich are able to garner all the resources because they have the wherewithal to do so and they have the greed to over-consume, making the poor poorer. The disparity grows and with it grows conflict. Living simply so that others can simply live was one of Gandhi's dreams. Another Truth that Gandhi cherished was that the world can provide for everyone's needs but not for everyone's greed.

In a manner of speaking, trusteeship and constructive action are two sides of the same coin. As an example of what people can do, there is the story of the young student at the University of Southern California in Los Angeles. In his first year at the university he realized there was a high school adjoining the downtown campus and that the school students were predominantly of a minority ethnicity and appeared to come from economically challenged families. The student spoke to the high school principal and offered to mentor one or two young men during his free periods. A few hours every week made a big difference in the lives of two young men who found someone who would not only help them through their difficulties but who listened to their woes and guided them. This act of compassion moved other students at the university to also become mentors so that now it is a full-fledged program.

On a different scale, in a different country, another small group of middle-class friends in Mumbai, India, aware of the distress of millions of their compatriots living in subhuman conditions on the sidewalks of the city, decided to use trusteeship and constructive action as an experiment. They spent several weeks in almost daily dialogue with the homeless people to understand and come to know the plight of poverty, to evaluate their strengths and determine their needs. It became clear that the homeless had migrated from their village huts to the city in search of survival. With economic development concentrated mostly in cities, the villages provided no economic opportunities to their residents except agriculture, which at best provided seasonal employment.

Some of the homeless worked as laborers in the city textile industry, the very industry that generations ago deprived them of their handloom industry. Many others labored at odd jobs to earn less than a dollar a day. Ever since their traditional handloom industry became a victim of modernization, these people were reduced to penury and virtual destitution.

The group of seven Samaritans organized a few hundred homeless and made it very clear to them that they had evolved a scheme to help that would require each of the participants to make a sacrifice every day and save a coin. This cooperative endeavor would help create a fund with which an economic program would be undertaken. This was an unusual approach since one would normally go to a funding agency and get a grant to quickly create economic opportunities for the poor. However, the Samaritans concluded that this quick approach did not help build the self-respect and self-confidence of the poor. It made them dependent on society, or the government, and the dependence turned out to be more oppressive.

The Samaritans spent many weeks teaching the homeless the value of trust, honesty, cooperation, and all the positive values of the culture of nonviolence. Arrangements were made to collect the coins every day and deposit them. Some six hundred individuals participated in this experiment and in less than two years the homeless collected the equivalent of eleven hundred dollars. This money was used to buy ten secondhand power looms and build a little tin shed in Vita village, which became the nucleus of their first cooperatively owned textile factory. Seventy homeless were chosen to go back to Vita to run this cooperative factory round-the-clock so that all those who had contributed to the fund could be provided employment or additional income. The homeless, of course, had no idea of how to run a business, but the Samaritans guided and trained them until they became confident enough to run it on their own. A program that was started in 1970 grew to five factories with more than six hundred power looms by 1989.

The homeless continued their small savings habit and in 1978 opened a cooperative bank in Mumbai city, which now has seven branch offices and total assets worth two million dollars. Through the bank they give small loans at low interest to the needy and homeless to start economic programs so that they can attain a better standard of living.

These are a few examples of the trusteeship and constructive action that Gandhi promoted as part of the program to establish a culture of nonviolence. There are many such programs conducted by individuals and groups in the United States and in other countries but, sadly, the media does not often take note of their activities. The reason Gandhi called for constructive programs was because any program undertaken should help rebuild the self-respect and self-confidence of the poor. If the poor become dependent on charity then the program is not constructive.

The world can be saved from certain destruction, Gandhi said, only if each one of us makes a concerted attempt to establish a comprehensive culture of nonviolence by looking at and eliminating every aspect of violence. Working for peace is not simply working to eliminate wars; we must work to eliminate all forms of exploitation of people. Only then can true harmony prevail. It must also be remembered that since violence to some extent is an integral part of

human life we may not be able to create a perfectly nonviolent society, but that does not mean we cannot reduce the level of violence
that is slowly consuming human society.

Dr. Arun Gandhi

PREFACE

This book is intended to explain, with documentary evidence, the main principles and ideas for which Mahatma Gandhi has stood in the course of his eventful career. On account of the mass of material it has been necessary to make a limited selection from the speeches and writings which he himself has addressed to the public. In the choice of such passages I have carefully avoided consulting beforehand the opinions of other writers about him, because I felt it best to give the one single impression that had become clear to me from long and intimate personal experience.

After writing the different chapters it was encouraging to me to find later that the outline of my own picture was not far removed in its special light and shade and contour from the character which Romain Rolland had drawn when his own study of the "Gandhi literature" had been made at an earlier date. Quite unconsciously my personal reading of Mahatma Gandhi's ideas has in a great measure coincided with his. In one sense this present book may be said to offer material supplementary to that which has already appeared in Rolland's great book. As a work of genius that study of Gandhi remains unparalleled in any language. I hope, however, that what I have written may have a special value of its own as an individual portrait, with a background of close personal knowledge about one who has been my friend for over fifteen years.

I have ventured to abbreviate certain passages quoted, in order to conserve as carefully as possible the limited space at my disposal. A short list of those Indian words which come frequently in the narrative will be found at the beginning of this volume, and I have explained in footnotes any further difficulties that may remain for the Western reader.

My dear companions, Principal Robert Russa Moton and his staff at Tuskegee, Alabama, have done me much kindly service in helping me to prepare this manuscript for the press while staying with them at Tuskegee. It is a great joy to me to dedicate this volume to them. Their love for Mahatma Gandhi is sincere and deep. It is a pleasure to me to express at the same time my gratitude to Miss Storey, Raghunath and Juliette Rao at Geneva, and also in this new world of America to Bishop and Mrs. Paddock, Kirby Page, Richard Gregg, Dr. Anson Phelps Stokes, Dr. Jesse Jones, Charles Gilkey, Wilbur Thomas, Haridas Muzumdar, Ben and Edith Cherrington, Mrs. Ruth Cranston, Dr. Helen Reid, and Kartar Singh.

It will be seen from this long list, which could have been made much longer, how much I have had to rely on the loving service of friends to get through the whole work in the time required.

Mr. H. S. L. Polak, Mahatma Gandhi's lifelong friend and my own, has generously undertaken to correct the proofs in England during my absence in British Guiana.

If what I have written gains acceptance, I shall hope to take up at a later date the life and work of the poet, Rabindranath Tagore; for it is through the close study of these two outstanding personalities that modern India can best be appreciated in the West.

C. F. Andrews
Halifax, Nova Scotia

INTRODUCTION

Mohandas Karamchand Gandhi was born at a little seaport town on the coast of Kathiawar, called Porbunder, in the year 1869. His father had been Prime Minister of the State, and this office had been made hereditary for some generations past. The family was, therefore, one of the most important in that part of the country, and its members were noted for their firmness and integrity of character. A story has become famous in India about the father of Mohandas Gandhi, that when he had been for a time dismissed from his own State and had taken service in another, he refused to salute the second Rajah with his right hand, saying that in spite of his dismissal his right hand was reserved for his former chief and could not be used in saluting any other.

The young boy's mother was a devout Hindu, who had a deep religious faith penetrating and inspiring her whole personal life and character. From his mother more than anyone else the child gained his own religious nature. It becomes clear from his autobiography that no one so profoundly affected him in childhood as she did.

The Indian States in Kathiawar more than fifty years ago were almost entirely unchanged by their contact with the West. The people have a rugged, independent nature, and though the West had fascinated them by its novelty, they did not think fit to change their own manners and customs. The young boy, therefore, was brought up in a Hindu environment which had little connection with the outside world.

More than once I have visited this corner of India in order, if possible, to find out the secret that lies behind such outstanding characters as those of Mahatma Gandhi and Swami Dayananda Saraswati, the founder of the Arya Samaj; for it is a truly remarkable thing that two of the greatest social and religious reformers of Modern

India, Dayananda and Gandhi, were both born in the comparatively small peninsula of Kathiawar.

Porbunder differs from Morvi, where Swami Dayananda was born. It is on the seacoast, jutting out into the sea, and has all the infinite variety and charm of the expanse of ocean around it. Mists of extraordinary beauty constantly rise from the sea and encompass the land. The sea itself is usually a brilliant ultramarine, with liquid green where the shoals lie. I have sat above it and watched its changing hues for hours as the sunlight plays upon it. The little town where Mohandas Gandhi was born rises almost out of the sea and becomes a vision of glory at sunrise and sunset, when the slanting rays beat upon it, turning its turrets and pinnacles into gold.

Morvi, on the other hand, lies inland, not far away from the desolate waste of the Rajputana Desert, which stretches unbroken to the north for hundreds of miles. The land at Morvi is rocky and the country is rugged. It is not perhaps a mere fancy to credit the childhood of each of these two great reformers with having been affected by his surroundings.

Gandhi, with the sea forever sounding with its waves upon the coast near his home, has a mystical side to his nature which is not so clear in Dayananda. Both are puritan in character and have little regard for the luxuriant symbolism of Hindu India to the south; but, while Dayananda in his fervour of reform rejected idolatry altogether, Mohandas Gandhi has left a place for it in his own religious scheme of things. He is more conservative than Dayananda.

One further thought has come to me while staying in Kathiawar. The desert is always very near. We have come, in this western corner of India, very close to Arabia. The most thoughtful and sensitive natures among the Hindus who live thus on the edge of the great deserts of Asia have no difficulty in appreciating the mystical side of Islam and its absorbing central truth of the unity and majesty of God. The saints of Hinduism in Sind, which is still farther to the west and also on the border of the desert, sing songs that are difficult to distinguish from those of the Sufi mystics of Islam.

In this Introduction I do not wish to enter into details with regard to Mahatma Gandhi's life and personality, but only to sketch the

barest outline of his career as an introduction to the chapters that
follow. In a subsequent book it is my great hope to be able to comment on and edit the account which he himself has written with
regard to his own *Experiments with Truth*. In that autobiography he
has revealed with marvellous candour and humility his own personal
character. There is no authentic account of him so singularly revealing
as this, and it greatly needs editing for the West.

The turning-point in Mohandas Gandhi's early days came when he
was able at last to go to England to finish his education and obtain a
full training as a barrister-at-law. Those years in England were among
the most eventful in his whole life. The change from Kathiawar to
London was extreme; he suffered terribly from solitude and nearly
lost his bearings time after time. But his mother's influence and her last
injunctions to him when he left for England kept him straight in the
midst of temptations. His life was lived with an asceticism and simplicity that made his character stronger morally as the years went by.

Mohandas Gandhi's father had died during his boyhood, when he
was living with him in Kathiawar. The young boy had been married
without any choice in the matter at an early age. He was already a
father himself when he left home for England. Thus he reached
manhood prematurely and had to battle with the world almost
alone. His mother had died just before his return to India; it was the
greatest shock of all in his young life.

On his arrival once more in his own country from England he
struggled to make an income at the Bar, both in Bombay and in
Kathiawar. His temperamental shyness was against him, and his
rugged honesty prevented his adopting the various devices whereby
young barristers obtained their clients. After some years of comparative failure in India, as far as worldly affairs were concerned, he was
invited to go to South Africa in order to undertake a lawsuit on
behalf of a Muhammadan client, a resident of Kathiawar who had
made a fortune as a merchant in South Africa. When he reached
South Africa on that occasion he had no intention whatever of staying there beyond the time necessary to complete the lawsuit; but the
hard conditions under which his own countrymen were suffering
induced him to remain with them and share their hardships. He was

admitted to the Bar in South Africa, and became one of the best-known practitioners for conducting Indian cases. At one time his income rose to over £3,000 a year. It was in the very midst of this worldly prosperity and outward success that the moral ideal put forward by Tolstoy, which had been exercising his mind for a long time, came home with such inner strength of conviction that he determined at last to abandon everything and give himself up to a life of poverty wherein he could practise ascetic self-control and entire non-violence in all his actions.

Tolstoy's teaching had drawn him on to read the Sermon on the Mount, and this made his own inner ideal still clearer and brighter. He linked this Sermon with the precepts which he had received as a Vaishnava from his mother in his childhood. The way in which this happened will be evident from his own words, quoted in various parts of the present volume.

With regard to the direct teaching of Tolstoy and of the Sermon on the Mount, Mahatma Gandhi has always declared that, while he found in these nothing new or strange, yet at the same time Christ's words came to him with a living inspiration and a spiritual power that had meant much to his personal life at the most critical period of all, when he was almost giving way to atheism in London. He had been saved from that abyss.

During the years while he remained in South Africa, from this time forward, he was entirely occupied in putting these new principles into practice—on the one hand through inner self-discipline and purification, and on the other hand through taking up the cause of his own countrymen and fighting a moral warfare of passive resistance.

My own first meeting with Mahatma Gandhi was towards the end of the passive-resistance struggle in Natal. It was then that I came to know him intimately and lived side by side with him, sharing his ideals and also inquiring from him as an earnest seeker after truth concerning his own thoughts and aspirations. This friendship has been one of the greatest blessings I have had in a singularly happy life. It has enabled me to study his principles and methods so closely that it has become in some measure possible for me to judge which of his writings reveal most clearly his thoughts.

After he went back to India, at the beginning of the year 1915, it was again my privilege to live with him for considerable periods on different occasions. This was especially the case when he had any dangerous illness. On two such occasions—in the year 1918 and in 1924—I was with him night and day while he was very near to death. On both these occasions, during his convalescence, the pressure of ordinary daily routine was diminished and talks of a personal character were more frequent than could be expected at other times, when he was in the midst of his public engagements. The great dividing-line in Mahatma Gandhi's political life came in the year 1920, when, after repeated failure to obtain any clear sign of repentance for the wrongs that had been done to his country at Amritsar, and for the broken promises made to the Indian Mussalmans during the War, he declared that he could no longer co-operate with the British Government. Therefore he started what was called the non-co-operation movement. The partial failure of that movement, owing to an outbreak of violence at Bombay and Chauri Chaura, brought with it a reaction, and he was himself prepared to retire from the struggle. But he was arrested and imprisoned almost immediately after this outbreak of violence, and was released in 1924 owing to the fact that his health had become very seriously impaired. He had been obliged to undergo, whilst still in prison, a dangerous operation for appendicitis, from which he very slowly recovered.

The outstanding event after this was the fast of twenty-one days which he undertook at Delhi towards the end of the year 1924, in order to stop the rioting between Hindus and Mussalmans. Blood had been shed in these riots and Mahatma Gandhi took upon himself the sins of his own people. No more impressive event has happened in recent Indian history than this fast. It was a solemn occasion, not only for the little band of his faithful followers, who gathered round him during the fast, but for the whole of India. One of the results which followed was the deep and sustained effort on the part of the leaders of both religions in India to find a common solution for their difficulties on a spiritual basis.

More recent events need hardly be told in this introduction. The weakness of health which has pursued Mahatma Gandhi in recent years has often become extreme, and he is now in his sixtieth year, an age which, for climatic reasons, is comparatively older in the East than in the West. Yet he has determined at the call of duty to take up work once more in the strenuous political field.

One thing needs to be said to correct a wrong impression which I have found prevalent in the West. It is not at all true to say that Mahatma Gandhi's influence has waned in recent years. His retirements from active participation in current politics have only made his spiritual hold on the masses of the Indian people still firmer than ever. I have been with him on recent tours in different parts of India and can vouch for this fact from my own observation.

A Short List of Common Indian Words

Two Titles of Reverence

Mahatma: A title of Gandhi meaning Great Soul
Gurudeva: A title of Tagore meaning Revered Teacher

Two Religious Institutions

Sabarmati Ashram: The religious institution of Mahatma Gandhi near Ahmedabad
Santiniketan Ashram: The religious institution of Rabindranath Tagore near Calcutta

Terms Used in Passive Resistance

Ahimsa: Non-violence
Satya: Truth
Satyagraha: Truth-force or soul-force
Satyagrahi: One who practices soul-force

Mahatma Gandhi's Hand-Spinning Movement

Charka: The spinning-wheel
Khaddar: Home-spun cloth

Muhammadan Religious Terms

Islam: The religion of the Prophet Muhammad
Muslim: Belonging to Islam
Mussalman: Follower of Islam
Khilafat: The office of Caliph
Caliph or Khalifa: The religious head of Islam

Sacred Sanskrit Books

Vedas: The earliest religious hymns
Upanishad: The earliest religious philosophy
Puranas: The sacred Hindu legends

Hindu Religion

Dharma: Religion or religious duty
Varnashrama Dharma: Religion of Caste
Sanatana Dharma: Orthodox Hindu religion
Sanatani: An orthodox Hindu

The Four Castes

Brahman: The first Caste (knowledge)
Kshattriya: The second Caste (rule)
Vaishya: The third Caste (trade, agriculture)
Shudra: The fourth Caste (labour)

The Four Religious Stages

Brahmacharya: The first stage of the religious life (chastity)
Grihastha: The second stage of the religious life (householder)
Vanaprastha: The third stage of the religious life (gradual retirement)
Sanyas: The fourth stage of the religious life (complete retirement)

The Two Great Epics

Mahabharata: The national epic wherein Krishna is the divine hero. The Bhagavad Gita is part of this epic.
Ramayana: The sacred epic of North India wherein Rama is the divine hero

Political Terms

Swadeshi: Belonging to, or made in, one's own country
Swaraj: Self-government

Indian Coinage

Anna: Very slightly more than one penny ⎱
Rupee: About one shilling and six-pence ⎰ 16 annas = 1 rupee
Lakh: About 7, 500 pounds sterling
Crore: About 750, 000 pounds sterling

Gandhi in South Africa circa 1900

Part I

THE RELIGIOUS
ENVIRONMENT

1

THE BACKGROUND OF HINDUISM

There are few things perhaps more difficult to accomplish than to put oneself in sympathetic touch with a religion which is not one's own by birth-inheritance. The effort that has to be made is far more sustained than that of understanding a poem in a foreign tongue. There is a strangeness about every mood and tone of worship, as well as in the words of the sacred texts of Scripture and the revealed doctrines held to be orthodox. [See Appendix 1.]

An easy way of realizing this is to consider the instance of a Hindu reading certain passages of the Old Testament for the first time; or being told about the Holy Communion Service, with its consecrated elements of bread and wine representing the Body and Blood of Christ; or having explained to him St. Paul's doctrine of election and predestination, or the clauses in the Creed concerning the Descent into Hell, the Ascension into Heaven, and the Resurrection of the Body. We have become accustomed from childhood to the peculiar phraseology of Christian ceremonies and sacred texts, but others have not. I remember how the poet Rabindranath Tagore once told me that he could not go on reading some of the descriptions of enemy-slaughter in the Psalms to which he had turned on opening the Bible. His elder brother, who was one of the most saintly old men I have ever known, told me that the symbol of the slain "Lamb of God" presented to his mind a picture that was altogether revolting, and that he detested the sentence of the hymn, "Washed in the Blood of the Lamb."

I have taken these illustrations because in a similar manner there are bound to be aspects of Hindu Religion contained in Mahatma Gandhi's definition that at first sight will appear strange in the West. Therefore it may be well to offer some explanations before I quote his words about his Hindu belief and practice.

There are two elements in Hinduism which are very difficult to understand until one has lived a long time in India and found out their importance in that country.

1. "Caste," considered as a social and religious system.

In the original social organization of India there were evidently three main orders of higher society. We meet with these among all the leading Aryan peoples. They are clearly defined, for instance, in Ancient Persia and in Ancient Greece, where Aryan languages, akin to Sanskrit, were in daily use. First of all, there was the priestly or Brahman Caste, whose members studied the ritual and preserved the sacred texts. Secondly, there were the warriors and public administrators, called Kshattriyas, who ruled the different clans. Thirdly, there were the agricultural settlers, or Vaishyas, who tilled the soil and made wealth.

Last of all, much below these (and probably representing in origin a different, conquered race), there were the Shudras, who did the labourers' work. This class was represented by the *helots* in Ancient Greece, and was not reckoned with the Aryan race at all.

In India the vast majority of the conquered non-Aryan inhabitants were admitted into the Shudra class. But these were never allowed to wear the sacred thread, or to go through the ceremony of initiation as "twice-born." Only the first three ranks of society, which were of pure Aryan stock, were allowed to have this sacred privilege of initiation and to belong by birthright to the original community as its leading citizens.

Later on, attached to the Shudras but separated from them, as being lower still in the social scale, came the Namashudras. These were also named Panchamas, or Pariahs. These words, denoting a rank even below the Shudras, are used for that lowest social class which was called "untouchable." For these lowest conquered peoples, very dark of skin, began to be altogether despised and were given only the menial duties of scavengering, sweeping, tanning of animal hides, etc., which were regarded as "unclean" occupations. They were offered in return the leavings of food which otherwise would be cast to the dogs; they were reduced to eat even carrion flesh to keep themselves alive. Thus their very occupations made them filthy; their food was impure; and public neglect constantly added to their wretched plight. At last their touch itself, and in some parts of South India even their shadow, became regarded as polluting, and they were called as a class "untouchables."

While Mr. Gandhi, in his definition of Hinduism, declares that he believes in the ancient Caste system, he entirely refuses to have anything to do with "Untouchability." He also refuses to regard any Caste, such as that of the Brahmin, as superior in rank. He regards all men and women equally as his brothers and sisters, treating them in every single act of life as equals. I have seen him day after day living with the "untouchables" in the closest possible friendliness and fellowship. They love him as a father, and his name is revered from one end of India to another as their friend.

Along with this Caste system, and closely connected with it, there arose at a very early date in India, among the Aryans, the idea of marriage as a religious sacrament, which the higher Castes especially regarded as sacred. As an aristocracy they thought much about heredity and observed certain regulations in order to keep their stock pure. Marriage had to take place within the Caste and always according to Hindu sacred law and ceremony. Little by little, in process of time, this marriage within the Caste became the strictest of all the Caste obligations. Thus each Caste became one marriage-brotherhood. The question of marriage was so intimately bound up with Caste, and Caste with marriage, that those who have studied the whole question most thoroughly and scientifically have declared as an aphorism "Caste is marriage, and marriage is Caste, in Hindu Religion."

Just as marriage within the same Caste became obligatory and the obligation was never transgressed, so also there were solemn occasions, especially at marriages, when the dining together of all Caste fellows in one place at a common meal was of the highest social importance. To be refused or forbidden a seat at this common Caste meal was to be outcaste. It represented a social punishment of the most drastic and severe character; and nothing was more terrifying than this possibility of being turned out of Caste; for it meant that no one in the Caste would then give in marriage any of his children to such an outcaste person.

A number of moral actions were originally settled by each community in this manner; but, above all, the strict marriage relations were thus sanctified by Hindu religion. The Castes lived together, side by side, as independent units, in all their marriage relations. Inter-Caste marriages became practically unknown.

One more point must be noted. The original "Four Castes" have long ago become subdivided. Some of these subdivisions are comparatively small, and this has led to great hardships, for marriage has for long been virtually confined, in most parts of India, to the sub-Caste. The difficulty of finding a suitable marriage for a daughter within the sub-Caste has often become very great; and therefore a father may sometimes have a marriage ceremony performed at a very early age in order to ensure a bridegroom being found within the same sub-Caste. Such marriages correspond with betrothals in the West, but they often lead to consummation at far too early a date. Nevertheless, recent tendencies have been to raise both the age of marriage and that of consummation, and adult marriage is more common than is frequently supposed.

2. Cow Protection as a religious duty.

It is perhaps even more difficult in the West to understand this reverence paid to the cow than to understand the Hindu Caste System. For with us in the West there is always something stupid associated with the cow, as the epithet "bovine" clearly denotes.

But here, again, we must remember that we are dealing with a very ancient and profoundly religious people, whose traditions have never been snapped and broken asunder. We go back to those first beginnings of settled human history when agricultural life took the place of the nomad life of the hunter. It was at this early stage in India that the cow, which provided milk for daily food and helped every day in the tilling of the soil, became a valued companion of the household, to be cherished beyond all other treasures. From this began the religious reverence for the cow in Hindu India. It is a primitive belief intimately connected with the culture of the soil.

Let me give an analogy which may appeal to us in the West from the Old Testament. Among the ancient Hebrew people we can see clearly how a sacred meaning became attached to each one of those common acts which might preserve the growing Hebrew Community from social injury. We admire today the laws of Moses with their sanitary regulations. But perhaps we do not realize sufficiently that it was their religious sanction which made these sanitary laws so scrupulously observed.

In the same manner a religious sanction was given from the first in India to the protection of the cow. By investing this one animal of the household—so supremely necessary for a primitive agricultural society—with a sacred character, Ancient India really preserved one of the main sources of her own healthy life. Even today, among the Hindus of India, who are vegetarians, milk is the only food that goes along with the grain foods as a nutrient to preserve life. There are practically no other food-stuffs that are taken in any large daily quantities.

But the reverence for the cow thus inculcated by Hindu religion has been only the beginning of a reverence for all the lower animals, as we call them. They have gained a place close to the hearts of the Hindu people, as being hardly sub-human at all but practically human. Here again it is difficult for us to understand the Hindus, just as it is hard for them to understand us. For example, the slaughter of animals for sport or for food, accompanied by much bloodshed and suffering, which goes on thoughtlessly amongst ourselves, is looked on with utter repulsion by the Hindus. For sub-human life is comparatively free from injury by man in India over large areas. Little birds and squirrels and other tiny animals, which we call "wild" in the West, are so tame in India that they never fear at all the presence of mankind. Combined with this unfortunately runs parallel a neglect of animals in their suffering, which is due to the callousness of extreme poverty. But such callousness is not confined to animals; it is extended to human life owing to the same cause.

One further fact is noticeable. This reverence for the cow, which has been boldly established in the midst of other religious sanctions, has attached the people of the land to the soil. It has kept Hindus predominantly agricultural in character. Among no other people perhaps is this attachment to the soil so close and intimate. There is a pathetically anomalous sight today when Hindus within town areas will positively insist, against all conception of strict municipal regulations, on having cows near to them in the streets and lanes of the city, reminding them by their very presence of the country which is their birthright.

Where in other countries there has been a strong pressure and drag towards an urban civilization, this reverence for the cattle, which is centuries deep in every orthodox Hindu's heart, has proved an equally strong attraction in India in the opposite direction. If a symbol of the rural life were needed for the religious heart of man to fix his gaze upon in worship, the Hindu symbol of the cow may not be so irrational as at first sight appears. Among the many symbols that Christians associate with the Nativity in the Gospel story, the one symbol of Christ being born in a manger, with the patient, lowly cattle standing by and gazing with their great big eyes at the new-born Child, whose name is "Wonderful, the Prince of Peace," is probably most near of all to the heart of India.

It would not be feasible to go farther in explaining beforehand the different parts of Mahatma Gandhi's definition of Hinduism, where they are foreign to Western minds; but one thing may be stated—he himself and every instructed orthodox Hindu believes in one Supreme God. The word "God"—without any further connotation—is well known in every Indian language and is constantly on every Hindu's lips. The name of God is written on every Hindu's heart, and when he thinks of God he thinks of Him as One and Supreme. In all my many intimate talks on religion with Mahatma Gandhi, amid many divergences and shades of contrast, I have never felt that there was any real difference between us with regard to this ultimate belief. Here we were on common ground. In this sense Mr. Gandhi is a theist and so am I; to both of us this belief in God is as certain and immediate as our own personal existence.

A few Sanskrit words still remain to be translated. The word "Sanatani," with which he begins, means literally eternal or unchanging. It may be used to describe the Hindu orthodox position. Mr. Gandhi does not belong to any of the new reforming sects of Hinduism. He is a conservative in religion.

The Vedas are the most ancient of the Hindu Scriptures commonly regarded by Hindus as infallible, in the same way that the Hebrew Scriptures are considered to be infallible by many Christian people. The Upanishads are the earliest philosophic treatises. The Puranas represent the legends of ancient Hinduism.

The words "Varnashrama Dharma" signify the religion of the Hindu Caste System. Varna in Sanskrit means "colour" or "caste"; Dharma signifies "Religion."

With these preliminary explanations the following is Mahatma Gandhi's most recent definition of his own Hindu faith:

I call myself a Sanatani Hindu because

1. I believe in the Vedas, the Upanishads, the Puranas, and all that goes by the name of Hindu Scriptures, and therefore in Avataras (divine incarnations) and rebirth.
2. I believe in Varnashrama Dharma in a sense strictly Vedic, but not in its present popular and crude sense.
3. I believe in "Cow Protection" in a much larger sense than the popular belief.
4. I do not disbelieve in "idol-worship."
5. I believe implicitly in the Hindu aphorism that no one truly knows the Scriptures who has not attained perfection in Innocence (Ahimsa), Truth (Satya), and Self-control (Brahmacharya), and who has not renounced all acquisition or possession of wealth.
6. I believe, along with every Hindu, in God and His Oneness, in rebirth and salvation.

That which distinguishes Hinduism from every other religion is its "Cow Protection," even more than its Varnashrama. Varnashrama is in my opinion inherent in human nature, and Hinduism has simply reduced it to a science. It attaches to birth. A man cannot change "Varna" by choice. Not to abide by Varna is to disregard the law of heredity. [See Appendix 2.]

I do *not* believe in the exclusive divinity of the Vedas. I believe the Bible, the Quran, and the Zend Avesta to be as much divinely inspired as the Vedas. My belief in the Hindu Scriptures does not require me to accept every word and every verse as divinely inspired. Nor do I claim to have any first-hand knowledge of these wonderful books. But I do claim to know and feel the truths of the essential teaching of the Scriptures. I decline to be bound by any interpretation, however learned it may be, if it is repugnant to reason or moral sense.

I do *not* believe that interdining, or even intermarriage, necessarily deprives a man of the Caste status that his birth has given him. The four divisions, Brahmin, Kshattriya, Vaishya, Shudra, define a man's calling; they do not restrict or regulate social intercourse. The divisions define duties; they confer no privileges. It is, I hold, against the genius of Hinduism to arrogate to oneself a higher status, or assign to another a lower status. All are born to serve God's creation—a Brahmin with his knowledge, a Kshattriya with his power of protection, a Vaishya with his commercial ability, and a Shudra with his bodily labour.

This, however, does not mean that a Brahmin is absolved from bodily labour, or the duty of protecting himself and others. His birth makes a Brahmin predominantly a man of knowledge, the fittest by heredity and training to impart it to others. There is nothing, again, to prevent the Shudra from acquiring all the knowledge he wishes. Only he will best serve with his body, and need not envy others their special qualities for service. But a Brahmin who claims superiority by right of knowledge falls, and has no knowledge. And so with the others, who pride themselves upon their special qualities. Varnashrama implies self-restraint, conservation, and economy of energy.

Though, therefore, Varnashrama is not affected by interdining or intermarriage, Hinduism does most emphatically discourage these things.

Hinduism has reached the highest limit of self-restraint. It is undoubtedly a religion of renunciation of the flesh, so that the spirit may be set free. By restricting a Hindu's choice of a bride for his son to a particular group he exercises rare self-restraint.

Hinduism does not regard the married state as by any means

essential for salvation. Marriage is a "fall" even as "birth" is a fall. Salvation is freedom from birth and hence from death also.

Prohibition against intermarriage and interdining is essential for a rapid evolution of the soul. But this self-denial is no test of Varna (Caste). A Brahmin may remain a Brahmin, though he may dine with his Shudra brother, provided he has not left off his duty of service by knowledge. It follows from what I have said above that restraint in matters of marriage and dining is not based upon notions of superiority. A Hindu who refuses to dine with another from a sense of superiority altogether misrepresents his Hindu religion.

Unfortunately, today Hinduism seems to consist merely in "eating" and "not eating." Hinduism is in danger of losing its substance; it is resolving itself into a matter of elaborate rules as to what and with whom to eat. Abstemiousness from meat is undoubtedly a great aid to the evolution of the spirit; but it is by no means an end in itself. Many a man eating meat and dining with everybody, but living in the fear of God, is nearer to his salvation than a man religiously abstaining from meat and many other things, but blaspheming God in every one of his acts.

The central fact of Hinduism, however, is "Cow Protection." "Cow Protection" to me is one of the most wonderful phenomena in all human evolution; for it takes the human being beyond his species. The cow to me means the entire sub-human world. Man through the cow is enjoined to realize his identity with all that lives. Why the cow was selected for apothesis is obvious to me. The cow was in India the best companion. She was the giver of plenty. Not only did she give milk, but she also made agriculture possible. The cow is a poem of pity. One reads pity in the gentle animal. She is the "mother" to millions of Indian mankind. Protection of the cow means protection of the whole dumb creation of God. The ancient seer, whoever he was, began in India with the cow. The appeal of the lower order of creation is all the more forcible because it is speechless. "Cow Protection" is the gift of Hinduism to the world; and Hinduism will live so long as there are Hindus to protect the cow.

Hindus are enjoined to protect the cow by self-purification, by self-sacrifice. The present day "Cow Protection" has degenerated into a perpetual feud with the Mussalmans, whereas true cow protection means conquering the Mussalmans by our love.

A Mussalman friend sent me some time ago a book detailing the inhumanities practised by us on the cow and her progeny: how we bleed her to take the last drop of milk from her; how we starve her to emaciation; how we ill-treat the calves; how we deprive them of their portion of milk; how cruelly we treat the oxen; how we castrate them; how we beat them; how we over-load them. If they had speech they would bear witness to our crimes against them which would stagger the world. By every act of cruelty to our cattle we disown God and Hinduism; I do not know that the condition of the cattle in any other part of the world is so bad as in unhappy India. We may not blame the Englishman for this; we may not plead poverty in our defence. Criminal negligence is the only cause of the miserable condition of our cattle. Our cow-shelters, though they are an answer to our instinct of mercy, are a clumsy demonstration of its execution. Instead of being model dairy farms and great profitable national institutions they are merely depots for receiving decrepit cattle.

Hindus will be judged, not by their correct chanting of sacred text, not by their pilgrimages, not by their most punc-tilious observance of Caste rules, but by their ability to protect the cow. Whilst professing the religion of "Cow Protection" we have enslaved the cow and her progeny and have become slaves ourselves.

I can no more describe my feeling for Hinduism than for my own wife. She moves me as no other woman in the world can. Not that she has no faults; I dare say she has many more than I see myself. But the feeling of an indissoluble bond is there. Even so I feel for and about Hinduism with all its faults and limitations. Nothing elates me so much as the music of the Gita or Tulsidas's Ramayana, the only two books in Hinduism I may be said really to know. When on one occasion I fancied I was taking my last breath the Gita was my solace.

I know the vice that is going on today in all the great Hindu shrines, but I love them in spite of their unspeakable failings. There is an interest which I take in them and in no other. I am a reformer through and through. But my zeal never leads me to the rejection of any of the essential things of Hinduism.

I have said I do not disbelieve in idol-worship. An idol does not excite any feeling of veneration in me. But I think that idol-worship is part of human nature. We hanker after symbolism. Why should one be more composed in a church than elsewhere? Images are an aid to worship. No Hindu considers an image to be God. I do not consider idol-worship sin.

It is clear from the foregoing that Hinduism is not an exclusive religion. In it there is room for the worship of all the prophets of the world. It is not a missionary religion in the ordinary sense of the term. It has no doubt absorbed many tribes in its fold, but this absorption has been of an evolutionary, imperceptible character. Hinduism tells everyone to worship God according to his own faith, and so it lives at peace with all the religions.

That being my conception of Hinduism, I have never been able to reconcile myself to "untouchability." I have always regarded it as an excrescence. It is true that it has been handed down to us from generations; but so are many evil practices even to this day. I should be ashamed to think that dedication of temple girls to virtual prostitution was a part of Hinduism; yet it is practised by Hindus in many parts of India.*

Again, I consider it positive irreligion to sacrifice goats to Kali and do not consider it a part of Hinduism....There was, no doubt, at one time sacrifice of animals offered in the name of religion; but it is not true religion, much less is it Hindu religion.

So, also, it seems to me that when "Cow Protection" became an article of faith with our ancestors, those who persisted in eating beef were excommunicated. The civil strife must then

---

* Since the above statement, legislation for the abolition of this practice has been introduced in the Madras Legislative Council.

have been fierce. Social boycott was applied not only to the recalcitrants, but their sins were visited upon their children also. The practice of boycott, which had probably its origin in good intentions, hardened into harsh usage; and even verses crept into our sacred books giving the practice of boycott a permanence wholly undeserved and still less justified.

Such is my own theory of the origin of "untouchability." Whether it is correct or not, "untouchability" is repugnant to reason and to the instinct of pity or love. A religion that establishes the worship of the cow cannot possibly countenance or warrant a cruel and unhuman boycott of human beings; and I should be content to be torn to pieces rather than disown the suppressed classes. Hindus will certainly never deserve freedom, nor get it, if they allow their noble religion to be disgraced by the retention of the taint of untouchability; and, as I love Hinduism dearer than life itself, the taint has become for me an intolerable burden. Let us not deny God by denying to a fifth of our race the right of association on an equal footing.

Certain parts of this statement of Hindu belief would be challenged historically by such a thinker and philosopher as Rabindranath Tagore. The most important point, which cannot be left without comment, is Mahatma Gandhi's description of marriage as a "fall." Tagore, in a famous letter, refers to this side of Gandhi's ascetic disposition as akin to Buddhism rather than to the Upanishad teaching of early Hinduism. He points also to the early ideal of Hindu life contained in the four different stages which have to be passed through for the completion of human experience. Among these the second stage, that of the married householder, is the most important.*

Though there is a strain of asceticism running through many forms of popular Hinduism which appear to regard marriage as an evil necessity, yet the sacredness attached to marriage as a sacrament

---

* See Chapter 15, page 193, where the letter is quoted in connection with Non-Cooperation. Tagore regards Mahatma Gandhi's idea of marriage as having the same negative aspect. See also the short list of common words at the beginning of this book, where the four stages are given.

in the Hindu religion makes it difficult to believe that the negative
ideal of celibacy has ever been fundamental in India, except during
the Buddhist ascendancy. The Indian people finally rejected
Buddhism as their own religious creed. There are hardly any
Buddhists remaining in India proper today.

With regard to Mahatma Gandhi's thoughts on the deeper aspects
of the spiritual life, we have passages in his writings which may supplement the somewhat external character of his religious opinion of
Hinduism given above. The two which follow deal with the mystery
of God and the instinct of faith whereby God is apprehended. The
former runs thus:

> There is an indefinable mysterious Power that pervades every-
> thing. I feel it, though I do not see it. It is this unseen Power
> which makes itself felt and yet defies all proof, because it is so
> unlike all that I perceive through my senses. It transcends the
> senses. But it is possible to reason out the existence of God to
> a limited extent.
>
> Even in ordinary affairs we know that people do not know
> who rules or why and how he rules; and yet they know that
> there is a power that certainly rules. In my tour last year in
> Mysore I met many poor villagers, and I found upon inquiry
> that they did not know who ruled Mysore; they simply said
> some god ruled it. If the knowledge of these poor people was
> so limited about their ruler, I who am infinitely lesser in respect
> to God than they to their ruler need not be surprised if I do
> not realize the presence of God, the King of kings.
>
> Nevertheless I do feel, as the poor villagers felt about Mysore,
> that there is orderliness in the universe; there is an unalterable
> Law governing everything and every being that exists or lives.
> It is not a blind law; for no blind law can govern the conduct
> of living beings; and thanks to the marvellous researches of Sir
> J. C. Bose, it can now be proved that even matter is life.
>
> That Law, then, which governs all life is God. Law and the
> law-giver are one. I may not deny the Law or the Law Giver
> because I know so little about It or Him. Just as my denial or

ignorance of the existence of an earthly power will avail me nothing, even so my denial of God and His law will not liberate me from its operation; whereas humble and mute acceptance of divine authority makes life's journey easier even as the acceptance of earthly rule makes life under it easier.

I do dimly perceive that whilst everything around me is ever-changing, ever-dying, there is underlying all that change a Living Power that is changeless, that holds all together, that creates, dissolves, and re-creates. That informing Power or Spirit is God; and since nothing else that I see merely through the senses can or will persist, He alone is.

And is this power benevolent or malevolent? I see it as purely benevolent. For I can see that in the midst of death life persists; in the midst of untruth, truth persists; in the midst of darkness, light persists. Hence I gather that God is Life, Truth, Light. He is Love. He is the supreme Good.

But He is no God who merely satisfies the intellect, if He ever does. God, to be God, must rule the heart and transform it. He must express Himself in every smallest act of His votary. This can only be done through a definite realization more real than the five senses can ever produce. Sense perceptions can be, and often are, false and deceptive, however real they may appear to us. Where there is realization outside the senses it is infallible. It is proved, not by extraneous evidence, but in the transformed conduct and character of those who have felt the real presence of God within.

Such testimony is to be found in the experiences of an unbroken line of prophets and sages in all countries and climes. To reject this evidence is to deny oneself.

This realization is preceded by an immovable faith. He who would in his own person test the fact of God's presence can do so by a living faith; and since faith itself cannot be proved by extraneous evidence, the safest course is to believe in the moral government of the world, and therefore in the supremacy of the moral law, the law of Truth and Love. Exercise of faith will be the safest where there is a clear determination summarily to reject all that is contrary to Truth and Love.

I confess that I have no argument to convince through reason.
Faith transcends reason. All I can advise is not to attempt the
impossible. I cannot account for the existence of evil by any
rational method. To want to do so is to be co-equal with God. I
am therefore humble enough to recognize evil as such; and I call
God long-suffering and patient precisely because He permits evil
in the world. I know that He has no evil in Himself; and yet if
there is evil He is the author of it and yet untouched by it.

I know, too, that I shall never know God if I do not wrestle
with and against evil, even at the cost of life itself. I am fortified
in the belief by my own humble and limited experience. The
purer I try to become the nearer to God I feel myself to be.
How much more should I be near to Him when my faith is not
a mere apology, as it is today, but has become as immovable as
the Himalayas and as white as the snows on their peaks?
Meanwhile I pray with Newman, who sang from experience:

Lead, kindly Light, amid the encircling gloom,
Lead Thou me on;
The night is dark and I am far from home,
Lead Thou me on;
Keep Thou my feet, I do not ask to see
The distant scene; one step enough for me.

The second passage relates Mahatma Gandhi's own belief in the
following manner:

To me God is Truth and Love; God is ethics and morality; God
is fearlessness; God is the source of Light and Life, and yet He
is above and beyond all these. God is conscience. He is even the
atheism of the atheist. For in His boundless love God permits the
atheist to live. He is the searcher of hearts. He transcends speech
and reason. He knows us and our hearts better than we do ourselves. He does not take us at our word; for He knows that we
often do not mean it, some knowingly and others unknowingly.

God is personal to those who need His personal presence.

He is embodied to those who need His touch. He is all things to all men. He is in us and yet above and beyond us. Man may banish the word "God" in taking an oath, but he has no power to banish the Thing itself.

God cannot cease to be because hideous immoralities or inhuman brutalities are committed in His name. He is long-suffering. He is patient, but He is also terrible. He is the most exacting personage in the world and the world to come. He metes out the same measure to us that we mete out to our neighbours—men and brutes. With Him ignorance is no excuse. And withal He is ever-forgiving; for He always gives us the chance to repent. He is the greatest Democrat the world knows, for He leaves us "unfettered" to make our own choice between evil and good. He is the greatest Tyrant ever known, for He often dashes the cup from our lips and under cover of free will leaves us a margin so wholly inadequate as to provide only mirth for Himself at our expense.

Therefore it is that Hinduism calls it all His sport—Lila; or else calls it all an illusion—Maya. We are not, He alone Is.

In these last sentences it must be understood that Mahatma Gandhi is speaking in the poetical language of paradox, seeking in dim imagery to portray the Unimaginable. This aspect of God's nature, which is beyond human imagination in its deep mystery, is often called in popular Hinduism God's play (lila) or His illusion (maya). But this to Mahatma Gandhi, is no contradiction of His divine essence as Truth (Satya) and Harmlessness (Ahimsa).

In a third passage, which I have selected out of many which he has written, we find how Mahatma Gandhi himself in his own person prefers the active to the contemplative life; how he is able to find the greatest satisfaction in prayer to God through service to mankind. He writes thus:

Worshipping God is singing the praise of God. Prayer is a confession of one's own unworthiness and weakness. God has a
thousand names, or, rather, He is nameless. We may worship or
pray to Him by whichever name we please. Some call Him

Rama, some Krishna, others call Him God. All worship the same Spirit. But as all foods do not agree with all, so all names do not appeal to all. Each chooses the name according to his own associations; and He being the In-Dweller, the All-Powerful, the Omniscient, knows our innermost feelings and responds to us according to our deserts.

Worship and prayer, therefore, are not to be performed with the lips but with the heart. That is why they can be performed equally by the dumb and the stammerer, by the ignorant and the stupid; and the prayers of those whose tongues are nectared, but whose hearts are full of poison, are never heard. He, therefore, who would pray to God must cleanse his heart. The divine name Rama was not only on the lips of Hanuman;* He was enthroned in his heart. Rama gave Hanuman exhaustless strength. In Rama's strength Hanuman lifted the mountain and crossed the ocean. It is faith that steers us through the stormy seas, faith that moves mountains, and faith that jumps across the ocean. That faith is nothing but a living, wide-awake consciousness of God within. He who has achieved that faith wants nothing.

"But how is the heart to be cleansed to this extent?"

Only the true devotee knows this and can teach it. The Gita has defined the true devotee in three places, and talked of him generally everywhere. But a knowledge of the definition of a devotee is hardly a sufficient guide. They are rare on this earth. I have therefore suggested the Religion of Service as the means. God of Himself seeks for His seat the heart of him who serves his fellowmen. That is why the poet who "saw and knew" sang, "He is a true Vaishnava who knows how to melt at another's woe." Such was Abu Ben Adhem. He served his fellow-men, and therefore his name topped the list of those who served God.

But who are the suffering and the woebegone? The suppressed and the poverty-stricken. He who would be a devotee, therefore, must serve these by body, soul, and mind. He who

---

* Hanuman in the legend was the king of the monkey tribes who served Rama, the incarnate Hero-God, and worshipped him with true devotion.

does not even condescend to exert his body to the extent of spinning for the sake of the poor, and trots out lame excuses, does not know the meaning of service. He who spins before the poor, inviting them to do likewise, serves God as no one else does. The Lord says in the Gita: "He who gives me even a tri- fle, such as a fruit or a flower or even a leaf, in the spirit of devo- tion, is my servant. And He hath His footstool where live 'the poorest and the lowliest and lost.'"* The work of spinning, therefore, for such is the greatest prayer, the greatest worship, the greatest sacrifice. A prayerful heart is the vehicle, and service makes the heart prayerful. Those Hindus who in this age serve the "untouchables" from a full heart, they truly pray; those who spin prayerfully for the poor and the needy, they truly pray.

On no single day of his long fast at Delhi, [see chapter 18] in spite of his extreme weakness, did Mahatma Gandhi cease to perform his allotted task at the spinning-wheel in order to realize his oneness with the poor. Thus what he has here set down is not a matter of theory but of practical experience.

---

* From Tagore's *Gitanjali,* x.

2

THE HINDU–MUSLIM PROBLEM

With such a conception of Hinduism as that which Mahatma Gandhi has always carried with him in his daily life the question arises: What method of approach would he have towards Islam from such an angle of vision?

The contrasts between Hinduism and the creed of the Arabian Prophet are extreme. Hinduism accepts whole-heartedly the worship of God, symbolized in images and elaborate temple worship: Islam rejects absolutely all idolatry. Hinduism makes its appeal to the multitude through religious music and ritual: Islam is sternly austere in its Puritan rejection of music at the time of prayer. Hinduism, by its metaphysical speculations and its accommodation to the crude ideas of the masses, makes room for a Pantheon of deities and heroes in its conception of the Unseen and Eternal. Islam, arising from the bare solitude of the Arabian Desert, has avoided metaphysical subtlety and insisted on the majestic Unity of God, transcendent and omnipotent.

Thus, not only in their outward appeal to the masses, but also in their inner philosophy, it would be difficult to find two religions more diverse than these two which have divided the North of India. Out of an agelong struggle compromises have been reached; and (as I shall show later) Eastern mystics from either side have endeavoured tentatively to bridge over the gulf. Hinduism, indeed, with its assimilative traditions and antecedents, has even been ready to come to terms with Islam, if terms could be offered. But the Monotheism of Islam has remained intractable.

Islam had presented in India from the very first the victorious creed of the conquering race. It has been singularly free from racial and marriage distinctions. It has set great store by the conversion of those who were outside the fold of the faithful. Essentially it has been a proselytizing religion and has made converts until its numbers have reached to over seventy millions out of a population of three hundred and twenty millions. It is true that during one comparatively brief period the early Moghul Emperors had acted with notable toleration. But the zeal of the Emperor Aurangzeb made him revert to the more primitive method of fighting against the idolators. He arrogantly built his own mosque, with its towering minarets in the heart of the Holy City of the Hindus, at Benares. After his death, even when the decrepitude of the Emperors prevented their carrying out this intransigent policy of Aurangzeb, the bitter hatred between the two communities smouldered like a hidden fire, ready to break out at any moment into a conflagration. The ultimate problem of modern India is the reconciliation of these two opposing religions.

No one, of course, would dream of condoning the brutalities of the earlier Muhammadan invasions of India under Mahmud of Ghazni and his successors. Muslim historians in India have been the first to condemn them. But when we contemplate India as a whole today, in the north as well as in the south, we can see how, in certain matters that are vital and essential, the north of India has been truly purged by the presence of Islam from the accumulation of dead and decaying matter which was unwholesome and even poisonous. If the miasma of "untouchability" and some of the lower mists of idol-worship have been lifted from the atmosphere of Northern India more than from the South, it is not a little due to the constant presence of a faith which swept aside the luxuriant ritual growth that had encumbered the pure worship of the One God, and insisted at the same time that in His presence all believers are equal.

Thus Islam has been in India, wherever it has held sway, a cleansing medium. One of its greatest blessings to East and West alike has been the emphasis which at a critical period in human history it placed upon the Divine Unity. For during those Dark Ages both in East and West, from A.D. 600 to 1,000, this doctrine was in danger of being overlaid and obscured in Hinduism and in Christianity itself, owing to the immense accretion of subsidiary worships of countless saints and demigods and heroes. Islam has been, both to Europe and to India, in their darkest hour of aberration from the sovereign truth of God's unity, an invaluable corrective and deterrent. Indeed, without the final emphasis to this truth which Islam gave from its central position—facing India and facing Europe—it is doubtful whether this idea of God as One could have obtained that established place in human thought which is uncontested in the intellectual world today, and also widely spread among the common people. It reinforced in a vital manner the witness which the Jewish Religion has perpetually borne.

Furthermore, this divine truth, which has thus been preserved by Islam and Judaism alike, is not merely an abstract postulate of scientific thought: rather it is the most vital of all experiences and the very soul of pure religion. More perhaps than anything else in Islam it has been this aspect of the Divine Unity which has profoundly affected Northern India. The note that is struck is a Puritan note; but it is as a purifying element in religion that Islam has brought the greatest benefit to mankind.

It will be understood from what I have written that one of the gravest difficulties to be overcome in India in order to obtain national unity has always been this direct antagonism between Hinduism and Islam. While the latter religion has acted as a purge, it has also stirred up bitter hatreds; and these have gone deep into the heart of the Hindu people. Perhaps there is no more acute religious strife in the East today than that between Hindus and Mussalmans. During long periods this bitterness may fall into abeyance among the masses. The natural kindliness and good-nature of the people of India may reassert itself. But sooner or later, as past history has shown, a wave of fanatical hatred seems to sweep over the country and then all the deep-seated passions come back to the surface in terrible forms.

It may be well to set out in a tabular form some of the major controversies which divide Hinduism from Islam:

1. Islam regards all idolators as sinful. It refuses to allow any image-worship whatsoever, and condemns idolators as subject to the Divine Wrath.
2. Islam enjoins the sacrifice of an animal, on a certain religious festival, as a matter of religious obligation. This animal is not infrequently a cow. It is true that some other animal may be substituted; but

cows are still not uncommonly slaughtered in the name of Islam, and this has incensed the illiterate Hindus almost beyond endurance. I have seen with my own eyes their indignation, and it is something that I can never forget.

3. Orthodox Hinduism regards it as sinful to take food at the hands of a Mussalman. To do this would imply the breaking of Caste. No intermarriage is allowed for the same reason. This idea of pollution, which is not seldom present to the Hindu mind, is often a cause of offence to Mussalmans.

4. Popular Hinduism insists on music being played in the street, even before mosques, when religious ceremonies are being observed. Pious Mussalmans have become deeply incensed when the idols of Hindu gods and goddesses have been carried at these religious festivals with obtrusive ceremony past the doors of their own mosques. This not infrequently takes place in Northern India at the sacred hour of prayer, accompanied by loud drum-beating and the clanging of cymbals. Such music before mosques interrupts the silent worshippers, and often raises the spirit of fanatical hatred to a deadly point. I have talked on this subject with an old saintly Mussalman whose prayers had been thus interrupted. He was drawing near to the hour of death, and all bitterness had departed from his heart; but the wound that had been left in his own beautiful spirit was evident.

Thus, on either side, these antagonisms have become most painful subjects to the devotees of both religions. Among the illiterate masses, who are chiefly impressed by outward observances, such irritations when actually paraded in the street become wellnigh intolerable. When the followers of Islam lead a cow in sacrifice along the main street with a sacrificial garland round its neck, marking it out for slaughter, or when the followers of Hinduism beat their drums with pompous idol-worship before the doors of the mosques, riots may take place and bloodshed ensue. It was to stop such shedding of blood and to atone for such sins of murder that Mahatma Gandhi undertook his famous Fast at Delhi which I have recorded elsewhere.

During all the centuries that have intervened since the first Mussalman invasion immense efforts have been made by good people on both sides to overcome these profound incompatibilities. In the Middle Ages the great saints of Hinduism throughout the whole extent of the North of India, from Bengal in the East to Sind in the West, made the most earnest and sustained effort to appreciate Islam. They interpreted the fundamental doctrine of the Unity of God as in accord with their own Upanishad teaching. They even treated idolatry and Caste as matters of supreme indifference. Furthermore, they paid respect to Islam along such lines of pure devotion and goodness that the Mussalman saints from their side—especially those who were called Sufis—welcomed Hindu religious philosophy and appropriated its ideals. Thus in different earlier generations it seemed almost possible that a harmony between Hinduism and Islam could be attained. But the crude orthodoxy on either side has continually stood in the way and thrown things back again into riot and confusion.

During one period of Mahatma Gandhi's career in India, which is called the Non-Co-operation Movement, he made the nearest approach to Islam that has ever been made by Hinduism in recent times. He found that the devout followers of Islam, who reverenced the Caliph at Constantinople as the Head of their religion, had been outraged by the ignominious terms of surrender imposed upon the Commander of the Faithful at the end of the War. For the victorious Allies threatened the Caliphate itself and were ready to destroy much of the Caliph's temporal authority, thus threatening Islam at its very centre.

For centuries past this sacred office of the Caliph had been filled by the Sultan of Turkey. The Indian Mussalmans, who number over seventy millions, had claimed from the Allies that if they took part in the war against the Turks the temporal and spiritual power of the Caliph should not be injured. They also claimed that there should be no interference with the Caliph's guardianship of the two holy cities, Mecca and Medina, which are visited by thousands of devout pilgrims every year. An official statement made by Mr. Lloyd George, the Prime Minister of Great Britain, in January, 1918, was regarded by all Indian Mussalmans as a satisfactory promise to them that these two matters of vital religious importance would be granted.

But when the War was over the conduct of the Allies in their treatment of the Sultan of Turkey was such that Mr. Lloyd George was immediately charged with flagrantly breaking his word. The Mussalman population of North India was deeply agitated, and a movement in favour of the Caliph, called the Khilafat Movement, was started in order to obtain better treatment for Turkey and to restore the power of the Caliph as Head of the Muslim Faith.

At this point Mahatma Gandhi, whose one intense longing had always been to unite Hindus and Mussalmans together in one common Indian Nation, seized the psychological opportunity of supporting the Mussalmans in what he held to be a righteous cause. He promised them his entire devotion on behalf of their Caliph and gave himself whole-heartedly to them. Thus this Khilafat question, which was agitating Islam in India, became for a time the direct means of a cordial reconciliation.

It has been necessary to narrate in plain terms this situation in North India at the end of the War in order to elucidate what lies behind the quotation which follows from Mahatma Gandhi's writing on the subject of "Hindu Muslim Unity." It will be seen just how far he was prepared to go and where he was obliged to draw the line. He writes:

> I have been asked whether, if I was sincere in my profession of Hindu-Muslim Unity, I would eat and drink with Mussalmans and give my daughter in marriage to a Muhammadan. This question has been put again by some friends in another form as follows: "Is it necessary for Hindu-Muslim Unity that there should be interdining and intermarrying?"
>
> The questioners say that if the two are necessary real unity can never take place, because many millions of orthodox Hindus would never reconcile themselves to interdining, much less to intermarriage.
>
> I am one of those who do not consider Caste to be a harmful institution. In its origin Caste was a wholesome custom and promoted national well-being. In my opinion the idea that interdining and intermarrying are necessary for national growth is a superstition borrowed from the West. Eating is a process just as vital as the other sanitary necessities of life; and if mankind had

not, much to its harm, made of eating a fetish and indulgence, we should have performed the operation of eating in private even as one performs the other necessary functions of life in private. Indeed, the highest culture in Hinduism regards eating in that light; and there are thousands of Hindus still living who will not eat their food in the presence of anybody else. I can recall the names of several cultured men and women who always eat their food in entire privacy, but who have never had any ill will against anybody and live on the friendliest terms with all.

Intermarriage is a still more difficult question. If brothers and sisters can live on the friendliest footing without ever thinking of marrying each other, I can see no difficulty in my daughter regarding every Mussalman as a brother and vice versa. I hold strong views on religion and on marriage. The greater the restraint we exercise with regard to our appetites, whether about eating or marrying, the better we become from a religious standpoint. I should despair of ever cultivating amicable relations with the world if I had to recognize the right or propriety of any young man offering his hand in marriage to my daughter, or to regard it as necessary for me to dine with anybody and everybody. I claim that I am living on terms of friendliness with the whole world. I have never quarrelled with a single Mussalman or Christian. For years past I have taken nothing but fruit in their households.* But the restraint, or exclusiveness, exercised in these matters by me has never affected the closest companionship with them.

The fact is that intermarriage and interdining are not necessary factors in friendship and unity, though they are often emblems thereof. But insistence on either the one or the other can easily become a bar to Hindu–Muslim Unity. If we make ourselves believe that Hindus and Mussalmans cannot be one unless they interdine and intermarry, we create an artificial barrier between us which could hardly be removed at all.

---

* Even conservative Hindus will often take uncooked fruit from the hands of Mussalmans and Christians. But to go farther and take *cooked* food is regarded as breaking Caste.

I hold it to be utterly impossible for Hindus and Muhammadans to intermarry and yet retain intact each other's religion; and the true beauty of Hindu–Muslim Unity lies in each remaining true to his own religion and yet being true to each other; for we are thinking of Hindus and Muhammadans, even of the most orthodox type, being able to regard one another no longer as natural enemies as they have done hitherto.

What, then, does the Hindu–Muslim Unity consist in, and how can it be best promoted? The answer is simple. It consists in our having a common purpose, a common goal, and common sorrows. It is best promoted by cooperating in order to reach the common goal, by sharing one another's sorrows and by mutual toleration. A common goal we have. We wish this great country of ours to be greater and self-governing. We have enough sorrows to share; and today, seeing that the Muhammadans are deeply touched on the question of the Khilafat and their cause is just, nothing can be so powerful for winning Muhammadan friendship for the Hindu as to give his whole-hearted support to the claim.

And mutual toleration is a necessity for all time and for all races. We cannot live in peace if the Hindus will not tolerate the Muhammadan form of worship of God and his manners and customs; or if the Muhammadans will be impatient of Hindu idolatry or cow-worship. It is not necessary for toleration that I must approve of what I tolerate. I heartily dislike liquor-drinking, meat-eating, and smoking; but I tolerate all these in Hindus, Muhammadans, and Christians, even as I expect them to tolerate my total abstinence from all these, although they may dislike it. All our quarrels have arisen from each wanting to force the other to his view.

The more we study Mahatma Gandhi's own life and teaching the more certain it becomes that the Hindu Religion has been the greatest of all influences in shaping his ideas and actions. He is in no sense a literalist or a fundamentalist in his adherence to the Hindu Scriptures. His extraordinary tolerance of and sympathy with other faiths colours his whole outlook on human life, and makes him at

times seem nearer to the acceptance of an indeterminate position
than he really is. But his mother's influence, as a devout and gentle
Hindu saint, perpetually returns to his mind and conscience, making
the fragrance of the ancient Hindu texts so sweet that nothing else
in the world can compare with them, to his own imagination, in
beauty and truth and sweetness. I have noticed this again and again
when living intimately with him and sharing his deepest thoughts
about religion.

This very fact of his conservative orthodoxy—running side by
side with a truly remarkable spiritual freedom—has been his strength
with the masses of common people. They have been able to understand him through this avenue of familiar Hindu Scriptures. His
homely speech in Hindi is everywhere replete with imagery and
illustration from the Hindu sacred books. His fasts and penances, his
vows and renunciations, are anxiously marked and quickly understood by the millions of simple villagers—those singularly devout
and prayerful people who flock everywhere to meet him.

On one such occasion, during the night of an eclipse of the
moon, I watched an audience of nearly one hundred thousand peasant
people, men and women, who had gathered from all the country-
side to listen to his simple words. They had collected together on
that night partly also with a view to perform some religious ceremony at the time of the eclipse; but so deep was their concentration
on the speaker that not one of them moved. The sight of Mahatma
Gandhi was regarded by each and all of them as itself a purification
and an act of religion. Just in the same manner as he never fails to
understand them, so they in turn never fail to understand him and
implicitly follow his guidance.

Thus Mahatma Gandhi remains rooted in the soil of India. He is
not *déraciné,* like so many of those who have stayed for a long time
away from India and have adopted wholesale Western customs. His
mind stretches out in ever wider and wider circles, as we shall notice
in subsequent writings; but the centre of his being ever remains
fixed in Hinduism itself, which is his first and only love.

Again and again, as I watched him, my thoughts have gone back
to Wordsworth's description of the skylark, so different from Shelley's

marvellous poem. In some respects Shelley's thought comes nearer to the surging flights of song of the poet Rabindranath Tagore. But with Mahatama Gandhi there is always the strong gravitation towards the soil of India, even in his boldest essays in idealism. He does not "despise the earth where cares abound," even while he remains ever at heart a "pilgrim of the sky." His "love-prompted strain," wherewith he mounts "to the last point of vision,"

Thrills not the less the bosom of the plain.

At all times and in all emergencies, to quote the last line of the sonnet, he abides

True to the kindred point of Heaven and Home.

If it be asked in conclusion what Mahatma Gandhi himself has owed consciously to Islam as a religious faith, in the same way that he has owed much to Buddhist and Christian teachings, the direct answer at first is not altogether plain; though it is obvious to those who know him personally in intimate ways that the contact with Islam has made an immense difference to his own life.

This much is certain: his profound admiration for the character of the Prophet Muhammad, as a man of faith and action, and also for his son-in-law Ali, as a man of tender love and suffering, has deeply affected him. He has studied very closely indeed the historical record of the rise of Islam, and has been impressed to a remarkable degree by the nobility of the early Caliphate and the fervent faith of the first followers of the Prophet. The bare simplicity with which they lived, their chivalrous devotion to the poor, their intense belief in God's overruling majesty—all these things have had a great effect upon him; for there is a Puritan strain in Mahatma Gandhi to which such things as these most forcibly appeal.

Furthermore, following the example set by the Prophet of Islam, Mahatma Gandhi has never for a moment separated the political from the spiritual, or failed to deal directly with the social evils which stood out before his eyes. Thus the Prophet's supreme, practical instinct as a Reformer, combined with his intense faith in God as the sole Creator and Director of the Universe, has been a constant strength and support to Mahatma Gandhi himself in his own struggle. All this I know personally from intimate experience. There is no one at his own home at Sabarmati to whom he goes more surely for quiet counsel, sympathy, and help in a time of prayer than to the Imam, who has accompanied him from South Africa and has taken up his abode with him at his own Ashram. Their mutual regard has remained constant and unchanging for over thirty years.

Furthermore, whenever Mahatma Gandhi has turned from this political aspect of the struggle, in order to gain strength for the great conception of suffering injury without retaliation, he has constantly taken the character of the Prophet's son-in-law Ali, and of Hasan and Husain, for his example. The story of the suffering of these descendants of the Prophet, which is recited annually at each Muharram celebration, is indeed full of the deepest pathos. It illustrates how the human heart is most profoundly moved by stories of heroic endurance meekly and silently borne. There is a verse of William Blake, which deserves to be more widely known in this connection, where he writes

A tear is an intellectual thing,
And a sigh is the sword of an angel King.
And the bitter groan of a martyr's woe
Is an arrow from the Almighty's bow.

It is this "irresistible might of meekness"—as Milton calls it—which has always appealed most to Mahatma Gandhi, and it is interesting to see where he finds it exemplified in the religion of Islam.

If it be further asked whether the same characteristic can be found in the life of the Prophet himself, Mahatma Gandhi in his writings often refers to the early days of the Prophet's mission, when he was despised and rejected by his own countrymen and was fain to submit to every form of humiliation in silence. He has also related the story of the first days of Islam, when both the Prophet and his followers were content to live in the most self-denying manner and were accessible to the humblest of mankind. The Caliphs who directly succeeded the Prophet remained equally lowly in outward circumstance while their armies were conquering great kingdoms. In these aspects of true humility Mahatma Gandhi has continually set before the whole of India an illustration of the power of suffering to overcome the hardest heart. Thus in his own way he has found the teaching of the Prophet of Islam fully compatible with the principle of Ahimsa, or Non-violence, whereon he lays such stress.

Gandhi as a law-student in London

3

THE CHRISTIAN CONTACT

Mahatma Gandhi may be described, as the previous chapters will have shown, as an orthodox, conservative Hindu, with a deep sense of spiritual freedom and an equally deep passion for inward reform in Hinduism itself. His own religious principle of "Swadeshi," which he has defined as carefully as possible in precise words, has always prevented him from contemplating any abandonment of his ancestral faith. [See Chapter 6.] The nearest approach to such a possibility, even in the vague realm of contemplation, has been when he has said repeatedly that, if he was forced to believe that "untouchability" was an integral part of Hinduism, he would at once abandon such a faith. But in practice he has demonstrated that the Hindu Religion, both in its origin and in its practice, carries with it no such inhuman doctrine.

With regard to Mahatma Gandhi's relationship with Christians and the Christian Religion, I am fortunately able to draw upon abundant material from his own speeches and writings. There is also a valuable conversation with him in Johannesburg in early days, when his mind had been detached in a great measure from the outward ceremonials of Hinduism and he had constantly taken a silent part in acts of Christian worship by attending different churches and conventions. It will be the simplest course to quote in full a vivid description of his views at that time, as given by the Rev. J. J. Doke, of Johannesburg, one of his closest Christian friends, whose faithful record Mahatma Gandhi himself endorsed. He wrote as follows:

> One night, when the house was still, we argued out the matter into the morning, and these are the results.
>
> His conviction is that old Hinduism was a pure faith, free from idolatry; that the spiritual faith of India has been corrupted by

33

materialism, and because of this she has lost her place in the vanguard of the progressive nations; that through the ages God, pervading all, has manifested Himself in different forms, becoming incarnate, for the purpose of salvation, with the object of leading men back into the right path. The Gita makes Krishna say:

"When religion decays and when irreligion prevails, then I manifest myself. For the protection of the good, for the destruction of evil, for the firm establishment of religion, I am born again and again."

"But," said I, "has Christianity any essential place in your theology?"

"It is part of it," he said. "Jesus Christ is a bright revelation."

"But not the unique revelation he is to me," I replied immediately, with feeling.

"Not in the sense you mean," he said frankly. "I cannot set him on a solitary throne, because I believe God has been incarnate again and again."

To him Religion is an intensely practical thing. It underlies all action. Politics, morals, commerce—all that has to do with conscience must be Religion. He can only think in this way.

Naturally his imagination is profoundly stirred by the Sermon on the Mount. The idea of self-renunciation pictured there, as well as in the Bhagavad Gita and *The Light of Asia,* wins his complete assent. Self-mastery, self-denial, self-surrender, under the guidance of the Spirit of God, are, in his conception of life, stepping-stones to the ultimate goal of all, complete absorption of redeemed Man in God.

I question whether any religious creed would be large enough to express his views, or any church system ample enough to shut him in and enfold him.

An incident will illustrate what I have said. Mr. Gandhi suggested that we should visit the sick wife of Thambi Naidu, who was in prison as a passive resister. On our way we were joined by the Muhammadan Maulvi and a Jewish helper in the struggle, together with the Imam of the Mosque. There we were—two Mussalmans, a Jew, and a Christian—visiting this Hindu lady.

She was within a few days of the suffering of motherhood. After we had all bent together in silent prayer, the Maulvi spoke a few words to comfort her. It was one of the many glimpses we have had lately of that Divine Love which mocks at the boundaries of creeds and limits of colour and race. It was a vision of Mr. Gandhi's own ideal.

Owing chiefly to his sense of the sacredness of life, vegetarianism is with Mr. Gandhi a deep religious principle. The battle was fought out in childhood under his mother's influence. But since that time abstinence from all animal food has become a matter of strong conviction with him and he preaches it zealously. When in these Transvaal prisons the authorities persisted in cooking the crushed mealies of the prisoners in animal fat, his followers preferred to starve rather than to touch it.

It is also part of his creed to live simply. He believes that all luxury is wrong. He teaches that a great deal of sickness, and most of the sins of our day, may be traced to this source. To curb and discipline the flesh with a strong hand, to crucify it, to bring the needs of his own life—Thoreau- and Tolstoy-like—within the narrowest limits, are positive delights to him, only to be rivalled by the joy of guiding other lives into the same path.

I write this in the house in which he usually lives when in Johannesburg. Yonder is the open stove; there is the rolled-up mattress on which he sleeps. It would be difficult to imagine a life less open to the assaults of pride or sloth than the life lived here; everything that can minister to the flesh is abjured.

Mr. Gandhi is not a Christian in any orthodox sense. Perhaps orthodox Christianity has itself to blame for this. There is little inducement in South Africa for an Indian to recognize the Loveliness of Christ under the disguise in which Christianity clothes the Lord. What interest has the Christian Church in Johannesburg shown in these thousands from India and China who for years have been residents in our midst? Practically none. Are they encouraged to believe that they, too, are souls for whom Christ died? By no means.

Here and there individual efforts have been made, and some

few Indians attend Christian places of worship, but for the most part they have been left severely alone; while the few men who have tried to show that there is still a heart of love in the Church of Christ, and have dared to speak a word on behalf of a suffering people, have been subjected to all manner of abuse and have been made to suffer with them. It is this discrepancy between a beautiful creed and our treatment of the Indian at the door which repels the man who thinks.

We have failed also to realize the inwardness of the Passive Resistance Movement. It is their claim, put forward in suffering, to be treated by Christians in a Christian way.

Meanwhile, although according to my thinking the seeker has not yet reached the goal, I cannot forget what the Master Himself said, "Not everyone that saith unto Me, Lord, Lord, shall enter into the Kingdom of Heaven, but he that doeth the will of My Father which is in Heaven."

We have another record, in Mr. Gandhi's own words, of a friendship with a Quaker, named Mr. Coates, which may be quoted to complete the story of those times. It should be mentioned that both Gandhi and Tagore regard the Society of Friends as the nearest representation of what they themselves have read about the Christian life in the Gospels. He writes thus:

Mr. Coates had a great affection for me. We went out walking together and he also took me to other Christian friends. In pure faith I consented to read the books he sent me, and as I went on reading them we discussed them. I do not remember the names of them all; but they included the *Commentary* of Dr. Parker of the City Temple, Pearson's *Many Infallible Proofs,* and Butler's *Analogy.* Parts of these were unintelligible to me. I liked some things in them, while I did not like others. *Many Infallible Proofs* were proofs in support of the religion of the Bible as the author understood it; the book had no effect on me. Parker's *Commentary* was morally stimulating, but it could not be of any help to one who had no faith in the prevalent Christian beliefs. Butler's *Analogy* struck me as being a very profound and difficult book, which should be read four or five times to be understood properly. It seemed to me to be written with a view to converting atheists to Theism. The arguments advanced in it regarding the existence of God were unnecessary for me, as I had then passed the stage of unbelief; but the arguments in proof of Jesus being the only Incarnation of God and the Mediator between God and man left me unmoved.

But Mr. Coates was not the man easily to accept defeat. He had great affection for me. He saw, round my neck, the Vaishnava necklace of Tulasi-beads. He thought it to be superstition, and was pained by it. "This superstition does not become you. Come, let me break the necklace."

"No, you will not. It is a sacred gift from my mother."

"But do you believe in it?"

"I do not know its mysterious significance. I do not think I should come to harm if I did not wear it. But I cannot, without sufficient reason, give up a necklace that she put round my neck out of love and in the conviction that it would be conducive to my welfare. When with the passage of time it wears away and breaks of its own accord, I shall have no desire to get a new one. But this necklace cannot be broken."

Mr. Coates could not appreciate my argument, as he had no regard for my religion. He was looking forward to delivering me from the abyss of ignorance. He wanted to convince me that no matter whether there was some truth in other religions salvation was impossible for me unless I accepted Christianity, which represented *the* truth, and that my sins would not be washed away except by the intercession of Jesus, and that all good works were useless.

Mr. Gandhi then goes on to describe his contact at this time with a Plymouth Brother, who argued with him that it was impossible to live in this world sinless, and therefore Jesus suffered and atoned for all the sins of mankind. Only he who accepted Christ's great redemption could have continual peace, even while he went on sinning: otherwise life was restless and uncertain in this world of sin.

Mahatma Gandhi continues his story as follows:

This argument utterly failed to convince me. I humbly replied:

"If this be the Christianity acknowledged by all Christians, I cannot accept it. I do not seek redemption from the consequences of my sin; I seek to be redeemed from sin itself, or rather from the very thought of sin. Until I have attained that end I shall be content to be restless."

To which the Plymouth Brother rejoined: "I assure you your attempt is fruitless. Think again over what I have said."

And the Brother proved as good as his word. He voluntarily committed transgressions, and showed me that he was undisturbed by the thought of them.

But already I knew, before meeting with these friends, that all Christians did not believe in such a theory of Atonement. Mr. Coates himself walked in the fear of God. His heart was pure, and he believed in the possibility of self-purification. Others also shared his belief. Some of the books that came into my hands were full of devotion. So, although Mr. Coates was very much disturbed by this latest experience of mine, I was able to reassure him and tell him that the distorted belief of a Plymouth Brother could not prejudice me against Christianity.

My difficulties lay elsewhere. They were with regard to the Bible and its accepted interpretation.

We are able to connect this passage from his *Autobiography* with a remarkable address which Mahatma Gandhi delivered to the Christian missionaries assembled in Calcutta at the Y.W.C.A. on July 28, 1925.

Not many of you know that my association with Christians— not Christians so-called but *real* Christians—dates from 1889, when as a lad I found myself in London; and that association has grown riper as years have rolled on. In South Africa, where I found myself in the midst of inhospitable surroundings, I was able to make hundreds of Christian friends. I came in touch with the late Mr. Spencer Watton, Director of the South Africa General Mission, and later with the great divine, the Rev.

Andrew Murray, and several others.

There was even a time in my life when a very sincere and intimate friend of mine, a great and good Quaker, had designs on me. He thought that I was too good not to become a Christian. I was sorry to have to disappoint him. One missionary friend of mine in South Africa still writes to me and asks me, "How is it with you?" I have always told him that so far as I know it is all well with me. If it was prayer that these friends expected me to make, I was able to tell them that every day the heartfelt prayer within the closed door of my closet went to the Almighty to show me light and give me wisdom and courage to follow that light.

In answer to promises made to one of these Christian friends of mine, I thought it my duty to see one of the biggest of Indian Christians, the late Kali Charan Banerjee. I went to him with an absolutely open mind and in a receptive mood, and I met him also under circumstances which were most affecting. I found that there was much in common between Mr. Banerjee and myself. His simplicity, his humility, his courage, his truthfulness—all these things I have all along admired. He met me when his wife was on her death-bed. You cannot imagine a more impressive scene, a more ennobling circumstance. I told Mr. Banerjee: "I have come to you as a seeker"—this was in 1901—"I have come to you in fulfilment of a sacred promise I have made to some of my dearest Christian friends that I will leave no stone unturned to find out the true light." I told him that I had given my friends the assurance that no worldly gain would keep me away from the light if I could but see it. Well, I am not going to engage you in giving a description of the little discussion that we had between us. It was very good, very noble. I came away, not sorry, not dejected, not disappointed, but I felt sad that even Mr. Banerjee could not convince me. This was my final, deliberate striving to realize Christianity as it was presented to me.

Today my position is that, though I admire much in Christianity, I am unable to identify myself with orthodox

Christianity. I must tell you in all humility that Hinduism as I know it entirely satisfies my soul, fills my whole being, and I find a solace in the Bhagavad Gita and Upanishads that I miss even in the Sermon on the Mount. Not that I do not prize the ideal presented therein; not that some of the precious teachings in the Sermon on the Mount have not left a deep impression upon me; but I must confess to you that when doubt haunts me, when disappointments stare me in the face, and when I see not one ray of light on the horizon, I turn to the Bhagavad Gita, and find a verse to comfort me; and I immediately begin to smile in the midst of overwhelming sorrow. My life has been full of external tragedies, and if they have not left any visible and indelible effect on me, I owe it to the teachings of the Bhagavad Gita.

I have told you all these things in order to make absolutely clear to you where I stand, so that I may have, if you will, closer touch with you. I must add that I did not stop studying the Bible and the commentaries and other books on Christianity that my friends placed in my hands; but I said to myself that if I was to find my satisfaction through reasoning, I must study the scriptures of other religions also and make my choice. And I turned to the Quran. I tried to understand what I could of Judaism as distinguished from Christianity. I studied Zoroastrianism, and I came to the conclusion that all religions were right, and every one of them imperfect, because they were interpreted with our poor intellects, sometimes with our poor hearts, and more often misinterpreted. In all religions I found to my grief that there were various and even contradictory interpretations of some texts, and I said to myself, "Not these things for me. If I want the satisfaction of my soul I must feel my way. I must wait silently upon God and ask Him to guide me." There is a beautiful verse in Sanskrit which says, "God helps only when man feels utterly helpless and utterly humble." When I was studying Tamil I found in one of the books of Dr. Pope a Tamil proverb which means, "God helps the helpless." I have given you this life-story of my own experience for you to ponder over.

You, the missionaries, come to India thinking that you come to a land of heathen, of idolators, of men who do not know God. One of the greatest Christian divines, Bishop Heber, wrote two lines which have always left a sting with me: "Where every prospect pleases and only Man is vile." I wish he had not written them. My own experience in my travels throughout India has been to the contrary. I have gone from one end of the country to the other, without any prejudice, in a relentless search after Truth, and I am *not* able to say that here in this fair land, watered by the great Ganges, the Brahmaputra, and the Jumna, man is vile. He is *not* vile. He is as much a seeker after truth as you and I are, possibly more so. [See Appendix 3.]

This reminds me of a French book translated for me by a French friend. It is an account of an imaginary expedition in search of Knowledge. One party landed in India and found Truth and God personified in a little pariah's hut. I tell you there are many such huts belonging to the "untouchables" where you will certainly find God. They do not reason, but they persist in their belief that God is. They depend upon God for His assistance and find it, too. There are many stories told throughout the length and breadth of India about these noble "untouchables." Vile outwardly as some of them may be, there are noblest specimens of humanity in their midst.

But does my experience exhaust itself merely with the "untouchables"? No, I am here to tell you that there are non-Brahmins, there are Brahmins, who are as fine specimens of humanity as you will find in any place on the earth. There are Brahmins today in India who are embodiments of self-sacrifice, godliness, and humility. There are Brahmins who are devoting themselves body and soul to the service of "untouchables," but with execration from orthodoxy. They do not mind it, because in serving pariahs they are serving God.

I can quote chapter and verse from my experience. I place these facts before you in all humility for the simple reason that you may know this land better, the land which you have come to serve. You are here to find out the distress of the people of

India and remove it. But I hope you are here also in receptive mood; and if there is anything that India has to give you, you will not stop your ears, you will not close your eyes and steel your hearts, to receive all that may be good in this land. I give you my assurance that there is a great deal of good in India.

Do not flatter yourselves with the belief that a mere recital of that celebrated verse in St. John makes a man a Christian. If I have read the Bible correctly, I know many men who have never known the name of Jesus Christ, men who have even rejected the official interpretation of Christianity, but would nevertheless, if Jesus came in our midst today in the flesh, be probably owned by Him more than many of us. I therefore ask you to approach the problem before you with open-heartedness and humility.

It has often occurred to me that a seeker after truth has to be silent. I know the wonderful efficacy of silence. I visited a Trappist monastery in South Africa. A beautiful place it was. Most of the inmates of that place were under a vow of silence. I inquired of the Father the motive of it, and he said that the motive is apparent. We are frail human beings. We do not know very often what we say. If we want to listen to the still small voice that is always speaking within us, it will not be heard if we continually speak. I understand that precious lesson. I know the secret of silence.

I have told my missionary friends, "Noble as you are, you have isolated yourselves from the people whom you want to serve." I cannot help recalling to you the conversation I related in Darjeeling at the Missionary Language School. Lord Salisbury was waited upon by a deputation of missionaries in connection with China, and this deputation wanted protection. I cannot recall the exact words, but give you the purport of the answer Lord Salisbury gave. He said: "Gentlemen, if you want to go to China to preach the message of Christianity, then do not ask for assistance of the temporal power. Go with your lives in your hands, and if the people of China want to kill you, imagine that you have been killed in service of God!" Lord

Salisbury was right. Christian missionaries come to India under the shadow, or, if you like, under the protection of a temporal power, and it creates an impassable bar.

If you give me statistics that so many orphans have been reclaimed and brought to the Christian faith, I would accept them; but I do not feel convinced thereby that this is your mission. In my opinion your mission is infinitely superior to that. You want to find true men and women in India; and if you want to do that you will have to go to the lowly cottages—not to give them something, but it might be to take something from them. A true friend, as I claim to be of the missionaries of India and of the Europeans, I speak to you what I feel from the bottom of my heart. I miss receptiveness, humility, willingness on your part to identify yourselves with the masses of India. I have talked straight from my heart. May I find a response from your hearts?

It has come to my mind, while putting together this chapter, that I cannot do better than supplement Mahatma Gandhi's views about Christianity with his own beautiful description of the Rev. J. J. Doke, who had remained his personal friend and helper during the long Passive Resistance Struggle in South Africa. Mahatma Gandhi always recognized in him his ideal of what a Christian ought to be. The story that leads up to the description of Mr. Doke may be quickly told. Mr. Gandhi had been assaulted, owing to a grievous mistake, by some of his fellow-countrymen, called Pathans, who wrongly imagined that he was betraying their cause. Mr. Doke had found him lying wounded in the streets of Johannesburg, and, like a good Samaritan, had rescued him at the most critical moment of all and had taken him to his own house. Mr. Gandhi's description begins at this point as follows:

Mr. Doke and his good wife were anxious that I should be perfectly at rest and peaceful, and were therefore pained to witness my mental activity after the assault. They were afraid that it might react in a manner prejudicial to my health. They therefore, by making signs and similar devices, removed all persons

from near my bed, and asked me not to write or do anything.
I made a request in writing that before and in order that I
might lie down quietly their daughter Olive, who was then
only a little girl, should sing for me my favourite English hymn,
"Lead, Kindly Light." Mr. Doke liked this very much and
acceded to my request with a sweet smile. He called Olive by
signs and asked her to stand at the door and sing the hymn in
a low tone. The whole scene passes before my eyes as I dictate
this, and the melodious voice of little Olive reverberates in my
ears. How shall I describe the service rendered to me by the
Doke family?

Mr. Joseph Doke was a Baptist minister, then forty-six years
old, and had been in New Zealand before he came to South
Africa. Some six months before this assault he came to my
office and sent in his card. On seeing the word "Reverend"
before his name I wrongly imagined that he had come, as some
other clergymen did, to convert me to Christianity, or to advise
me to give up the struggle, or perhaps to express patronizing
sympathy with the movement. Mr. Doke entered, and we had
not talked many minutes before I saw how sadly I had misjudged
him and mentally apologized to him. I found him familiar with
all the facts of the struggle which we published in newspapers.
He said:"Please consider me as your friend in this struggle. I consider it my religious duty to render you such help as I can. If I
have learned any lesson from the life of Jesus it is this, that one
should share and lighten the load of those who are heavily
laden." We thus got acquainted with each other, and every day
marked an advance in our mutual affection and intimacy.

Now after I was injured, while I was lying in his house, all
day and night, one or other member of the family would be
waiting upon me. The house became a sort of caravanserai so
long as I stayed there. All classes of Indians flocked to the place
to inquire after my health and to see me, from the humble
hawker, basket in hand with dirty clothes and dusty boots, right
up to the Chairman of the Transvaal British Indian Association.
Mr. Doke would receive all of them in his drawing-room with

uniform courtesy and consideration, and so long as I lived with the Dokes all their time was occupied either with nursing me or with receiving the hundreds of people who looked in to see me. Even at night Mr. Doke would quietly peep twice or thrice into my room. While living under his hospitable roof I never so much as felt that it was not my home, or that my nearest and dearest could have looked after me better than the Dokes.

And it must not be supposed that Mr. Doke had not to suffer for according public support to the Indians in their struggle and for harbouring me under his roof. Mr. Doke was in charge of a Baptist church, and depended for his livelihood upon a congregation of Europeans, not all of whom entertained liberal views, and among whom dislike of the Indians was perhaps as general as among the other Europeans. But Mr. Doke was unmoved by it. I had discussed this delicate subject with him in the very beginning of our acquaintance; and he said: "My dear friend, what do you think of the religion of Jesus? I claim to be a humble follower of Him who cheerfully mounted the Cross for the faith that was in Him, and whose love was as wide as the world. I must take a public part in your struggle if I am at all desirous of representing Christ to the Europeans, who, you are afraid, will give me up to punishment. I must not complain if they do thus give me up. My livelihood is indeed derived from them, but you certainly do not think that I am associated with them for living's sake, or that they are my cherishers. My cherisher is God; they are but the instruments of His Almighty will. It is one of the unwritten conditions of my connection with them that none of them may interfere with my religious liberty. Please therefore stop worrying on my account. I am taking my place beside you in this struggle not to oblige the Indians, but as a matter of duty. The fact, however, is that I have fully discussed this question with my deacon. I gently informed him that if he did not approve of my relations with the Indians he might permit me to retire and engage another minister instead. But he not only asked me not to trouble myself about it; he even spoke some words of encouragement. Again, you must not imagine that all Europeans alike entertain hatred against your people. You can have no idea of the silent sympathy of many with your tribulations, and you will agree with me that I must know about it, situated as I am.

After this clear explanation I never referred to the subject again; and later on, when Mr. Doke died in the pursuit of his holy calling in Rhodesia, at a time when the Satyagraha struggle was still in progress, the Baptists called a meeting in their church, to which they invited the late Mr. Cachalia and other Indians as well as myself, and which they asked me to address.

About ten days afterwards I had recovered enough strength to move about fairly well, and I then took my leave of this godly family. The parting was a great wrench to myself no less than to the Dokes.

It will not be difficult to gather from these quotations, taken from Mahatma Gandhi's own writings, how profoundly impressed he has been in his own heart by the inner truth of the Christian message in its moral aspect. He has also witnessed at close quarters that message lived out in action by those who truly believed in it and felt its vital power. How deeply that sight had entered into his own life I experienced personally when I went with him to Johannesburg after the signing of the Gandhi-Smuts Agreement in January 1914. There were a thousand things to be done there which had been kept waiting for many months; but at the very first moment after our arrival he said to me, "Charlie, I want to take you on a pilgrimage."

"What do you mean?" I said to him—not following his thought. "Where do you want to go on pilgrimage?"

"I want to go with you," he explained, "to the house of Mrs. Doke, who nursed me like a mother back to health when I was injured here."

We walked together to Mrs. Doke's house, and each step of the way he related to me this same touching incident that has been told in his own language above. When he came to the house it was difficult for him to control his emotion as he saw Mrs. Doke in her widow's dress with her face pale and worn with suffering. She on her part treated him with all the tenderness of a mother, forgetting her own suffering in her anxiety about his health and that of Mrs. Gandhi. She went on asking questions about the latter, who was very ill at the time.

Then at last, after a little while, she told us the story of the death of her husband from a malignant fever, far away in the interior of Africa, in Rhodesia. He had gone there, long after middle age had come upon him, in order to carry, to those who had never heard the Gospel, the "unsearchable riches of Christ." It was a narrative full of tragic pathos—how they had tried to carry the dying saint into a hospital-station, where he could receive the best medical help, and how his life had suddenly ebbed away. Mrs. Doke had set out herself at once, in order to rejoin him and nurse him; but she had not been able to meet him before death came. The simplicity with which she spoke added to the sadness of her words. Mr. Gandhi, who had himself gone through far more suffering than most people, was clearly overcome, and the tears were in his eyes as he listened.

For many years since that day in Johannesburg I have lived in close companionship with him, and whenever he has spoken concerning Mr. and Mrs. Doke and their children, his reverence for that truly Christian family has been abundantly evident in every word he has uttered.

Another incident may be mentioned. Towards the end of the twenty-one days' Fast at Delhi, which will be recorded elsewhere, I had come back from the Holy Communion service at St. James's Church, and had still in my mind the recollection of a hymn which we had just sung in church. So I sang it to him:

I am not worthy, cold and bare
The lodging of my soul!
How canst Thou deign to enter there?
Lord, speak, and make me whole.

While I was explaining to him the Gospel setting from which the hymn was taken he said to me: "You need not tell me about the story, Charlie, for I know it quite well; and also I have often heard that hymn. Perhaps you have not yet understood how very often I used to attend the Sunday services in Johannesburg, and what a pleasure it was to me at that time to do so. Some of the truest friends I have had in the world were the Christian friends I made there. That hymn was one of those I heard, and it is very sweet to me to hear it now at such a time as this. It reminds me of those days long gone by when I was in South Africa."

Whenever I have been present in Sabarmati Ashram, it has always been his custom to ask me, towards the close of his prayers, to sing a Christian hymn. The two which he himself nearly always chooses are

Lead kindly Light, amid the encircling gloom,

and one which sometimes he puts first of all,

When I survey the wondrous Cross.

Further hymns which I have sung with acceptance have been

Nearer my God to Thee, nearer to Thee;
E'en though it be a cross that raiseth me,

and the evening hymn,

Abide with me. Fast falls the eventide.
The darkness deepens, Lord with me abide.

At one time, also, he told me that the hymn

Rock of Ages cleft for me

had been a very great comfort in hours of darkness and despondency.*

---

* For further quotations from Mahatma Gandhi's writings on this subject see Appendix 4 and Appendix 5.

4

"THE PLACE OF JESUS"

The title I have given to this chapter is the heading of an article included in it which Mahatma Gandhi contributed to his own paper, *Young India*. It will describe still further the position which organized Christianity holds in India today and Mr. Gandhi's relation to it.

The overlapping of Christian Missionary work by the forceful and pervasive environment of the British administration in India—so that in many missionary stations there is very little outward sign of any distinction between the British civil rule and the Mission work—has led to a painful and almost universal confusion about the essential meaning of the Christian Religion among orthodox Hindus and Muhammadans. This confusion has been acutely apparent for the last fifty years or more, and has been heartily disliked by every earnest missionary who has come out to work in India. It is only just beginning to break down today.

This tragic situation, in which earnest and sincere men and women are forced into a false position, has been dramatically represented in a recent remarkable play by Edward Thompson, the University Lecturer in Bengali at Oxford. The play is called *Atonement*. The crisis comes in the drama when Gregory, the Principal of the Missionary College, becomes obliged to take up his rifle and join with the rest of the British in the station (who are all officials) in order to put down, by military force, a sudden political riot in the village. The actual circumstance here dramatized might be considered exceptional, but it depicts a desperately impossible situation for a missionary of the Gospel of Christ in India.

No one who has only lived in Europe or America, in complete inexperience of this worldly entanglement, can realize what it has led to, and how exotic the Indian Christian community has become in consequence, over large areas of India and Ceylon. There could not be found in the world a kinder or gentler critic than Mahatma Gandhi. Therefore the very restraint of many of the things that he has written on this subject should only serve to make all the more obvious to those who read them in the West what intense bitterness those Indians who are ardent and exclusive nationalists feel when they witness this identification of the Indian Christian community with the foreign political power. Not everyone has the large-hearted charity of Mr. Gandhi.

It is quite true that orthodox Hindus were themselves greatly to blame for outcasting noble men like Kali Charan Banerjee, Piary Mohan Rudra, Nilakantha Goreh, and others, who were among the greatest Indian patriots of their own generation, and men of conscience, sincerity, and truth. Such converts as these only became Christians out of utter conviction of soul, and their sincere convictions ought to have been sincerely respected. The almost complete social boycott that pursued them was surely wrong. Therefore Hindu orthodoxy must share some part of the pitiful result.

But today, in India, the Indian Christians could easily win back their rightful position in the life of the body politic if only they would follow the sound advice that Mahatma Gandhi has so often given. Let me add at once that a transformation is now taking place very rapidly indeed. Dr. S. K. Datta, K. T. Paul, and others have already pointed the way forward.

The following passages from his writings appear to me of deep and living interest in this connection, and they demand careful study. He writes this about his own childhood in Kathiawar, referring to an almost incredible state of things which has long since passed away:

> Only Christianity found little toleration as a creed from my father, who was tolerant towards all other faiths. I developed myself a sort of dislike for it. And for a reason. In those days Christian missionaries used to stand in a corner near the High School and hold forth, pouring abuse on Hindus and their gods. I could not stomach this. I must have stood there to hear

them once only, but that was enough to dissuade me from repeating the experiment. About the same time I heard of a well-known Hindu having been converted to Christianity. It was the talk of the town that when he was baptized he had to eat beef and drink liquor, that he also had to change his clothes, and that thenceforth he began to go about in European costume, including a hat. These things got on my nerves. Surely, thought I, a religion that compelled one to eat beef, drink liquor, and change one's own clothes did not deserve the name. I also heard that the new convert had already begun abusing the religion of his ancestors, their customs, and their country. All these things created in me a dislike for Christianity.

Mr. Scott, who was a missionary in Rajkot, Kathiawar, during those early days, sent a very kindly letter to Mahatma Gandhi, pointing out that the actual stories about beef-eating and liquor-drinking, at the time of becoming a Christian, were mere bazaar rumours and even wilful inventions. To this Mr. Gandhi replied:

Though the preaching took place over forty years ago, the painful memory of it is still vivid before me. What I have heard and read since has but confirmed that first impression. I have read several missionary publications, and they appear able only to see the dark side, and to paint it darker still. The famous hymn of Bishop Heber's, "From Greenland's Icy Mountains," in its second verse is a clear libel on Indian humanity. I was favoured with some literature, even in the Yerawada prison, by well-meaning missionaries, which seemed to be written as if merely to belittle Hinduism. About beef-eating and wine drinking at baptism I have merely stated what I *heard,* and I have said as much in my Autobiography. Whilst I accept Mr. Scott's repudiation, I must say that, though I have mixed freely among thousands of Christian Indians, I know very few who have scruples about eating beef or other flesh-meats and drinking intoxicating liquors.

When I have gently reasoned with them they have quoted to me the celebrated verse, "Call thou nothing unclean"—as if it referred to eating and drinking, and gave a licence for indulgence.

I know that many Hindus eat meat; some eat even beef and
drink wine. They are not converts. Converts are those who are
"born again," or should be. A higher standard is expected of
those who change their faith, if the change is a matter of the
heart and not of convenience. But I must not enter into these
deeper waters. It is a matter of pleasure to me to be able to say
that, if I have had painful experiences of Christians and
Christian missionaries, I have pleasant ones also which I treasure. There is no doubt that among them the spirit of toleration
is growing. Among individuals there is also a deeper study of
Hinduism and other faiths, and an appreciation of their beauties, and among some even an admission that the other great
faiths of the world are not false. One is thankful for the growing liberal spirit; but I have the conviction that much still
remains to be done in that direction.

A further revealing passage in the Autobiography records a conversation with one of the leaders of the South African Indian
Community, Abdulla Sheth, a sturdy Muhammadan patriot.

"But," said I, "there are so many young Indians born and educated here. Do not they help you?"

"They!" exclaimed Abdulla Sheth in despair. "They never
care to come to us; and, to tell you the truth, we care less to recognize them. Being Christians, they are under the thumb of the
white clergymen, who in their turn are subject to the
Government."

This opened my eyes. I felt that this class should be claimed
as our own. Was this the meaning of Christianity? Did they
cease to be Indians because they had become Christians?

There are, besides these different personal reminiscences, two very
important recent speeches, delivered in India and Ceylon by
Mahatma Gandhi on those long tours throughout the country, during
which he addressed in turn every single community. In Calcutta he
spoke to the Christians as follows:

When I wander about throughout the length and breadth of India I see many Christian Indians almost ashamed of their birth, certainly of their ancestral religion and of their ancestral dress. The aping of Europeans on the part of Anglo-Indians is bad enough; but the aping of them by Indian converts is a violence done to their country, and, shall I say, even to their new religion.

There is a verse in the New Testament to bid Christians avoid meat if it would offend their neighbours. Meat here, I presume, included drink and dress. I can appreciate uncompromising avoidance of all that is evil in the old; yet where there is not only no question of anything evil, but where an ancient practice may be even desirable, it would be a crime to part with it when one knows for certain that the giving up would deeply hurt relatives and friends.

Conversion must not mean denationalization. Conversion should mean a definite giving up of the evil of the old, adoption of all the good of the new, and a scrupulous avoidance of everything evil in the new. Conversion, therefore, should mean a life of greater dedication to one's own country, greater surrender to God, greater self-purification.

Years ago I met the late Kali Charan Banerjee. Had I not known before I went there that he was a Christian, I should certainly not have noticed from the outward appearance of his home that he was one. It was no different from an ordinary modern Hindu home, simple and meagre in furniture. That great man was dressed like an ordinary un-Europeanized Hindu Bengali.

I know that there is a marvellous change coming over Christian Indians. There is on the part of a large number of them a longing to revert to original simplicity, a longing to belong to the nation and to serve it; but the process is too slow. There need be no waiting. It requires not much effort. Even as I write I have a letter from a Christian Indian before me telling me that he and his friends find it difficult to make the change because of the opposition of their superiors. Some of them tell me that they are even jealously watched, and any movement on their part to identify themselves with national movements is strongly condemned.

The late Principal Rudra and I used often to discuss this evil tendency. I well remember how he used to deplore it. I am offering a tribute to the memory of a dead friend when I inform the reader that he used often to express his grief that it was too late in life for him to change some of the unnecessary European habits to which he was brought up. Is it not truly deplorable that many Christian Indians discard their own mother tongue and bring up their children only to speak in English? Do they not thereby completely cut themselves adrift from the nation in whose midst they have to live?

But they may answer in self-defence that many Hindus and even Mussalmans have become denationalized. The *tu quoque* argument serves no useful purpose. I am writing not as a critic but as a friend, who has enjoyed for the past thirty years the closest intimacy with hundreds of Christian Indians.

On a still later occasion, at Colombo, Mr. Gandhi delivered an address, which was much commented on at the time, called "The Place of Jesus." From this address I have taken the title of the present chapter. It contained the following passages:

> For many years I have regarded Jesus of Nazareth as one among the mighty teachers that the world has had, and I say this in all humility. I claim humility for this expression because this is exactly what I feel. Of course, Christians claim a higher place for Jesus of Nazareth than I, as a non-Christian and a Hindu, am able to feel. I purposely use the word "feel" instead of "give" because I consider that neither I nor anybody else can possibly arrogate to himself the claim of *giving* a place to a great man.
>
> For the great teachers of mankind have not had their places *given* to them. That place has belonged to them as a matter of right, as a matter of service; but it is the privilege of the lowest and humblest amongst us to *feel* certain things about them. The relation between ourselves and the great teachers is somewhat after the style of the relation between wife and husband. It

would be a terrible thing, a tragic thing, if I were to argue out intellectually for myself what place I was to give to the wife of my heart. It is not, indeed, a matter of my *giving* at all. She takes the place that belongs to her as a matter of right in my heart. It is a matter purely for feeling. Thus I can say that Jesus occupies in my heart the place of one of the great teachers who have made a considerable influence on my life.

I say to the 75 percent of Hindus receiving instruction in this college that your lives also will be incomplete unless you reverently study the teaching of Jesus. I have come to the conclusion in my own experience that those who, no matter to what faith they belong, reverently study the teaching of other faiths, broaden instead of narrowing their own hearts. Personally I do not regard any of the great religions of the world as false. All have served to enrich mankind, and are now even serving their purpose. A liberal education should include, as I have put it, a reverent study of all other faiths.

The message of Jesus is contained in the Sermon on the Mount, unadulterated and taken as a whole. Even in connection with the Sermon on the Mount my own humble interpretation of the message is in many respects different from the orthodox. When I was prematurely discharged from jail C. F. Andrews, than whom I do not own on this earth a closer friend, showed me a letter addressed by the bishops to their flock. It may be presumptuous for me to say so, but I did not agree with their interpretation of Christ's words.

One's own religion is after all a matter between oneself and one's Maker. But if I feel impelled to share my thoughts with you it is because I want to enlist your sympathy in my search for truth, and because so many Christian friends are deeply interested in my thoughts on the teachings of Jesus and wish to know what place I give to Jesus in my heart.

If, then, I had to face only the Sermon on the Mount and my own interpretation of it, I should not hesitate to say, "Oh yes, I am a Christian." But I know that at the present moment if I said any such thing I would lay myself open to the gravest misinterpretation.

But negatively I can tell you that to my mind much of that which passes for Christianity is a negation of the Sermon on the Mount. Please mark my words carefully. I am not at the present moment speaking especially of Christian conduct; I am speaking of Christian belief, of Christianity as it is understood in the West. I am painfully aware of the fact that conduct everywhere falls far short of belief. Therefore I do not say this by way of criticism. I know from the treasures of my own experience that, although I am every moment of my life trying to live up to my professions, nevertheless my conduct falls short of these professions. Far therefore be it from me to say this in a spirit of criticism. But I am placing before you my fundamental difficulties with regard to the appearance of Christianity in the world and the formulation of Christian beliefs.

There is one thing which came forcibly to me in my early studies of the Bible. It seized me immediately when I read one passage. The text was this: "Seek ye first the Kingdom of God and His righteousness, and all other things will be added unto you." I tell you that if you will understand, appreciate, and act up to the spirit of this passage, then you will not even need to know what place Jesus, or any other teacher, occupies in your heart or my heart. If you will do this moral scavenger's work, so as to clean and purify your hearts and get them ready you will find that all these mighty teachers will take their places without any invitation from us. That, to my mind, is the basis of all sound education. The culture of the mind must be subservient to the culture of the heart. May God help you to become pure!

When I began as a prayerful student to study Christian literature in South Africa in 1893, I asked myself again and again, "Is this Christianity?" And I could only say, "No, no. Certainly this that I see is not Christianity." And the deepest in me tells me that I was right; for it was unworthy of Jesus and untrue to the Sermon on the Mount.

I claim to be a man of faith and prayer, and even if I were to be cut to pieces I trust God would give me the strength not to deny Him, but to assert that He is. The Mussalman says, "He is, and there is no one else." The Christian says the same thing, and so does the Hindu. If I may venture to say so, the Buddhist also says the same thing, only in different words. It is true that we may each of us be putting our own interpretation on the word "God." We must of necessity do so; for God embraces, not only this tiny globe of ours, but millions and billions of such globes and worlds beyond worlds. How can we, little crawling creatures, possibly measure His greatness, His boundless love, His infinite compassion? So great is His infinite love and pity that He allows man insolently to deny Him, to wrangle about Him, and even to cut the throat of his fellow-man!

Thus, though we may utter the same words about God, they may not bear the same meaning for us all. But what does that matter? We do not need to proselytize either by our speech or by our writing. We can only do so really with our lives. Let our lives be open books for all to study.

Would that I could persuade all my missionary friends to take this view of their mission. Then there would be no distrust, or suspicion, or jealousy, or dissension amongst us in these religious matters, but only harmony and peace.

Because of its Western, external appearance we in India have come to distrust the Christian missionary endeavour that has reached us from the West.

The one deduction I would like you students to draw from all this is that you yourselves should not be torn from your moorings; and those from the West should not consciously or unconsciously lay violent hands upon the manners and customs of this country in so far as they are not repugnant to fundamental morality. Do not confuse Jesus's teaching with what passes as modern civilization. I ask you who are missionaries, pray do not do unconscious violence to the people among whom you cast your lot. It is no part of your call, I assure you, to tear up the lives of the people of the East by their roots. Tolerate whatever is good in them. As Christ said to us all: "Judge not, that ye be not judged. Forgive, and it shall be forgiven you. For with what measure ye mete, it shall be measured to you again."

In spite of your belief in the greatness of Western civilization, and in spite of your pride in all your achievements, I plead with you to exercise humility. I ask you to leave some little room for honest doubt. Let us simply each one live our life; and if ours is the right life, where is the cause for hurry? It will react of itself.

By all means drink deep of the fountains that are given to you in the Sermon on the Mount; but then you will have to take up sackcloth and ashes also with regard to failure to perform that which is taught in Christ's Sermon. For the teaching of the Sermon was meant for each and every one of us. You cannot serve both God and Mammon. God the Compassionate and the Merciful, who is Tolerance incarnate, allows Mammon to have his nine days' wonder. But I say to you students and youths, fly from that self-destroying but destructive show of Mammon, which I see around me today. For you cannot serve Mammon and God together.

It must not be thought from what I have here related that Mahatma Gandhi's attitude towards Indian Christians and towards European missionaries is always critical. On the contrary he has many of his most devoted followers and friends among them. In South Africa some of the noblest of the Passive Resisters were Indian Christians. No guests are more welcomed than certain loved European missionaries at Sabarmati. I have watched them with joy sharing the life of the Ashram—the European ladies helping Mrs. Gandhi in her household works and sharing her motherly affection.

Perhaps the best way in which I can explain this whole-hearted appreciation of Indian Christianity at its best by Mahatma Gandhi is by quoting in full his deeply touching tribute to the late Principal Susil Kumar Rudra of Delhi. My own name comes in it, but I have felt that I must leave it intact. He wrote as follows:

I would ask the reader to share my grief over the death of an esteemed friend and silent public servant, Principal Susil Kumar Rudra, who died on Tuesday, June 30th. India, whose chief disease is her political servitude, recognizes only those who are fighting publicly to remove it by giving battle to a bureaucracy that has protected itself with a treble line of entrenchment—army and navy, money, and diplomacy. She naturally does not know her selfless and self-effacing workers in other walks of life, no less useful than the purely political. Such a humble worker was Susil Rudra, late Principal of St. Stephen's College. He was a first-class educationist. As Principal he had made himself universally popular. There was a kind of spiritual bond between him and his pupils. Though he was a Christian, he had room in his bosom for Hinduism and Islam, which he regarded with great veneration. His was not an exclusive Christianity, that condemned to perdition everyone who did not believe in Jesus Christ as the only saviour of the world. Jealous of the reputation of his own, he was tolerant towards the other faiths. He was a keen and careful student of politics. Of his sympathies with the so-called extremists, if he made no parade, he never made any secret either. Ever since my return home in 1915 I had been his guest whenever I had occasion to go to Delhi. It was plain sailing enough so long as I had not declared Satyagraha in respect of the Rowlatt Act. He had many English friends in the higher circles. He belonged to a purely English Mission. He was the first Indian Principal chosen in his college. I therefore felt that his intimate association with me and his giving me shelter under his roof might compromise him and expose his college to unnecessary risk. I therefore offered to seek shelter elsewhere. His reply was characteristic:

"My religion," he said, "is deeper than people may imagine. Some of my opinions are vital parts of my being. They are formed after deep and prolonged prayer. They are known to my English friends. I cannot possibly be misunderstood by keeping you under my roof as an honoured friend and guest. And if ever I have to make a choice between losing what influence I may have among Englishmen and losing you, I know what I would choose. You cannot leave me."

"But what about all kinds of friends," I asked, "who come to see me? Surely you must not let your house become a caravanserai when I am in Delhi."

"To tell you the truth," he replied, "I like it all. I like the friends who come to see you. It gives me pleasure to think that in keeping you with me I am doing some little service to my country."

The reader may not be aware that my open letter to the Viceroy giving concrete shape to the Khilafat claim was conceived and drafted under Principal Rudra's roof. He and Charlie Andrews were my revisionists. Non-Co-operation was conceived and hatched under his hospitable roof. He was a silent but deeply interested spectator at the private conference that took place between the Ali Brothers, other Mussalman friends, and myself.

Religious motive was the foundation for all his acts. There was, therefore, no fear of temporal power, though the same motive also enabled him to value the existence and the use and the friendship of temporal power. He exemplified in his life the truth that religious perception gives one a correct sense of proportion, resulting in a beautiful harmony between action and belief.

Principal Rudra drew to himself as fine characters as one could possibly wish for. Not many people know that we owe C. F. Andrews to Principal Rudra. They were twins. Their relationship was a study in ideal friendship. Principal Rudra leaves behind him two sons and a daughter, all grown up and settled in life. They know their grief is shared by the numerous friends and admirers of their noble-hearted father.*

* For further reference to this subject see Appendix 4 and Appendix 5.

5

The Ashram of Soul-Force

It is impossible to understand Mahatma Gandhi's principles in their entirety without studying their embodiment in his Ashram, or place of religious retreat. In India every great moral and spiritual leader sooner or later founds what is called an Ashram for the sake of giving a concrete expression to his own creative ideas. Thus Gopal Krishna Gokhale—one of the greatest statesmen that India has ever produced—founded the Servants of India Society at Poona. The poet Rabindranath Tagore has created a unique Ashram at Santiniketan in Bengal. The late Swami Shraddhananda founded the Gurukula at Kangri, Hardwar, in connection with the Arya Samaj.

It is a profoundly interesting experience to live as an inmate of such Ashrams as these. Only thus can one appreciate the spirit and personality of the founder. While the religious leader himself is still living the interest is all the greater, because we are then able to see the creative ideal actually shaping itself round the personality of the saintly life itself, which is thus finding its own extension in other lives.

The power of discipleship is common all over the East, and young ardent spirits gravitate to such Ashrams as surely as water finds its own level; for there is a spiritual law of gravitation which is no less constant than the natural law which binds together the physical world around us. During all the twenty-five years that I have lived in the East there have been few things that have impressed me more than the natural attraction of the human mind in India towards religion, and the reverence freely given to truly spiritual personalities when they seek to express their own ideals in action.

We are helped in our understanding of Mahatma Gandhi's religious ideals, as they are being put into practice, by having a full description of those special features of his religious life which he himself has desired to be carried out literally in his own Ashram. At the time when these were drawn up he sent a copy in manuscript to me for criticism. In reply I wrote out for him a long statement very earnestly asking him to withdraw the vow of celibacy, which appeared to me to be one of those short cuts, foreign to the Hindu religion, bringing inevitable evil in its train. But he was adamant on this point at that time, though I have gathered from his writings since that he has now in certain circumstances modified it in accordance with the wish of the majority of the residents of the Ashram.

His whole statement reads as follows:

> No work done by any man, however great, will really prosper unless it has a distinct religious backing. But what is Religion? I for one would answer: "Not the Religion you will get after reading all the scriptures of the world. Religion is not really what is grasped by the brain, but a heart grasp."
>
> Religion is a thing not alien to us. It has to be evolved out of us. It is always within us: with some, consciously so; with others, quite unconsciously. But it is always there. And whether we wake up this religious instinct in us through outside assistance or by inward growth, no matter how it is done, it has got to be done, if we want to do anything in the right manner, or to achieve anything that is going to persist.
>
> Our Scriptures have laid down certain rules as maxims of human life. They tell us that without living according to these maxims we are incapable of having a reasonable perception of Religion. Believing in these implicitly, I have deemed it necessary to seek the association of those who think with me in founding this Institution. The following are the rules that have been drawn up and have to be observed by everyone who seeks to be a member.
>
> The first and foremost is

> ### The Vow of Truth

> Not simply as we ordinarily understand it, not truth which merely answers the saying, "Honesty is the best policy," implying

that if it is not the best policy we may depart from it. Here
Truth as it is conceived means that we may have to rule our life by
this law of Truth at any cost; and in order to satisfy the definition
I have drawn upon the celebrated illustration of the life of
Prahlad.* For the sake of Truth he dared to oppose his own
father; and he defended himself, not by paying his father back
in his own coin. Rather, in defence of Truth as he knew it, he
was prepared to die without caring to return the blows that he
had received from his father, or from those who were charged
with his father's instructions. Not only that, he would not in
any way even parry the blows; on the contrary, with a smile on
his lips, he underwent the innumerable tortures to which he was
subjected, with the result that at last Truth rose triumphant. Not
that he suffered the tortures because he knew that some day or
other in his very lifetime he would be able to demonstrate the
infallibility of the Law of Truth. That fact was there; but if he
had died in the midst of tortures he would still have adhered to
Truth. That is the Truth which I would like to follow. In our
Ashram we make it a rule that we must say "No" when we
mean No, regardless of consequences.

Then we come to the

Doctrine of Ahimsa

Literally speaking, Ahimsa means "non-killing." But to me it has
a world of meaning, and takes me into realms much higher,
infinitely higher. It really means that you may not offend anybody; you may not harbour an uncharitable thought, even in
connection with one who may consider himself to be your
enemy. To one who follows this doctrine there is no room for
an enemy. But there may be people who consider themselves to
be his enemies. So it is held that we may not harbour an evil
thought even in connection with such persons. If we return
blow for blow we depart from the doctrine of Ahimsa. But I go

---

* The story of the young boy Prahlad, who suffered for the Truth's sake, is one of the most
famous in ancient Indian literature. It is well known by every Indian child—just as the
story of George Washington is famous in the West.

farther. If we resent a friend's action, or the so-called enemy's action, we still fall short of this doctrine. But when I say we should not resent, I do not say that we should acquiesce: by the word "resenting" I mean wishing that some harm should be done to the enemy; or that he should be put out of the way, not even by any action of ours, but by the action of somebody else, or, say, by divine agency. If we harbour even this thought we depart from this doctrine of Non-Violence. Those who join the Ashram have literally to accept that meaning.

This does not mean that we practise that doctrine in its entirety. Far from it. It is an ideal which we have to reach, and it is an ideal to be reached even at this very moment, if we are capable of doing so. But it is not a proposition in Geometry; it is not even like solving difficult problems in higher mathematics—it is infinitely more difficult. Many of us have burnt the midnight oil in solving those problems. But if you want to follow out this doctrine you will have to do much more than burn the midnight oil. You will have to pass many a sleepless night, and go through many a mental torture, before you can even be within measurable distance of this goal. It is the goal, and nothing less than that, which you and I have to reach, if we want to understand what a religious life means.

A man who believes in the efficacy of this doctrine finds in the ultimate stage, when he is about to reach the goal, the whole world at his feet. If you express your love—Ahimsa—in such a manner that it impresses itself indelibly upon your so-called enemy, he must return that love. Under this rule there is no room for organized assassinations, or for murders openly committed, or for any violence for the sake of your country, and even for guarding the honour of precious ones that may be under your charge. After all, that would be a poor defence of their honour. This doctrine tells us that we may guard the honour of those under our charge by delivering our own lives into the hands of the man who would commit the sacrilege. And that requires far greater courage than delivering of blows. If you do not retaliate, but stand your ground between your charge and the opponent, simply receiving the blows without retaliating, what happens? I give you my promise that the whole of his violence will be expended on you, and your friend will be left unscathed. Under this plan of life there is no conception of patriotism which justifies such wars as you witness today in Europe.

Then again there is

The Vow of Celibacy

Those who want to perform national service, or to have a gleam of the real religious life, must lead a celibate life, whether married or unmarried. Marriage only brings a woman closer to man, and they become friends in a special sense, never to be parted either in this life or in the lives to come. But I do not think that, in our conception of marriage, our lusts should enter. Be that as it may, this is what is placed before those who come to the Ashram. I do not deal with it at any length.

Then we have, further,

The Vow of the Control of the Palate

A man who wants to control his animal passions easily does so if he controls his palate. I fear this is one of the most difficult vows to follow. Unless we are prepared to rid ourselves of stimulating, heating, and exciting condiments we shall certainly not be able to control the overabundant, unnecessary, and exciting stimulation of the animal passions. If we do not do that we are likely to abuse the sacred trust of our bodies that has been given us, and to become less than animals and brutes, eating, drinking, and indulging in passions which we share with animals. But have you ever seen a horse or cow indulging in the abuse of the palate as we do? Do you suppose that it is a sign of civilization, a sign of real life, that we should multiply our eatables so far that we do not even know where we are; and seek dishes until at last we have become absolutely mad and run after the newspaper sheets which give us advertisements about these dishes?

Then we have once more

The Vow of Non-Thieving

I suggest that we are thieves in a way. If I take anything that I do not need for my own immediate use and keep it, I thieve it from somebody else. It is the fundamental law of Nature, without exception, that Nature produces enough for our wants from day to day; and if only everybody took enough for himself and nothing more there would be no pauperism in this world, there would be no man dying of starvation. I am no Socialist, and I do not want to dispossess those who have got possessions; but I do say that personally those of us who want to see light out of darkness have to follow this rule. I do not want to dispossess anybody; I should then be departing from the rule of Non-Violence. If somebody else possesses more than I do, let him. But so far as my own life has to be regulated I dare not possess anything which I do not want. In India we have got many millions of people who have to be satisfied with one meal a day, and that meal consisting of a chapatti* containing no fat in it and a pinch of salt. You and I have no right to anything that we really have until these many millions are clothed and fed. You and I, who ought to know better, must adjust our wants, and even undergo voluntary privation, in order that they may be nursed, fed, and clothed.

Then there is the "Vow of Non-Possession," which follows as a matter of course, and needs no further explanation at this point, where only a brief summary of various difficulties and their answer is being given.

Then I go to

The Vow of Swadeshi

The vow of Swadeshi is a necessary vow. We are departing from one of the sacred laws of our being when we leave our neighbourhood and go out somewhere else in order to satisfy our wants. If a man comes from Bombay and offers you wares, you are not justified in supporting the Bombay merchant so long as you have got a merchant at your very door, born and bred in Madras.

---

* Bread made without yeast—somewhat like a pancake.

That is my view of Swadeshi. In your village you are bound to support your village barber to the exclusion of the finished barber who may come to you from Madras. If you find it necessary that your village barber should reach the attainments of the barber from Madras you may train him to that. Send him to Madras by all means, if you wish, in order that he may learn his calling. Until you do that you are not justified in going to another barber. That is Swadeshi. So when we find that there are many things that we cannot get in India we must try to do without them. We may have to do without many things; but, believe me, when you have that frame of mind you will find a great burden taken off your shoulders, even as the Pilgrim did in that inimitable book *Pilgrim's Progress*. There came a time when the mighty burden that the Pilgrim was carrying unconsciously dropped from him, and he felt a freer man than he was when he started on the journey. So will you feel freer men than you are now, if immediately you adopt this Swadeshi life. We have also

The Vow of Fearlessness

I found, through my wanderings in India, that my country is seized with a paralysing fear. We may not open our lips in public: we may only talk about our opinions secretly. We may do anything we like within the four walls of our house; but those things are not for public consumption.

If we had taken a vow of silence I would have nothing to say. I suggest to you that there is only One whom we have to fear, that is God. When we fear God, then we shall fear no man, however high-placed he may be; and if you want to follow the vow of Truth, then fearlessness is absolutely necessary. Before we can aspire to guide the destinies of India we shall have to adopt this habit of fearlessness.

And then we have also

The Vow Regarding the "Untouchables"

There is an ineffaceable blot that Hinduism today carries with it. I have declined to believe that it has been handed down to

us from immemorial times. I think that this miserable,
wretched, enslaving spirit of "untouchableness" must have
come to us when we were at our lowest ebb. This evil has stuck
to us and still remains with us. It is, to my mind, a curse that has
come to us; and as long as that curse remains with us, so long I
think we are bound to consider that every affliction in this
sacred land is a proper punishment for the indelible crime that
we are committing. That any person should be considered
untouchable because of his calling passes my comprehension;
and you, the student world, who receive all this modern education, if you become a party to this crime, it were better that you
received no education whatsoever.

Education through the Vernaculars

In Europe every cultured man learns not only his own language, but also other languages.

In order to solve the problem of language in India we in this
Ashram must make it a point to learn as many Indian vernaculars as possible. The trouble of learning these languages is nothing compared to that of mastering English. How dare we rub
off from our memory all the years of our infancy? But that is
precisely what we do when we commence our higher life
through the medium of a foreign tongue. This creates a breach
for which we shall have to pay dearly. And you will see now the
connection between this education and untouchability—this
persistence of the latter in spite of the spread of knowledge and
education. Education has enabled us to see the horrible crime,
but we are seized with fear, and therefore we cannot take this
doctrine to our homes.

The Vow of Khaddar*

You may ask, "Why should we use our hands?" You may say,
"Manual work has got to be done by those who are illiterate. I

---

* Khaddar is home-spun and home-woven cloth. The vow of Khaddar would be to spin
with one's own hands and to wear nothing but home-spun garments.

can only occupy myself with reading literature and political essays."
We have to realize the dignity of labour. If a barber or shoe-
maker attends a college he ought not to abandon his profession.
I consider that such professions are just as good as the profession
of medicine.

Last of all, when you have conformed to these rules you may
come to

The Religious Use of Politics

Politics, divorced from religion, has absolutely no meaning. If
the student world crowd the political platforms of this country,
that is not necessarily a healthy sign of national growth; but this
does not mean that you, in your student life, ought not to study
politics. Politics are a part of our being; we ought to understand
our national institutions. We may do this from our infancy. So
in our Ashram every child is taught to understand the political
institutions of our country and to know how the country is
vibrating with new emotions, with new aspirations, with new
life. But we want also the steady light, the infallible light of religious faith; not a faith which merely appeals to the intelligence,
but a faith which is indelibly inscribed on the heart. First we
want to realize our religious consciousness, and immediately we
have done that the whole department of life is open to us; and
it should then be a sacred privilege of all, so that when young
men grow to manhood they may do so properly equipped to
battle with life. Today what happens is this: much of the political
life is confined to the students, but immediately they cease to be
students they sink into oblivion, seeking miserable employments,
knowing nothing about God, nothing of fresh air or bright
light, or of real vigorous independence, such as comes out of
obedience to those laws that I have placed before you on this
occasion.

An analysis of these different principles, underlying the life of
Mahatma Gandhi's Ashram, reveals the fact that there is a singular
blending in them of different inward acts of conscience which issue

in outward acts of observance. While Mahatma Gandhi would lay every stress on the inward principle as of primary importance (without which the outward act is of no value at all), at the same time he would bring the inward principle immediately to the test of action. This is in strict accordance with Christ's teaching in the Sermon on the Mount, where he says: "By their fruits ye shall know them. Do men gather grapes from thorns, or figs from thistles?"

Thus the vow of control of the palate follows upon the vows of truthfulness and non-stealing and non-possession as a simple means to reach those great ends. He would regard it as practically impossible for a man to indulge the appetite and yet remain for a long period strictly truthful, fearless, honest, and single-minded.

As representing the rules of an Ashram, where self-discipline is one of the main features of the life of religion, it is not difficult to trace the logical connection between the inward and the outward in this manner. But personally I had felt from the first that the vow of lifelong celibacy had imposed a slur on marriage; and therefore I had objected to this vow being included along with that of Truthfulness and Ahimsa. While ancient Buddhism had seemed to me to bear this negative aspect by regarding the celibate life as necessarily higher than the married life, Hinduism had always appeared to have the contrary tendency. For Hinduism has had in certain important directions a development which finds its parallel directly in the Christian religion. It lays stress on personal continence, called Brahmachary, during the early period of life before marriage, but encourages the married life and the bearing of children in the second stage as truly spiritual. Thus Hinduism, as far as I have been able to understand it, holds marriage to be a religious sacrament, which is *not* an indulgence but rather one of the highest forms of inward self-discipline. It was distressing to find what appeared to me to be an unnatural view concerning marriage set forward in the regulations of Mahatma Gandhi's Ashram of Soul-Force. This vow of celibacy for the whole Ashram appeared to sever one of the vital roots of the Hindu religion, and for this reason I wrote to him urging its withdrawal.

Some of the vows with which Mahatma Gandhi concludes the series are clearly rather of a local nature than of permanent and perpetual

value. "Education through the vernacular," the "removal of untouchability," the use of "politics," are obviously in their present setting
directed rather to the immediate needs of India than to any universal
human situation.

In respect to two other vows which have a direct external
aspect—namely, the Vow of Swadeshi and the Vow of Khaddar—
Mahatma Gandhi would by no means regard these as either local or
temporary. They go down very deep indeed into his whole conception
of human progress. But since they will be dealt with in two separate
chapters elsewhere, it will not be necessary to discuss them here.

Turning from the rules of the Ashram of Soul-Force to the life as
it is passed by the members who form this ideal community, the following account given by some visitors may make the picture vivid.
It has been necessary to abbreviate what has been written, but I have
tried to keep the personal touch and human interest of the narrative.
It runs as follows:

> Let me give my own impression of Mahatma Gandhi himself.
> Truth and sincerity are in every line of his face, and seem to
> demand the same truth and sincerity in return. One could
> never be artificial with such a man, for his keen vision pene-
> trates all outer wrappings. We had already met some of his clos-
> est friends and had admired each in turn. Now that we have
> met him we can fully appreciate why such love and devotion
> are extended to him. All residents upon the compound, from
> the oldest to the youngest, had been joyously looking forward
> to his return. Simply and quietly, unknown to all, he had slipped
> into his room, to emerge later into the very bosom of his fam-
> ily and friends. The children came flocking around him. No
> feeling of fear or awe comes within his environment. Any off-
> ishness or assumption of superiority in connection with him is
> unthinkable. All day he mixed freely with his friends and rela-
> tives, visiting homes and interesting himself in the veriest details
> of the Ashram.
>
> It is not too much to say that the feeling left by our first
> meeting is that of having come into contact with a man nearer to

the Christ-like ideal than any other living person. In the evening
we had a short walk and then went over for dinner. At 6.30 P.M.
we went to prayers, and when these were over, at his own invitation, we sang two hymns, first reading the words aloud.

Beautiful and impressive as the prayers had been on the previous evenings, there was a deeper feeling of joy this evening
because Mahatma Gandhi had once more returned to his
home. Everyone felt the benediction of his presence as he sat
facing us with a little grandniece nestling close to him. The few
words he spoke were for the children, who all sat in front.
Everyone was reluctant to break the silence which wrapped us
round; and as we slowly dispersed it was evident that each one
carried away a sense of peace. It was an unforgettable evening—
one of the precious memories which make existence worth
while.

After his return the whole of the next two days he observed
silence, so that he might prepare himself for the Kathiawar
Conference. This silence was broken just before prayers on
Tuesday evening, when we had the pleasure of another chat
with him, and he invited us to accompany him on his morning
walk as far as the jail gates. He refers to the jail as his second
home; and when we suggested that jail had no terrors for him
he replied, "No, indeed it has not."

The next day was a red-letter day. True to his promise he
came to our room for us at nine o'clock and we started off for
the walk. As we passed the compound of the jail we saw fine
vegetables growing; this turned our conversation to the question
of prison reform, and we agreed that such institutions should
give up the idea of punishment and replace it by reformation,
and that most crimes were the outcome of social conditions.

He told us of the test to which he had been put when starting
his Ashram. He was asked whether he was prepared to take
"untouchable," and had replied in the affirmative. His questioners
little knew that this test would be carried into effect within a
month; but when a married "untouchable" couple applied for
admittance he accepted them immediately. The man is now the

principal of a small Ashram, and his daughter has been adopted by Mr. Gandhi. She is one of the little folk who nestle up so lovingly to him during the time of prayer.

On Monday we continued our work in the weaving-shed and got all the thread ready to start weaving. After prayers in the evening two of our women friends carried us off to one of their homes. All mats were spread ready for our reception; an interpreter was called from an adjoining home, and he kindly spent a whole hour telling us of the wonderful story of our host and hostess, who had been in Fiji.

We went very early next morning to the carding-room, and then returned to our room to wait for Mahatma Gandhi's arrival. At 9.30 he came, and joyfully we joined him. We had decided that we would rather listen to his talking than speak ourselves. So to gain this end we had written down one or two questions.

We first asked him about his Spinning Franchise, as we wanted to know whether his aim was to raise the depressed classes, or was it to be used to level all classes? He said it was both a levelling up and levelling down; to prevent the exploitation of the depressed classes on the one hand, and to prevent swelled head upon the other. For a man to grow his own food and make his own wearing apparel from the product of his own land was just as necessary as breathing the air around him. No one should be fed or clothed without having worked towards the end himself. To Mahatma Gandhi this has absolutely universal application as the only way of saving the world.

When we asked him whether spinning and weaving were a means to an end or an end in itself, he said that mankind is only able to utilize the means; the ultimate goal is beyond us. As soon as we think that we have achieved one end, another arises. So all we are concerned with here are the simple means of life, the primal necessities; the rest we may leave in the hands of God. He did not care in the least for the accessories of life; its necessities alone were his concern. Until everyone was able to gain these for himself he would not consider his work finished; and in this way again his work was not for India alone, but for the whole world.

Then we asked him what he thought to be the real function in India of the British, and he replied promptly that it was to serve India. He has always been friendly towards the British; but it was not until his return from South Africa to work for the good of India that he found how patronizing and obstructive they could be. His friendship for them is as great and as true as ever; but he realizes the impossibility of any improvement in Indian affairs while the British continue in this attitude of patronage and obstruction. When they see that service, and not exploitation, should be their aim, then true friendship will arise and the harmonious working of the two nations ensue.

When asked if British rule was necessary to protect India from outside interference he replied: "No; but since they are here, my aim shall be to urge them to work with us as friends and equals." He went on to say that the British could give to India resourcefulness, energy, and initiative, which are such marked characteristics of our nation, and that these were just the qualities needed to help India rise from the lethargy into which she had sunk.

Morning and evening prayers form one of the features of the common life of the Ashram. All the men, women, and children are gathered together, the stars shining above, the river silver in the moonlight, Mahatma Gandhi as discipline personified and yet the very embodiment of love. After the verses were read and the singing finished he gave forth his message, which has been translated for us thus: "I do not want a kingdom, salvation, or heaven; what I want is to remove the troubles of the oppressed and the poor."

On Wednesday the waning moon and the three planets again made of the morning sky a picture which will long remain in our minds. Knowing that Mr. Gandhi was to leave by the morning train for Delhi, we went to him early. We found him sitting on the floor before his desk in his own room. Upon the floor was spread a Khaddar cloth, and as the rising sun lighted up the whole place he looked a wonderful figure in these bare yet characteristic surroundings. The room is absolutely devoid of all ornaments; a few bookshelves, a low desk, one deck-chair, which remains folded against the wall, a couple of spinning-wheels, and a low bench constitute its furniture.

He says that when he feels a thing is right and when he is really convinced that it must be, then he goes straight forward with it, never doubting, knowing that if he makes a mistake it is an honest one, and God will pardon him for it and help him to put it right; but if he is in doubt about a thing he refuses to have anything to do with it. That is, of course, what makes him irresistible; he is so convinced of the righteousness of his cause that others cannot help believing it too. "I know where I stand and have a strong belief in myself. So I go forward fearlessly."

He explained that Gujarat was more suited to take the lead in spinning and weaving than any other province, because here things had been well organized, and the result was that there were more persons capable of teaching both these arts than in any other part of the country. He expects to have to go over to the Madras side in connection with the question of the "untouchables"; for, as he put it, "I have to go wherever the people need me."

When we left the room he said, "I shall expect to see you here when I return." And as we went away we felt a great sense of emptiness and loss as we thought how few were the days left to us of this wonderful month.

For indeed when we thought of the whole atmosphere of the place and the ideals for which it stands—the joy of the workers in their work, the happy, contented homes, the education available to the children, the absence of any anxious thought for the morrow—our hearts ached to think that we were to leave it all so soon.

Here, more than ever before in our busy lives, have we felt the truth of the words "Laborare est orare"—to labour is to pray.

6

THE RELIGIOUS MEANING OF SWADESHI

There are few things in Mahatma Gandhi's religious experience that have struck me with more force, by their unexpectedness and individuality, than his insistence upon Swadeshi itself as a religious duty. The word "Swadeshi" is a compound meaning "one's own country." Swadeshi is so intimately linked up with Hinduism in his own mind that it is necessary to bring it in here as a part of his religious belief, though many earnest orthodox people would not hold it to be an integral Hindu doctrine. Perhaps it should be regarded as an idiosyncrasy of Mahatma Gandhi himself, representing his own individual way of expressing one aspect of his Hindu faith.

With Mahatma Gandhi, Swadeshi represents the principle that one's own surroundings are to be preferred to everything else; that the country of one's birth demands personal homage in preference to that of others. It means still further to him—that to change from one religion to another is an almost inconceivable thing. In Swadeshi he finds a principle which explains his relation to Christianity and other religions. There is to him a religious patriotism as well as a patriotism of national status.

This Swadeshi doctrine, which he holds so strongly as a religious article of faith, clearly makes for the birth-fixity of social condition. It compels men to remain "in that state of life to which it has pleased God to call them"—to quote the Church of England Catechism with its feudal background. It explains to some extent in his own mind how Caste, which he calls Varnashrama Dharma, may be justified as a reasonable system. It shows also why he desires to call himself an orthodox Hindu, holding to the principles underlying the traditional Hindu Scriptures. The extreme limit of this doctrine was reached in a book called *The Gospel of Swadeshi,* written by one of his followers, to which he wrote a preface, though he afterwards withdrew his approval of some of the narrow forms of the doctrine which the author himself had laid down and publicly expressed. It is necessary to repeat that many who are orthodox Hindus would entirely deny this doctrine of Swadeshi as a part of their Hindu faith. Others would also reject the birth-fixity implied in the Caste System, even while still upholding the refusal to intermarry under present conditions. But Mr. Gandhi's faith in these things as a Hindu appears to be fundamental. While upholding radical principles in other matters he is strongly conservative here.

That Swadeshi has the character of religious duty with him may be seen from the leading place which he gives to it in his vows at the Satyagraha Ashram at Sabarmati. This may be studied at greater length in the chapter describing the Ashram of Soul-Force. [See chapter 5.] The same fact is made still more clear by his choosing Swadeshi as his own special subject at the Christian Missionary Conference at Madras on February 14, 1916, when he was asked to address the missionaries assembled on some religious subject such as he himself regarded as of primary importance. He would never have chosen this subject of Swadeshi on such a unique occasion—when for the first time in India he was addressing an audience of devotedly earnest men and women whom he wished to convince about sovereign truth—unless he had felt that the religious principle he was propounding went down to the bed-rock spiritual experience of things divine. After many long and arduous discussions with him on this subject I can write words as strong as these about its religious significance with him; for in this matter he is inflexible and he has long ago thought the matter out. When I asked him what was the final word he had written on the subject, he gave me the following speech addressed to the missionaries at Madras:

> After much thinking I have arrived at a definition of Swadeshi that perhaps best illustrates my meaning:
> *Swadeshi is that spirit within us which restricts us to the use and service of our immediate surroundings to the exclusion of the more remote.*

Thus (i) in the matter of Religion I must restrict myself to my ancestral religion—that is, the use of my immediate surroundings in religion. If I find my religion defective I should serve it by purging it of its defects. (ii) In the domain of politics I should make use of the indigenous institutions and serve them by curing them of their proved defects. (iii) In the field of economics I should use only those things that are produced by my immediate neighbours, and serve those industries by making them efficient and complete where they might be found wanting.

(i) Hinduism has become a conservative religion, and therefore a mighty force, because of the Swadeshi spirit underlying it. It is the most tolerant creed because it is non-proselytizing, and it is as capable of expansion today as it has been found to be in the past. It has succeeded, not in driving out (as I think it has been erroneously held), but in absorbing Buddhism. By reason of the Swadeshi spirit a Hindu refuses to change his religion, not necessarily because he considers it to be the best, but because he knows that he can complement it by introducing reforms. And what I have said about Hinduism is, I suppose, true of the other great faiths of the world; only it is held that it is especially so in the case of Hinduism. But here comes the point I am labouring to teach.

If there is any substance in what I have said, will not the great missionary bodies of India, to whom she owes a deep debt of gratitude for what they have done and are doing, do still better and serve the spirit of Christianity better by dropping the goal of proselytizing while continuing their philanthropic work? I make the suggestion in all sincerity and with due humility.

I have endeavoured to study the Bible and consider it to be a part of my Scriptures. The spirit of the Sermon on the Mount competes almost on equal terms with the Bhagavad Gita for the domination of my heart. I yield to no Christian in the strength of devotion with which I sing "Lead, Kindly Light" and several other inspired hymns of a similar nature. I have come under the influence of noted Christian missionaries belonging to different denominations, and I enjoy to this day the privilege of friendship with some of them. Thus I have offered the above suggestion, not as a biased Hindu, but as a humble and impartial student of religion with great leanings towards Christianity.

May it not be that the "Go ye unto all the world" message has been somewhat narrowly interpreted and the spirit of it missed? It will not be denied—I speak from experience—that many of the "conversions" are only so-called. In some cases the appeal has gone not to the heart but to the stomach; and in every case a conversion leaves a sore behind it, which I venture to think is avoidable. Quoting again from experience, a new birth, a change of heart, is perfectly possible in every one of the great faiths.

I know I am now treading upon thin ice; but I do not apologize in closing this part of my subject by saying that the frightful outrage that is just now going on in Europe perhaps shows that the message of Jesus of Nazareth, the Son of Peace, has been little understood in Europe, and that light may have to be thrown upon it from the East.

(ii) Following out the Swadeshi spirit in political matters, I observe the indigenous institutions of India, and the village *panchayats* (committees) hold me. India is really a republican country, and it is for this reason that it has survived every shock hitherto delivered. Princes and potentates, whether they were Indian-born or foreigners, have hardly touched the vast masses except for the collection of revenue. The latter in their turn seem to have rendered unto Caesar what was Caesar's, and for the rest to have done much as they have liked. The vast organization of Caste answered not only the religious wants of the community, but also its political ends. The villagers managed their internal affairs through the Caste system, and through it also they dealt with any oppression from the ruling power. It is not possible to deny, with regard to a nation producing the Caste system, its wonderful powers of organization, One has but to attend the great Kumba Festival* at Hardwar to know how skilful that organization must have been which without any seeming effort

---

* A special Hindu bathing festival to which the village people gather in immense numbers.

was able effectively to cater for more than a million pilgrims.
Yet it is the fashion to say that we lack organizing ability. This is
true, I fear, to a certain extent of those who have been nurtured
in the new traditions. We have laboured under a terrible handicap
owing to an almost fatal departure from the Swadeshi spirit.

We, the educated classes, have received our education
through a foreign tongue. We have therefore not reacted upon
the masses. We want to represent the masses, but we fail. They
recognize us not much more than they recognize the English
officers. Their hearts are an open book to neither. Their aspirations are not ours. Hence there is a break; and you witness not
in reality failure to organize, but want of correspondence
between the representatives and the represented. If during the
last fifty years we had been educated through the vernaculars,
our elders and our servants and our neighbours would have
partaken of our knowledge; the scientific discoveries of J. C.
Bose and P. C. Ray would have been household treasures, as are
the Ramayana and the Mahabharata.

As it is, so far as the masses are concerned, those great discoveries made by Indians might as well have been made by foreigners. Had instruction in all the branches of learning been
given through the vernaculars they would have been enriched
wonderfully. The question of village sanitation would have been
solved long ago. The village *panchayats* would be now a living
force, and India would almost be enjoying self-government
suited to its requirements and would have been spared the
humiliating spectacle of organized assassination on its sacred soil.

(iii) Much of the deep poverty of India is due to the departure from Swadeshi in the economic life. If not a single article
of commerce had been brought from outside India she would
be today a land flowing with milk and honey. But that was not
to be.

We were greedy, and so was England. The connection
between England and India was based clearly upon an error.
But England did not remain in India owing to an error. It is her
declared policy that India is to be held in trust for the Indian

people. If this be true, Lancashire must stand aside; and if the Swadeshi doctrine is sound, Lancashire can stand aside without hurt, though it may sustain a shock for the time being.

I think of economic Swadeshi not as a boycott movement undertaken by way of revenge, but as a religious principle to be followed by all. I am no economist, but I have read some treatises which show that England could easily become a self-contained country, growing all the produce she needs.

India cannot live for Lancashire, or any other country, before she is able to live for herself; and she can live for herself only if she produces everything for her own requirements within her own borders. She need not be drawn into the vortex of mad and ruinous competition which breeds fratricide, jealousy, and many other evils.

The hand-loom industry in India is in a dying condition. I took special care during my wanderings last year to see as many weavers as possible, and my heart ached to find how much they had lost, how families had retired from this once flourishing and honourable occupation. If we follow the Swadeshi doctrine it will be your duty and mine to find out neighbours who can supply their wants, assuming that there are neighbours who are in need of healthy occupation. Then every village of India will almost be a self-supporting and self-contained unit, exchanging only necessary commodities with other villages where they are not locally producible.

This may all sound nonsensical. Well, India is a country of nonsense. It is nonsensical to parch one's throat with thirst when a kindly Muhammadan is ready to offer pure water to drink; and yet thousands of Hindus would rather die of thirst than drink water from a Muhammadan household. These non-sensical men can also, once they are convinced that their religion demands that they should wear garments manufactured in India only and eat food grown only in India, decline to wear any other clothing or eat any other food. I hate legislative interference in any department of life. At best it is a lesser of two evils. But I would welcome a stiff protective duty upon foreign goods.

Natal, a British Colony, protected its sugar by taxing the sugar that came from another British Colony, Mauritius. England has sinned against India by forcing Free Trade upon her. It may have been food for England but it has been poison for this country.

It has been urged that India cannot adopt Swadeshi in the economic life. Those who advance this objection do not look upon Swadeshi as a rule of life. With them it is a mere patriotic effort, not to be made if it involved any self-denial. But Swadeshi, as defined here, is a religious principle to be undergone in utter disregard of physical discomfort caused to individuals. A Swadeshist will learn to do without a hundred things which today he considers necessary.

There now remains for me to consider one more objection that has been raised against Swadeshi. The objectors consider it to be a most selfish doctrine without any warrant in the civilized code of morality. With them to practice Swadeshi is to revert to barbarism. I cannot enter into a detailed analysis of this proposition; but I would urge that Swadeshi is the only doctrine consistent with the law of humility and love. It is arrogance to think of launching out to serve the whole of India when I am hardly able to serve even my own family. It were better to concentrate my effort upon the family, and consider that through them I was serving the whole nation and, if you will, the whole of humanity. This is humility and it is love.

The motive will determine the quality of the act. For instance, I may wrongly serve my family, regardless of the sufferings I may cause to others; as, for example, I may accept an employment which enables me to extort money from people. I may enrich myself thereby and then satisfy many unlawful demands of my family. Here I am neither serving the family nor the State. Or I may recognize that God has given me hands and feet only to work with for my sustenance and for that of those who may be dependent upon me. I would then at once simplify my life and that of those whom I can directly reach. In this instance I would have served the family without causing injury to anyone else. Supposing that everyone followed this mode of

life, we should have at once an ideal State. All will not reach that
condition at the same time; but those of us who enforce it in
practice will clearly accelerate the coming of that happy day.

Under this plan of life, in seeming to serve India to the
exclusion of every other country I do not harm any other
country. My patriotism is both exclusive and inclusive. It is
exclusive in the sense that in all humility I confine my attention
to the land of my birth; but it is inclusive in the sense that my
service is not of a competitive nature. "Use your own property
in such a way that you hurt no one else's" is not merely a good
legal maxim, but a grand doctrine of life. It is the key to a proper
practice of Ahimsa, of Love. It is for us, who are the custodians of
a great Faith, to show that patriotism based on hatred "killeth,"
but that patriotism based on love "giveth life."

The careful study of this address on Swadeshi throws light on certain important details in Mahatma Gandhi's own religious position. It
is not of the type that ever looks forward (if I judge him rightly) to a
single World Religion and a single World State, but rather to separate
units working out their individual destiny in cordial, harmonized,
friendly relations. There will always be impassable barriers between
them which appear to him divinely ordained. Herein he differs, as
far as I can gather, from Tagore, to whom this limited aspect of patriotism and religion is unthinkable. To Tagore the overpassing of these
boundaries is all-important; to Gandhi their due observance appears
essential in this present stage of human existence. Holding strongly a
belief in reincarnation, he seems to have no anxiety about reaching
any further stage of unification in this present cycle of existence.

I remember a deeply interesting conversation which I had with
him concerning the relationship of Marriage. This brought out his
own theory of Swadeshi in an interesting form. During a sustained
argument I put to him the purely hypothetical case of a marriage
between our two families which should cross the boundaries of
Caste and institutional religion.*

---

* For the sake of clearness let me add that I am still unmarried and therefore have no children; Mahatma Gandhi has a family of four sons but no daughters.

"Suppose," I said to him, "simply for the sake of argument, that I myself had a daughter, who in every way was a suitable bride for your son, and that the two loved one another with devotion of the purest character. You have often told me that I am more than a blood-brother to you and the friend of your heart. Would you, then, stand in the way of such a marriage on the ground of difference of Caste or creed?"

Mahatma Gandhi answered in some such words as these: "Yes, I would never give my consent to such a marriage, because it would be contrary to my ideas of religion thus to transgress the boundaries wherein we were born. I would not personally agree to a marriage out of Caste; at the same time I do not believe in the artificial multiplication of Castes which has occurred in India. That evil and the evil of untouchability are both separable from the true ideal of Varna."

"What, then," I asked him, "is your own conception of the true Caste system, which you call Varnashrama Dharma?"

"It is not easy," he answered, "to explain it to you, because you have never come under its discipline. To one like myself, who believes in the four Varnas, human life, during this present birth on the planet, is only one of a series. There are other experiences which have to be gone through when this life is over. Our present existence is a discipline which has to be lived within certain rules suited to this special stage. We cannot choose at this stage, for instance, our own parents, or our own birthplace, or our own ancestry. Why, then, should we claim as individuals the right during this present brief life-period to break through all the conventions wherein we were placed at birth by God Himself? The Gita has very wisely said that the performance of one's own religious duty is preferable to the carrying out of the religious duty of others. This religious duty, which we call by the untranslatable word 'Dharma,' appears to me to include the environment wherein we were placed at birth by God. It connotes our seeking to live in harmony with those birth conditions and not rebelling against them, or seeking to overpass their limitations, either for individualistic or selfish reasons."

I have tried to put down, through the medium of my own interpretation, the ideas which Mahatma Gandhi had sought to express to me on that memorable morning. It was easy to see that his own thought about Swadeshi was very intimately related to his Hindu religious training in Varnashrama Dharma or Caste Religion; for while Tagore has abandoned the Caste system once for all, Gandhi still declares that he believes in the original four Castes, or Varnas, as natural divisions of society.

What I am trying to make clear is this, that "Swadeshi" with Mahatma Gandhi is not to be confused with the current belief in sovereign "nationalism" in the West, though it runs at certain points perilously along the edge of it and has actually been mistaken for it by some of his own more impulsive followers. Rather it is something much more elemental; it goes back to the Varnashrama Dharma itself, the Religion of Caste. Indeed, this Hindu Caste Religion still retains among orthodox people in India the name of Sanatana Dharma, the Eternal Religion.

7

THE TEACHING OF AHIMSA

Among Mahatma Gandhi's practical religious ideals the emphasis seems always placed upon Ahimsa, or Non-Violence. It is difficult in the West to realize how this has become to him the heart of all religion. It is bound up absolutely in his mind with Truth. He holds that the truth of all life on this planet and of God Himself is to be found in this principle of the sacredness of life and refusal to use violence. This principle he calls Ahimsa, which means literally Non-Violence. There is an early Christian saying in the Epistle to Diognetus: "Violence is not the attribute of God." This would have won his whole-hearted adherence.

In taking up this position Mahatma Gandhi is neither original nor revolutionary from the Hindu standpoint; for as early as the days of the ancient Epic, called Mahabharata, this one virtue of Ahimsa has all along been declared by the Hindu Religion to be the perfection of religious duty. The words of the Mahabharata, which may be translated "Ahimsa is the Supreme Religion," are well known all over India. They have obtained a currency among the common people equivalent to the most familiar texts of the Bible in the West. I have often heard this saying about Ahimsa quoted by the villagers themselves.

When we come to analyse what constitutes Ahimsa we find at once that it is not merely a negative virtue; it involves the positive doing of good quite as much as the negative refusal to do harm. This is made clear in the same passage from the Mahabharata, which goes on to say that Ahimsa is supreme kindness and supreme self-sacrifice.

It is true that among certain forms of Hinduism the negative aspect has become prominent; for instance, among the Jains, Ahimsa has been centralized in the refusal to take the life of even the smallest insect. It has thus become a burden to humanity almost impossible to bear. But this is only one example of the extreme application of a great sovereign truth. With Mahatma Gandhi there is no such purely literal interpretation. He would say, concerning the doctrine of Ahimsa, "The letter killeth, but the Spirit giveth life."

It is obvious that it will be impossible, within the compass of a single chapter, to deal with all the questions and difficulties of this doctrine in a world such as we have around us today. Yet it may be easily proved that Ahimsa underlies all Mahatma Gandhi's passive resistance campaigns, both in South Africa and in India. A technique has been worked out by him under this head. Many methods of passive resistance have been rejected because they were likely to lead to violence, or else because they contained some compromise with truth; others have been accepted because no violence was implied and no compromise with truth.

There are two aspects which may appeal to the conscience of Western readers with regard to Mahatma Gandhi's actions in relation to Ahimsa. The former of these describes him putting an end to the miserable suffering of a little calf which was lying in agony by administering to it an opiate poison. This slaughter of a cow, as it might almost be called, was an amazingly daring act in the citadel of Hindu India. It disillusioned with a shock the blind devotion towards him of the fundamentalists in Hindu Religion. It seemed to them to go directly contrary to the principle of Ahimsa itself. The question of violently driving away destructive monkeys from the Ashram, which he binds up with it, has also given rise to great heart-burning among his followers.

The second question has been Mahatma Gandhi's relation to the problems connected with War and with recruiting for military service. Here again there have been instances in his career which have terribly perplexed his followers; for in spite of the profession of Ahimsa Mahatma Gandhi at one time actually encouraged recruiting for the great World War. Personally I have never been able to reconcile this with his own conduct in other respects, and it is one of the points where I have found myself in painful disagreement. In the paragraphs which I shall quote later his detailed explanations will be given. These will relate his own justification for recruiting, and I have quoted him at considerable length.

In the succeeding chapters of this book, which deal with the different historical events of his career, there will be seen written in letters of gold those unselfish deeds wherein he has relied upon Soul-Force in order to obtain his object, and has refused to admit the use of any physical force whatever. These acts of his, which cover a whole lifetime, speak eloquently of that spiritual power which has become the deepest principle of his being. Men may hold different opinions about his recruiting for the War, but there can be no two opinions concerning the entire nobility of his line of action in one great Passive Resistance Movement after another, wherein he entirely abjured the use of any physical force to attain his spiritual end.

The first passage to be quoted below will describe what he calls the "fiery ordeal" through which he was compelled to pass at the time when he was obliged to put out of its sufferings the little maimed calf. He writes thus:

An attempt is being made at Sabarmati Ashram to run a small model dairy and tannery on behalf of the Cow Service Society. Its work in this connection brings it up at every step against intricate moral dilemmas that would not arise but for the keenness to realize the Ashram ideal of seeking Truth through the exclusive means of Ahimsa.

For instance, some days back a calf, having been maimed, lay in agony in the Ashram. Whatever treatment and nursing was possible was given to it. The surgeon whose advice was sought in the matter declared the case to be past help and past hope. The suffering of the animal was so great that it could not even turn on its side without excruciating pain.

In these circumstances I felt that humanity demanded that the agony should be ended by ending life itself. I held a preliminary discussion with the Managing Committee, most of whom agreed with my view. The matter was then placed before the whole Ashram. At the discussion a worthy neighbour vehemently opposed the idea of killing even to end pain and offered to nurse the dying animal. The nursing consisted, in co-operation with some of the Ashram Sisters, in warding the flies from the animal and trying to feed it. The ground of the friend's opposition was that we have no right to take away life, which we cannot create. His argument seemed to me to be pointless here. It would have point if the taking of life was actuated by self-interest. Finally, in all humanity, but with the clearest of convictions, I got in my presence a doctor kindly to administer the calf a quietus by means of a poison injection. The whole thing was over in less than two minutes.

I knew that public opinion would not approve of my action, and that it would read nothing but Violence in it; but I know, too, that performance of one's duty should be independent of public opinion. I have all along held that one is bound to act according to what appears to oneself to be right, even though it may appear wrong to others; and experience has shown that this is the only correct course.

I admit that there is always a possibility of mistaking right for wrong and vice versa; but often one learns to recognize wrong only through unconscious error. On the other hand, if a man fails to follow the light within for fear of public opinion, or any other similar reason, he would never be able to know right from wrong, and in the end lose all sense of distinction between the two. That is why the poet has sung

The pathway of love is the ordeal of fire;
The shrinkers turn away from it.

The pathway of Ahimsa—that is, of love—has often to be trodden all alone.

But the question may be very legitimately put to me: Would I apply to human beings the principle I have enunciated in connection with the calf? Would I like it to be applied in my own case? My reply is: Yes; the same law holds good in both cases. The law of "As with one so with all" admits of no exceptions; otherwise the killing of the calf was wrong and violent. In practice, however, we do not cut short the sufferings of our ailing dear ones by death, because as a rule we have always means at our disposal to help them, and because they have the capacity to think and decide for themselves. But supposing that in the case of an ailing friend I am unable to render any aid whatever, and recovery is out of the question, and the patient is lying in an unconscious state in the throes of fearful agony, then I would not see any violence in putting an end to his suffering by death.

Just as a surgeon does not commit violence, but practises the purest Ahimsa, when he wields his knife on the patient's body for the latter's benefit, similarly one may find it necessary, in certain imperative circumstances, to go a step farther and sever life from the body in the interest of the sufferer. It may be objected that, whereas the surgeon performs his operation to save the life of the patient, in the other case we do just the reverse. But on a deeper analysis it will be found that the ultimate object sought to be served in both cases is the same—namely, to relieve the suffering soul within from pain.

But the trouble with our votaries of Ahimsa is that they have made of it a blind fetish and put the greatest obstacle in the way of the spread of true Ahimsa in our midst. The current (and in my opinion mistaken) view of Ahimsa has drugged our conscience and rendered us insensible to a host of other and more insidious forms of violence, like harsh words, harsh judgments, ill-will, anger, spite, and lust of cruelty; it has made us forget that there may be far more violence in the slow torture of men and animals, the starvation and exploitation to which they are subjected out of selfish greed, the wanton humiliation and oppression of the weak and the killing of their self-respect that we witness all around us today, than in the benevolent taking of life.

It is this fundamental misconception about the nature and scope of Ahimsa—this confusion about the relative values—that is responsible for our mistaking mere nonkilling for Ahimsa, and for the fearful amount of violence that goes on in the name of Ahimsa in our country.

Let a man contrast the sanctimonious horror that is affected by the so-called votaries of Ahimsa at the very idea of killing an ailing animal, in order to cut short its agony, with their utter apathy and indifference to countless cruelties that are practised on our dumb-cattle world, and he will begin to wonder whether he is living in the land of Ahimsa or in that of conscious or unconscious hypocrisy.

I now come to the other crying problem confronting the Ashram today which brings in the principle of Ahimsa. The monkey nuisance has become very acute and an immediate solution has become absolutely necessary. The growing vegetables and fruit trees have become a special mark of attention of this privileged fraternity, and these are now threatened with utter destruction. In spite of all our efforts we have not yet been able to find an efficacious, and at the same time non-violent, remedy for this evil.

The idea of wounding monkeys to frighten them away seems to me unbearable, though I am seriously considering the question of killing them in case it should become unavoidable. But this question is not so simple or easy as the previous one.

I see a clear breach of Ahimsa even in driving away monkeys; the breach would be proportionately greater if they have to be killed; for any act of injury done from self-interest, whether amounting to killing or not, is doubtless violence.

All life in the flesh exists by some violence. Hence the highest religion has been defined by a negative word, Ahimsa. The world is bound in a chain of destruction. In other words, violence is an inherent necessity for life in the body. That is why a votary of Ahimsa always prays for ultimate deliverance from the bondage of the flesh.

None, while in the flesh, can thus be entirely free from violence, because one never completely renounces the "will to live." Of what use is it to force the flesh merely if the spirit refuses to co-operate? You may starve even unto death, but if at the same time the mind continues to hanker after objects of sense your fast is a sham and a delusion. What, then, is the poor, helpless slave to the "will to live" to do? How is he to determine the exact nature and the extent of violence he must commit?

Society has, no doubt, set down a standard and absolved the individual from troubling himself about it to that extent. But every seeker after Truth has to adjust and vary the standard according to his individual need, and to make a ceaseless endeavour to reduce the circle of violence. But the peasant is too occupied with the burden of his hard and precarious existence to have time or energy to think out these problems for himself; and the cultured class, instead of helping him, chooses to give him the cold shoulder.

Having become a peasant myself, I have no clear-cut road to go by, and must therefore chalk out a path for myself and possibly for fellow-peasants; and the monkey nuisance being one of the multitude of ticklish problems that stare the farmer in the face, I must find out some means by which the peasant's crops can be safeguarded against it with the minimum amount of violence.

I am told that the farmers of Gujarat employ special watch-men whose very presence scares away the monkeys and saves the peasant from the necessity of killing them. That may be, but it should not be forgotten that, whatever efficacy this method might have, it is clearly dependent upon some measure of destruction at some time or other; for these cousins of ours are wily and intelligent beings. The moment they discover that there is no real danger for them they refuse to be frightened even by gun-shots, and only gibber and howl the more when shots are fired.

None of the methods that I have known up to now is free from violence. Whilst, therefore, I would welcome any practical suggestions for coping with this problem, let the intending advisers bear in mind what I have said above, and send only such solutions as they have themselves successfully tried and have found to cause the minimum amount of injury.

The discussion which Mahatma Gandhi has thus carried on, revealing the torture of his own soul over the fact that as long as any human being remains in the flesh he cannot avoid acts of violence, gives us a clear idea of the supreme religious value that he attaches to this one virtue of Ahimsa. At the same time it shows us how far he is from being a mere literalist, and how entirely indifferent he is to being charged with inconsistency so long as his own conscience remains clear.

A second example wherein his action appears to me far more difficult to defend will now be brought forward. It gives his own self-defence for taking part in Red Cross work during different wars in which the British Commonwealth was engaged. These acts have been felt recently by many in Europe and America to be a vital contradiction of his own doctrine of Ahimsa. It will be best to give his explanation at some length in his own words. He does not defend himself, but rather takes up the same position as that enunciated above—namely, that all human existence is built up on evil, and that our choice is rather confined to taking the lesser of two evils than to the avoidance of evil altogether. He writes as follows:

There is no defence for my conduct in doing ambulance work, weighed only in the scales of Ahimsa. I draw no distinction between those who wield the weapons of destruction and those who do Red Cross work. Both participate in war and advance its course; both are guilty of the crime of war. But even after introspection, during all these years, I feel that in the circumstances in which I found myself I was bound to adopt the course I did, both during the Boer War and the Great European War, and for that matter the so-called Zulu "Rebellion" of Natal in 1906.

Life is governed by a multitude of forces. It would be smooth sailing if we could determine the course of action only by one general principle, whose application at a given time was too obvious to need even a moment's reflection. But I cannot recall a single act which could be so easily determined.

Being a confirmed war-resister, I have never given myself training in the use of destructive weapons, in spite of opportunities to take such training. It was perhaps thus that I escaped direct destruction of human life. But so long as I live under a system of Government based on force and voluntarily partook of the many facilities and privileges it created for me, I was bound to help that Government to the extent of my ability when it was engaged in a war, unless I non-co-operated with that Government and renounced to the utmost of my capacity the privileges it offered me.

Let me take an illustration. I am a member of an institution which holds a few acres of land whose crops are in imminent peril from the monkeys. I believe in the sacredness of all life, and hence I regard it as a breach of Ahimsa to inflict any injury on the monkeys. But I do not hesitate to instigate and direct an attack on the monkeys in order to save the crops. I would like to avoid this evil. I can avoid it by leaving or breaking up the institution. I do not do so because I do not expect to be able to find a society where there will be no agriculture, and therefore no destruction of some life. In fear and trembling, in humility and penance, I therefore participate in the injury inflicted on the monkeys, hoping some day to find a way out.

Even so did I participate in the three acts of war. I could not— it would be madness for me to sever my connection with the society to which I belong. And on those three occasions I had no thought of non-co-operating with the British Government. My position regarding that Government is totally different today, and hence today I should not voluntarily participate in its wars. I should risk imprisonment and even gallows if I were forced to take up arms or otherwise take part in its military operations.

But that still does not solve the riddle. If there were an Indian National Government, whilst I should not take any direct part in any military training of those who wish to take it, I should not oppose it. For I know that all its members do not believe in Non-Violence to the extent I do. It is not possible to make a person, or a society, nonviolent by compulsion.

Non-violence works in a most mysterious manner. Often a man's actions defy analysis in terms of non-violence; equally often his actions may wear the appearance of violence when he is absolutely non-violent in the highest sense of the term, and is subsequently found to be so. All I can then claim for my conduct is that it was, in the instance cited, actuated in the interests of non-violence. There was no thought of sordid national or other interests. I do not believe in the promotion of national or any other interest at the sacrifice of some other interest.

I may not carry my argument any farther. Language at best is but a poor vehicle for expressing one's thoughts in full. For me non-violence is not a mere philosophical principle. It is the rule and the breath of my life. I know I fail often, sometimes consciously, more often unconsciously. It is a matter not of the intellect but of the heart. True guidance comes by constant waiting upon God, by utmost humility, self-abnegation, by being ever ready to sacrifice one's self. Its practice requires fear-lessness and courage of the highest order.

But the light within me is steady and clear. There is no escape for any of us save through truth and non-violence. I know that war is wrong, is an unmitigated evil. I know, too, that it has got to go. I firmly believe that freedom won through bloodshed or fraud is no freedom. Would that all the acts alleged against me were found to be wholly indefensible rather than that, by any act of mine, Non-Violence was held to be compromised, or that I was ever thought to be in favour of violence or untruth in any shape or form. Not violence, not untruth, but Non-Violence! Truth is the law of our being!

I shall venture to quote a further explanation, which he himself has made, although it partly covers the same ground. He writes thus:

I did honestly believe that, in spite of the many disabilities my country, India, was labouring under, it was making its way towards freedom, and that on the whole the British Government from the popular standpoint was not wholly bad; and that the British administrators were honest, though insular and dense. Holding that view, I set about doing what an ordinary Englishman would do in the circumstances. I was not wise or important enough to take independent action. I had no business to judge or scrutinize ministerial decisions with the solemnity of a tribunal, I did not impute malice to the Ministers either at the time of the Boer War, the Zulu revolt, or the late European War. I did not consider Englishmen—nor do I now consider them—as particularly bad, or worse than other human beings. I considered, and still consider, them to be as capable of high motives and actions as any other body of men, and equally capable of making mistakes. I therefore felt that I sufficiently discharged my duties as a man and a citizen by offering my humble services to the Empire in the hour of its need, whether local or general. That is how I would expect every Indian to act by his country under Swaraj. I would be deeply distressed if on every conceivable occasion each one of us was to be a law unto himself and to scrutinize in golden scales every action of our future National Assembly. I would surrender my judgment in most matters to national representatives, taking particular care in making my choice of such representatives. I know that in no other manner would a democratic government be possible for one single day.

The whole situation is now changed for me. My eyes, I fancy, are opened. Experience has made me wiser. I consider the existing system of government to be wholly bad and requiring special national effort to end or mend it. It does not possess within itself any capacity for self-improvement. That I still believe many English administrators to be honest does not assist me because I consider them to be as blind and deluded as I was myself. Therefore I can take no pride in calling the Empire mine or describing myself as its citizen. On the contrary, I fully realize that I am a pariah of the Empire. I must therefore constantly pray for its radical reconstruction or total destruction; even as a Hindu pariah would be fully justified in so praying about Hinduism or Hindu society.

The next point, that of Ahimsa, is more abstruse. My conception of Ahimsa impels me always to dissociate myself from almost every one of the activities I am engaged in. My soul refuses to be satisfied so long as it is a helpless witness of a single wrong or a single misery. But it is not possible for me, a weak, frail, miserable being, to mend every wrong or to hold myself free of blame for all the wrong I see. The spirit in me pulls one way, the flesh in me pulls in the opposite direction. There is freedom from the action of these two forces, but that freedom

is attainable only by slow and painful stages. I cannot attain freedom by a mechanical refusal to act, but only by intelligent
action in a detached manner. This struggle resolves itself into an
incessant crucifixion of the flesh so that the spirit may become
entirely free.

I was again an ordinary citizen no wiser than my fellows,
myself believing in Ahimsa, and the rest not believing in it at
all, but refusing to do their duty of assisting the Government
because they were actuated by anger and malice. They were
refusing out of their ignorance and weakness. As a fellow-worker
it became my duty to guide them aright. I therefore placed
before them their clear duty, explained the doctrine of Ahimsa
to them, and let them make their choice, which they did. I do
not repent of my action in terms of Ahimsa. For under Swaraj,
too, I would not hesitate to advise those who *would* bear arms
to do so, and thus fight for the country.

I am obliged to leave his argument regarding war without discussion. It does not convince or satisfy me; yet it has been tested and
examined in his personal experience by his own pure spirit; and he
cannot as yet see a flaw in it. It was not possible for me to convince
him in this matter, when I tried to do so, any more than on a later
occasion concerning the violence of the "Burning of Foreign
Clothes." That second act of his, which appeared to me to be contrary to the spirit of Ahimsa, I have set forward in another chapter
and have quoted his own explanation.

8

THE ETHICS OF KHADDAR

The love of the poor and of the oppressed is deep in Mahatma Gandhi's nature. His whole attitude towards life ever since his great conversion, owing to the reading of Tolstoy and his study of the Sermon on the Mount along with the Bhagavad Gita, has been one of complete identification with those who are "the poorest, the lowliest, and the lost." He would literally live their life and share their fate, and his prayer that he may be born an "untouchable" has been no mere empty gesture, but the heart-longing of one who is himself the soul of sincerity and truth.

At the same time his nature is practical, and he is a poet in deeds rather than in words. His Caste inheritance as a member of the trading and agricultural community, called the Vaishya Caste, has given him this utilitarian side, which is almost unique in an idealist so uncompromising as Mahatma Gandhi.

It will be seen from this how natural it has been for him to make a practical economic programme for the help of the poor of his own country an essential part of his religion. This economic issue of Khaddar* (or homespun cloth) has shared with the Swadeshi principle and the doctrine of Ahimsa his moral allegiance. Indeed, in a singular way the three principles of Swadeshi, Khaddar, and Ahimsa combine in one, to his own kindled imagination, as offering the practical remedy for the suffering of the millions of village people who live in India on the border-line of famine and starvation. He has often explained to me how the Swadeshi principle makes for contentment with local conditions and with the things that God has

---

* R. B. Gregg's book, *Economics of Khaddar,* published by S. Ganesan, Triplicane, Madras, is the authoritative work on this subject from Mahatma Gandhi's own standpoint. It has received his strong approval.

provided for man's sustenance, instead of the ruthless exploitation of other countries to obtain unnecessary luxuries; thus overthrowing their own internal economic equilibrium and introducing discord. He has also shown me on many occasions how the cultivation of home-spinning and weaving is the one means of preventing the spirit of violence from spreading in India by giving the village people an industry that will occupy their idle time and lead onward to prosperous conditions. He has the strong basic instinct, which belongs to his own Vaishya Caste, that God is to be found in material things and through the satisfaction of economic needs, and that to preach God's love to starving people, while neglecting to improve their condition, is an insult to God Himself.

His own explanation of the Khaddar programme, which I quote below, is so full of detail that it will need no further explanation. He writes as follows:

> In order to understand properly what the Home-spinning movement means one must first have a clear idea of all that it does not mean. For instance, hand-spinning does not compete with, in order to displace, any existing type of industry; it does not aim at withdrawing a single able-bodied person who can otherwise find a more remunerative occupation from his work. To compare, therefore, the remuneration that hand-spinning offers with the earnings offered by any other occupation, to measure its economic value in terms of returns and dividends, can only serve to mislead. In a word, hand-spinning does not claim to satisfy the economics of "getting rich." The sole claim on its behalf is that it alone offers an immediate, practicable, and permanent solution of the problem of problems that confronts India—namely, the enforced idleness for nearly six months in the year of an overwhelming majority of India's population, owing to lack of a suitable occupation supplementary to agriculture and the chronic starvation of the masses that results therefrom. There would be no place for the spinning-wheel in the national life of India, comparatively small as the remuneration that can be derived from it is, if these two factors were not there.

A proper appraisement of the economic value of home-spinning would therefore involve a consideration of the almost incredible poverty of the Indian masses, and partly of its causes, inasmuch as the remedy is to be sought in the removal of the causes.

The gradual extinction of all of India's principal indigenous industries, without any new ones arising to take their place; the steadily growing ruralization of the country; the deterioration of the existing stock of cattle; scarcities and famines following in quick succession; the progressive pauperization of the agriculturist, rendering him incapable of making any improvement in the little bits of his minutely subdivided holding, which are in their turn unfit for the application of new implements and improved methods of agriculture; the control over agriculture of the money-lending agencies driving the agriculturist to concentrate on cotton and aggravating the evil of high prices of food-stuffs: all these and many other factors have combined to make poverty and unemployment the stupendous problem of today.

There are Dr. Buchanan's and Montgomery Martin's surveys of Northern India during the first quarter of the nineteenth century to bear eloquent testimony to the villages and towns smiling with plenty, to the vast voluntary organization that was at work in every town and village, keeping millions of spinners, tens of thousands of weavers, and thousands of dyers, bleachers, carpenters, smiths, and smaller handicraftsmen busy throughout the districts, all the year round, and bringing millions of rupees and distributing them equably in Bihar, Bengal, U.P., and Mysore. If official testimony were needed for the contrast which the picture of the present-day India bears to that of those days, enough is to be had in the Census Reports. The average size of an agricultural holding in the major provinces today is about three acres, except in Bombay, N.W.P., and the Punjab, where the average is ten and a half.

It is on these impoverished holdings that 72 percent of the whole population of India is supposed to subsist. "This," says the Census Report, "utilizes to the full neither the energy of the worker nor the productivity of the soil." Mr. Thompson (Bengal

Census) states: "The number of actual workers in cultivation ... in British Bengal is 11,060,629. This means 2.2 acres per worker. It is in such figures as these that the explanation of the poverty of the cultivator lies. The cultivation of less than two and a quarter acres of land cannot employ a man for more than a comparatively small number of days in the year. The cultivator works fairly hard for a few days when he ploughs his land and puts down his crops and again when he harvests them, but for most of the year he has little or nothing to do.

Mr. Edye (U.P. Census) describes the agriculture of the Province as involving "very hard work for certain short periods ... and almost complete inactivity for the rest of the year. These periods of inactivity are spent in idleness." Thus Mr. Houghton (C.P. Census): "The Kharif crop which is raised at the end of the rains is the only crop of importance that is grown, and when this crop is gathered there is a scarcity of employment until shortly before the break of the next monsoon." Mr. Calvert, in his book *The Wealth and Welfare of the Punjab,* estimates "that the work done by the average cultivator in the Punjab does not represent more than about 150 days' full labour for twelve months." When this is the state of things in a province where the average size of a holding is comparatively very large (9.18 acres), and where the percentage of irrigated area (which keeps the agriculturist better employed than dry areas) is the second highest in India, the state of other provinces can well be imagined.

It is thus clear that all these officials are unanimous on the point that the whole of the agricultural population remains without work for at least half of the year, and one or two have made pointed reference to that fact as the sole cause of the poverty of the agriculturist. When even in Lancashire, with an acreage of 21 per peasant, it is thought that "it would be a great boon if in bad weather and winter the agriculturists had something to do in their homes of a remunerative character as in days past,"* and in Italy, with an important textile trade of its own,

---

* Green, *Rural Industries of England.*

"the peasant women of almost every district where mulberry-
trees can be grown are fully occupied with spinning,"* the
importance of a subsidiary cottage industry connected with
agriculture in a country of the vast magnitude of India should
need no argument.

But what exactly that subsidiary industry should be has been
the subject of much argument—ever since, and only since, the
inception of the home-spinning movement. Let us hope that
critics will recognize that it was the Charkha** that first set
them a-thinking. Once they recognize it one might humbly
submit to them the fact that the Charkha is no new invention,
like Ford's motor-car; it is a rediscovery, like the discovery of its
own mother by a strayed child. The critic must not forget that
the child here is a vast multitude of people, the most conservative in the world, and scattered over a continent 1,900 miles
long and 1,500 miles broad, and the mother is the handicraft
that gave them all warmth and sustenance.

Once this fact is understood, no one will seriously press the
claims of any other industry. Industries there are enough and to
spare. Why not try dairying? Well, India is not Denmark, which
easily possesses 40 percent of the butter trade of England. In
1900 Denmark received 8 million pounds sterling from
England for butter, and 3 million for bacon, the raising of pigs
being an important adjunct of the dairy industry. But India
cannot find a bigger India to take its dairy products, and no one
will ask the India of Hindus and Mussalmans to engage in the
bacon-curing industry. Poultry-rearing and beekeeping may
also be dismissed on the same score, if not on the ground of
their novelty and their necessitating technical skill. India cannot
today develop her agriculture and increase the one acre per
inhabitant that it has today; for India is not Ireland, which has
its wonderful Department of Agriculture organizing numerous

---

* Bombay Mill-owners' statement to the Tariff Board.
** The word "Charkha" means the hand-spinningwheel. "Khaddar" means hand-spun and
   hand-woven cloth. "Khadi" is another word used with approximately the same meaning.

colleges and placing numerous experts at the disposal of County Councils. Nor will anyone suggest that the vast mass of people can take up sock-knitting, or cane-work, or basket-making. These do not and cannot command the ready and permanent market that yarn always does. Even today in parts of Bengal and Madras the old tradition of yarn markets continues. Why not have a jute-mill in the jute areas of Bengal, suggests a Bengal civilian with unconscious humour. Possibly he is wondering why none of his brother-civilians has suggested the establishment of more cotton-mills in cotton areas. He forgets the jute-mills employ today not more than 250,000 labourers, impoverish the jute-grower, and fatten a few capitalists and middlemen. After 70 years of cotton industry, and having some 50 crores of capital, the cotton magnates* only claim to have given their daily bread to 1 ½ million souls, representing the families of 370,000 mill-hands employed by them, and a handful of clerks and superior staff.

But, it is objected, spinning affords only a miserable pittance, and is thus an economic waste. It is forgotten that spinning has never been put forward as a principal occupation. It is offered to those who would otherwise waste their time in idleness. Whether two annas per day, or, let us say, an anna per day, or Rs. 24 yearly, is a miserable pittance,** is a matter that can only be judged by one who has seen the "chill penury" of the masses with his own eyes. This is no place to discuss the income per head in India. The Indian Economic Inquiry Committee cited the estimates of no less than fifteen authorities taken at different times. Ever since Dadabhai Naoroji started the chase of that golden hind† a number of others have pursued it, no one yet being recognized as having captured it. But assuming even what appears to be an estimate farthest wide of the mark as the correct

---

* Bombay Mill-owners' statement to the Tariff Board. A crore of rupees represents today about £750,000.

** An anna represents roughly a penny, and a rupee one shilling and sixpence.

† I.e. to discover the personal income of the whole population of India.

one, viz. that of Rs. 116 by Mr. Finlay Shirras, one may like to know if Rs. 24 is not a substantial addition to that income!

Whereas hand-spinning presents the following special features which render it pre-eminently suitable as a remedy for India's present economic distress:

1. It is immediately practicable because
    (a) It does not require any capital or costly implements to put in operation. Both the raw material and the implements for working it can be cheaply and locally obtained.
    (b) It does not require any higher degree of skill or intelligence than the ignorant and poverty-stricken masses of India possess.
    (c) It requires so little physical exertion that even little children and old men can practise it and so contribute their mite to the family fund.
    (d) It does not require the ground to be prepared for its introduction afresh, because the spinning tradition is still alive among the people.
2. It is universal and permanent, since, next to food, yarn alone can be sure of always commanding an unlimited and ready market at the very doorsteps of the worker, and thus ensures a steady, regular income to the impoverished agriculturist.
3. It is independent of monsoon conditions and so can be carried on even during famine times.
4. It is not opposed to the religious or social susceptibilities of the people.
5. It provides a most perfect ready means of fighting famine.
6. It carries work to the very cottage of the peasant, and thus prevents the disintegration of the family under economic distress.
7. It alone can restore some of the benefits of the village communities of India now wellnigh ruined.
8. It is the backbone as much of the hand-weaver as of the agriculturist, since it alone can provide a permanent and

stable basis for the hand-loom industry, which at present is supporting from eight to ten million people and supplies about one-third of the clothing requirements of India, but uses chiefly mill-made yarn.

9. Its revival would give a fillip to a host of cognate and allied village occupations, and thus rescue the villages from the state of decay into which they have fallen.

10. It alone can ensure the equitable distribution of wealth among the millions of the inhabitants of India.

11. It alone effectively solves the problem of unemployment, not only the partial unemployment of the agriculturist but of the educated youth aimlessly wandering in search of occupation. The very magnitude of the task requires the marshalling of all the intellectual forces of the country to guide and direct the movement.

We shall now consider how far the claims advanced on behalf of the Charkha movement have been realized. The Charkha movement began in 1920. The salient features may be noted.

1. *Organization.*—Instead of the scattered efforts of the beginning we have now a regular organization with branches in every province and with a capital of 15 lakhs,* collecting assets and distributing loans, publishing reports of production and sales in the various provinces month by month, collecting and publishing all valuable data; making experiments, in improving the Charkha, the carding-bow and the hand-gin, and popularizing them; receiving yarn from voluntary spinners, accurately testing its quality and directing so far as is possible the various producing centres in the matter of improving the yarn and cloth; training workers in all the technical processes, from the picking of cotton to the final weaving and dyeing of cloth and making it ready for the market, and organizing a Khadi Service.

---

* A lakh of rupees represents about £7,500.

2. *Work*.—The concrete work of the All-India Spinners' Association may be noticed under several heads:—

(a) The figures of production cover only that done under the supervision of the Board. They do not represent such production as has been traditionally in existence in parts of Assam, Rajputana, Punjab, and Madras, independent of the Charkha movement.

The figures for production for the year 1924 to 25 total Rs. 1,903,034 as against Rs. 949,348 in 1923 to 24. The figures for the year 1925 to 26 have shown a great advance on the previous year. It is not necessary to give the figures for sales, as they represent those for production, practically every yard of Khaddar that is produced being sold. Rs. 1,903,034 worth of cloth means 3,806,068 yards of cloth (the average price of a yard being 8 annas), which in its turn represents 1,522,427 lb. of yarn. This represents the fruit of two years' concentrated effort in a movement which only started five years ago.

(b) Improvement in the quality of yarn and cloth and decrease in the cost and price may be considered together.

Whereas five years ago yarn of high counts was a rarity, not only Madras, but Bihar and Bengal, both produce it now. The quality of ordinary yarn is being daily more and more standardized—15 to 20 counts being the usual quality spun everywhere except in Gujarat. Not that we have yet been able completely to perfect that yarn, but the defective yarn may be regarded as a passing phase. All Khaddar depots are now testing the yarn they receive, and have practically decided not to accept yarn under standard test.

(c) *Prices*.—Effective decentralization and integration of processes is the keynote of the economics of hand-spinning, just as centralization and the division of processes is the law in large-scale production. Thus in Gujarat, where ginning, carding, and spinning are done by different persons, the cost of production of yarn was Rs. 0-9-4 1/2 per lb.;

in Tirupur, where the spinner cards for himself, the cost was Rs. 0-6-10 ½; in parts of Bengal ginning and carding are both done by the spinner, bringing down the cost to Rs. 0-5-6.

The result of efforts in this direction has been a remarkable decrease in the cost of production in all provinces except perhaps in Gujarat. The cost and price in Madras and in the Punjab show today a 50 percent reduction over what they were in 1920; 25 percent over what they were in 1922. It may be remarked that the reduction of the price to the extent of 50 percent is really to the extent of 100 percent, as the quality of cloth is certainly 50 percent better than it was five years ago, though we recognize that the reduction is partly due to a fall in the price of cotton during the last two years.

(d) *Cotton.*—A final stage in the development of the economics of hand-spinning is reached when the spinner not only performs all the preliminary processes, but begins to stock his own cotton. This was done with wonderful results in Kathiawar last year. They not only had good cotton but saved a lot of waste and spun better quality of yarn. At the present time the whole cotton crop is controlled by middlemen or agents of the mill-owners, who take away the best of the harvest, leaving only indifferent cotton behind, which is mostly the cotton used by the hand-spinners, partly explaining the inferior quality of yarn. When the hand-spinning agriculturist understands his own interest better, as soon he must, he would automatically stock his own cotton and spin for personal use, not for wages.

3. *Famine Areas.*—It is difficult to indicate in brief the way in which Charkha came to be adopted as a relief measure in famine areas. Famines, some might say, occurred in the days of the Charkha, too. Indeed, they did, but with nothing like the frequency that they have occurred since 1864. Ever since that date there have been famine commissions which

have only emphasized the essential difficulty of State relief.
There is reluctance of those unaccustomed to famine to
seek relief; there is eagerness of those accustomed to famine
to accept relief; there is demoralization that follows when
families are broken up and half-starved masses become a
moving multitude. "The maintenance of the village system
is the only means of saving life by preserving order," said Sir
Edward Caird. By nothing could this be maintained so well
as by taking the means to earn relief to the very door of the
famine-stricken, namely, the Charkha. That is the only work
which can be done by young and old, decrepit and infirm,
day and night, and without any strain.

Dr. P. C. Ray first tried paddy-husking and other forms
of relief in the flood and famine areas of West Bengal in
1923 to 24. He found that they were of no avail, and then
tried the Charkha, which worked to perfection. What can
be called a signal achievement is that the Charkha has now
a permanent home in those areas, enabling the people to
supplement their slender means and to resist crop failures
and floods more effectively than ever before.

So far we have considered the actual work achieved.
That work in itself should contain the promise of its future
possibilities. But, it is said, we are not reckoning with the
competition of the machine-made cloth. Is it, however, fair
to say that there *is* competition between the home-made
and the machine-made cloth! There can be competition
between mills and mills—foreign mills and indigenous mills,
mills driven by steam power and those driven by electric
power. But how can there be, or rather why should there
be, any competition between one which is an essentially
vital industry and another which is not?

We shall make our meaning clear. Among the most crying
needs of the day is relief from economic distress of the millions
of the peasantry—removal of the partial unemployment of
the agricultural classes. The spinning-wheel is the only
industry that can give such relief and such employment. The

fifty crores of capital which the mills have sunk can only give their daily bread to 1½ million souls, representing the families of 370,000 mill-hands, who are largely drawn from the agricultural classes. Now, supposing that the mill industry expands to the extent of the total cloth consumption of India, will the matter be any the better so far as the starving millions, who are badly in need of a subsidiary industry, are concerned? Let us see. Our cloth consumption today is 4,661 million yards. To produce that amount about 1,165 million pounds of yarn will be needed. To have 1,165 million pounds of yarn it would be necessary to have about 11 million spindles, and to convert the yarn into cloth, 215,655 looms. To work these 11 million spindles and 215,655 looms the number of operatives will at an outside estimate be 600,000. This means that 2,500,000 people at the most can find their living from the industry, and these people are largely lost to the soil. Therefore the mill industry at best can only tear from their homes so many agriculturists. It cannot give a single one of them a supplementary industry. The mills and the spinning-wheel are, therefore, dissimilars admitting of no comparison.

Let us now see how many souls the same amount of cloth produced by our home industry can find employment for. The production of 1,165 million lb. of yarn would require at least 46,600,00 spinning-wheels producing 25 lb. a year. This means that 46,600,000 spinners would supplement their income by spinning. Add to these the additional thousands of ginners, carders, sizers, dyers, carpenters, smiths, and educated organizers, and 3,107,033 weavers necessary for the maintenance of the industry. This means (deducting 61.4 million children under 10 from the total 224 million agricultural people) not much less than half the agriculturist population of India.

So far as the consumer is concerned it has already been possible to secure his response to this vital industry, and for the industry to meet his wants in increasing proportion; for

a progressive improvement in quality and cheapness has
been steadily maintained. The industry is vital because its
conception is based on economics founded upon life.
"Nations," says a writer, "must have an economy that
enables them to live." Here is an industry which will enable
the Indian people not only to live as a nation, but to live as a
nation producing wealth which is real and equitably distrib-
uted; not wealth which in Ruskin's picturesque language
"may in verity be only the gilded index of far-reaching
ruin; a wrecker's handful of coin gleaned from the beach to
which he has beguiled an argosy."

Is it too much to expect the State to protect such a life-
giving industry? Is it too much to expect them to extend it
their exclusive protection, even as it is extended to a vital
service like the Postal Service? It is quite usual in some
countries to protect the "market rights" of municipalities;
and in protecting our "market rights" in respect of Khaddar,
Government will but expiate the sins of predecessors who
strangled the one vital industry of the land.

9

"OUR SHAME AND THEIRS"

As will be apparent later, I have kept Mahatma Gandhi's own title for this chapter on "Untouchability." At the same time I would wish to use it here in a sense that he never intended; for when we speak of the segregation of the "untouchables" in India we are really confronting at the same time our own Western race and colour problem, which is our own shame, in the same way that "untouchability" is the shame of India.

The Christian Church in the West, no less than the Hindu Religion, has sadly failed hitherto to deal justly and act generously with those of another race. It has today its own "untouchable" problem in Africa and elsewhere, which it has not yet solved.

Many of the noblest saints in Hinduism, such as Chaitanya and Nanak, have striven for racial equality. Gautama, the Buddha, five hundred years before Christ, proclaimed it and welcomed the out-caste into his Church. But the evil has been repeatedly revived in new forms of fear and hatred until racial segregation has ensued. The religious idea of ceremonial uncleanness or pollution has entered in besides, so that the segregation which took place originally from social causes has obtained a religious sanction. Thus the evil has grown like a canker in the heart of Hinduism, just in the same way that colour prejudice has sprung up in certain lands in the heart of the Christian Church.

Among the Hindus of Modern India more than fifty millions have only been admitted into the outermost fringe of Hinduism as outcastes or "untouchables." The latter word is used because, according to a theory which has grown up among the common people and has become in recent times regarded as a part of religion itself, it is necessary for a Caste Hindu, who by accident touches one of these outcastes, to purify himself by an ablution. The degradation into which these poor outcastes have fallen may be judged from the fact that a very large number of them now eat carrion and garbage and the leavings from the meals of the Caste people. Their houses, separated from the Caste people's dwellings, are hovels hardly fit for human habitation. In South India the conditions in which they live are the most terrible of all.

I can remember how, when I went near a poor "untouchable" woman in Malabar, who was crouching in her hut with three half-starved children by her side and with a mere skeleton of a baby in her arms, she screamed out in a terrible manner, even though I was wearing Indian home-spun clothes and could not possibly have been mistaken for an official. She was possessed with the horrible fear that she might pollute me by her presence, and that I might in return perhaps do her some bodily injury. The shock was to me so great when I saw her frightened face that it haunted me for many days.

I have told this simple story in order to make clear what an immense load of fear has to be lifted from these poor people before they can be set free and cherished as brothers and sisters.

The problem, as I have said, is not one that affects India alone. The treatment of the coloured races in different parts of the world, such as South Africa and the Southern States of America, has in it all the elements which have gone to make up in the past "untouchability" in India. The fear of lynching among the Negroes, wherever terrorism has done its evil work, is not altogether unlike the fear in that poor woman's face in Malabar. The psychology is the same in both cases. By an irony of fate the Indians who have gone to South Africa are segregated in various ways which are parallel to the social segregation between caste and outcaste in India. Mr. Gandhi is never tired of pointing out that this is the due retribution for the sin of "untouchability." In season and out of season he has declared that India cannot attain Swaraj until the people themselves have removed from their midst this curse. The following is one of his pointed utterances while making a speech in the presence of the "untouchables" themselves:

I regard "untouchability" as the greatest blot on Hinduism. This idea was not brought home to me simply by my bitter experiences during the South African struggle. It is not, again, due to the fact that I was once an agnostic. It is equally wrong to think, as some people do, that I have taken my views from my study of Christian religious literature. These views of mine on this subject date as far back as the time when I was neither enamoured of, nor was acquainted with, the Bible or the followers of the Bible.

I was hardly yet twelve when this idea had dawned on me. A scavenger named Uka, an "untouchable," used to attend our house for cleaning latrines. Often I would ask my mother why it was wrong to touch him and why I was forbidden to do so. If I accidentally touched Uka I was asked to perform the ablutions; and though I naturally obeyed, it was not without smilingly protesting that "untouchability" was not sanctioned by religion and that it was impossible that it should be so. I was a very dutiful and obedient child; but so far as was consistent with respect for my parents I often had tussles with them on this matter. I told my mother that she was entirely wrong in considering physical contact with Uka as sinful; it could not be sinful.

While at school I would often happen to touch the "untouchables"; and, as I never would conceal the fact from my parents, my mother would tell me that the shortest cut to purification, after the unholy touch, was to cancel it by touching any Mussalman passing by. Therefore simply out of reverence and regard for my mother I often did so, but never did so believing it to be a religious obligation.

The Ramayana* used to be regularly read in our family. A Brahmin used to read it. He was stricken with leprosy and was confident that a regular reading of the Ramayana would cure him; and indeed he was cured. "How can the Ramayana," I thought to myself, "in which one who is regarded nowadays as

---

* The Ramayana Epic, reciting the Divine Incarnation of Rama, was translated into Hindi by Tulsidas from Valmiki's original Sanskrit work. It has been called the "Bible" of North India among Hindus.

an 'untouchable' took Rama across the Ganges in his boat, countenance the idea of any human beings being 'untouchable' on the ground that they are polluted souls?"

The fact that we addressed God as "the purifier of the polluted" shows that it is a sin to regard anyone born in Hinduism as polluted—that it is Satanic to do so. I have hence been never tired of repeating that it is a great sin. I do not pretend that this thing had crystallized as a conviction in me at the age of twelve, but I do say that I did then regard "untouchability" as a sin.

I have always claimed to be an orthodox conservative Hindu. It is not that I am quite innocent of the Scriptures. I am not a profound scholar of Sanskrit. I have read the Vedas and the Upanishads only in translation. Naturally, therefore, mine is not a scholarly study of them. My knowledge of them is in no way profound, but I have studied them as a Hindu and I claim to have grasped their true spirit. By the time I had reached the age of twenty-one I had studied other religions also.

There was a time when I was wavering between Hinduism and Christianity. When I recovered my balance of mind I felt that to me salvation was possible only through the Hindu Religion, and my faith in Hinduism grew deeper and more enlightened. But even then I believed that "untouchability" was not for me.

So long as Hindus wilfully regard "untouchability" as part of their religion, so long as the mass of Hindus consider it a sin to touch a section of their brethren, Swaraj is impossible of attainment.

But I have faith in me still. I have realized that the spirit of kindness whereof the poet Tulsidas sings so eloquently, which forms the corner-stone of the Jain and Vaishnava religions, which is the quintessence of the Bhagavat* and behind every verse in the Gita—this kindness, this love, this charity is slowly but steadily gaining ground in the hearts of the masses of this country.

---

* One of the Hindu scriptures, much loved by village people for its spirit of generous love and forgiveness and devotion, and often recited in the villages.

I was at Nellore on National Day. I met the "untouchables" there, and I prayed as I have done today. I *do* want to attain spiritual deliverance. I do *not* want to be reborn. But if I have to be reborn I should wish to be born an "untouchable," so that I may share their sorrows, sufferings, and the affronts levelled at them, in order that I may endeavour to free myself and them from that miserable condition. Therefore I prayed that if I should be born again I should be so, not as a Brahmin, Kshattriya, Vaishya, or Shudra, but as an "untouchable."

I love scavengering. In my Ashram an eighteen-year-old Brahmin lad is doing the scavenger's work, in order to teach the Ashram scavenger cleanliness. The lad is no reformer. He was born and bred in orthodoxy. He is a regular reader of the Gita and faithfully performs his prayers. When he conducts the prayer his soft, sweet melodies melt one into love. But he felt that his accomplishments were incomplete until he had become also a perfect sweeper. He felt that if he wanted the Ashram sweeper to do his work well he must do it himself and set an example.

You should realize that you are cleaning Hindu society. You have, therefore, to purify your lives. You should cultivate the habits of cleanliness, so that no one may point his finger at you. Some of you are addicted to habits of drinking and gambling which you must get rid of.

You claim to be Hindus, you read the Scriptures; if, therefore, the Hindus oppress you, then you should understand that the fault does not lie in the Hindu religion, but in those who profess it. In order to emancipate yourselves you have to purify yourselves. You have to get rid of evil habits like drinking liquor and eating carrion. I have come in contact with the "untouchables" all over the country, and I have observed that immense possibilities lie latent in them, whereof neither they nor the rest of the Hindus seem to be aware. Their intellect is of virginal purity. I ask you to learn spinning and weaving; and if you take this up as a profession you will keep poverty from your doors.

You should now cease to accept leavings from plates, however clean they may be represented to be. Receive grain only—

good, sound grain, not rotten grain—and that too only if it is courteously offered. If you are able to do all that I have asked you to do, you will secure your emancipation.

The Hindus are not sinful by nature; they are sunk in ignorance. "Untouchability" must be extinct in this very year. Two of the strongest desires that keep me in the flesh are the emancipation of the "untouchables" and the protection of the cow. When these two desires are fulfilled, there is Swaraj; and therein lies my own soul's deliverance! May God give you strength to work out your own soul's salvation to the end!

Let me quote another dramatic incident. In the pages of *Young India* Mahatma Gandhi writes, with his own sincere and passionate accent, about a visit to Orissa, when I was his personal companion. Orissa is by far the most miserable and poverty-stricken part of India. He describes what happened as follows:

The long-deferred visit to Orissa has come to fill the bitter cup of sorrow and humiliation. It was at Bolgarh, thirty-one miles from the nearest railway station, that, whilst I was sitting and talking with Dinabandhu* Andrews, a pariah with a half-bent back, wearing only a dirty loin-cloth, came crouching in front of us. He picked up a straw and put it in his mouth, and then lay flat on his face with arms outstretched. He then raised himself, folded his hands, bowed, took out the straw, arranged it in his hair, and was about to leave.

I was writhing in agony whilst I witnessed the scene. Immediately the performance was finished I called out for an interpreter, asked the friend to come near, and began to talk to him.

He was an "untouchable" living in a village six miles away, and, being in Bolgarh for the sale of his load of faggots and having heard of me, he had come to see me. When asked why he had taken the straw in his mouth, he said that this was to honour me. I hung my head in shame. The price of such "honour" seemed to me to be far too great to bear. My Hindu spirit was deeply wounded.

---

* Literally, "Friend of poor people." A religious title.

I asked him for a gift. He searched for a copper about his waist.

"I do not want your copper," I said to him in my misery; "I want you to give me something better."

"I will give it," he replied.

I had ascertained from him that he drank liquor and ate carrion because it was the custom.

"The gift I want you to give me is a promise never again to take that straw in your mouth for any person on earth; it is beneath a man's dignity to do so; never again to drink, because it reduces man to the condition of a beast; never again to eat carrion, for it is against Hinduism, and no civilized person would ever eat carrion."

"But my people will excommunicate me if I do not eat carrion and drink," the poor man said.

"Then suffer the excommunication, and if need be leave the village."

The downtrodden, humble man made the promise. If he keeps it his threefold gift is more precious than all the rupees that generous countrymen entrust to my care.

This "untouchability" is our greatest shame. The humiliation of it is sinking deeper and deeper.

There could hardly have been a more tragic situation in his own life than when he had at last determined to take a little "untouchable" girl into his own house as his own adopted daughter, and Mrs. Gandhi at first was against it. The scene is told with amazing directness and frankness in his *Autobiography*, but it is too long to repeat in this chapter. It led to a dispute between husband and wife so acute that he declared he could not go on living in the house unless his wife were willing to receive the little "untouchable" child as his daughter. With many tears Mrs. Gandhi, who at that time did not share all his ideals, gave way.

On another occasion a somewhat similar dispute between husband and wife arose over the reception of a young clerk, who belonged to the "untouchable" class, in her house in South Africa. The question

of cleaning utensils which this "untouchable" had used was the cause
of the quarrel. It was one of the very rare occasions on which Mr.
Gandhi lost his temper with his wife, and his confession of this in
the *Autobiography* is told with deep humiliation. Such disputes as
these show to us with what strength of feeling these prejudices are
still held.

I have lived for a long time at different intervals in South Africa,
and nothing has struck me more than the similarity of these two
irrational, but fanatically potent, forces in human nature—the Caste
feeling in India and the race prejudice in South Africa.

One day I was asked in Travancore by the "untouchables" themselves, through a messenger, whether I would be willing to meet
them. They had heard of me as "Gandhi's brother," and they had sent
this message to me. When with joy I had accepted their invitation
and had reached the place at midday, I found that more than three
thousand of them had collected. Along with some devoted followers
of Gandhi who were with me we went up and down the rows of the
"untouchables," encouraging them and showing our friendship. It
was necessary thus to go moving slowly through their midst until
they had banished from their minds every last vestige of fear. What I
found out that day concerning the cruelty they received at the hands
of the landlords, and the oppression from which they suffered, was a
story of misery and wrong. Their faces told me by their lines of suffering the truth of their tale.

The following is another passage from Mahatma Gandhi's writing
on this subject:

> Surely when Hindus, by a deliberate and conscious effort, not
> by way of policy but for self-purification, remove the taint of
> "untouchability," that act will give the nation a new strength
> born of the consciousness of having done the right thing, and
> will therefore contribute to the attainment of Swaraj. We are
> powerless today because we have lost the power of cohesion.
> When we learn to regard these fifty millions of outcastes as our
> own we shall learn the rudiments of what it is to be one people.
> That one act of cleansing will probably solve also the Hindu-

Muslim question. For in it, too, the corrosive poison of "untouchability" is consciously or unconsciously working its way. Hinduism must be poor stuff if it requires to be protected by an artificial wall of this kind.

If "untouchability" and Caste are convertible terms, the sooner Caste perishes the better for all concerned. But I am satisfied that Caste is a healthy institution. The modern Caste, with its arrogant exclusiveness, is as good as gone. The innumerable subdivisions are destroying themselves with a rapidity of which we can have no conception.

It is our fault and shame that these suppressed classes are living outside towns and villages, and that they are leading a wretched life. Even as we rightly charge the British rulers with our helplessness and lack of initiative, so let us admit the guilt of the High-Caste Hindus in making the "untouchables" what they are today. The Alpha of our spiritual training must begin by our coming down from the Himalayan height and feeling one with them in love.

During the crisis of the Non-Co-operation Movement, in the year 1921, there was no subject that exercised the mind of Mahatma Gandhi so much as that of "untouchability." This movement has very often been misunderstood in the West as a purely negative, political revolt, born out of race bitterness and leading to the overthrow of the established order. On the contrary, the deepest note of all that was struck with perpetual response was the need of India's own self-purification and repentance for the national sin of regarding brothers and sisters as "untouchables." In no way would he allow the inescapable logic to be forgotten that if Indians treated their brothers and sisters so cruelly, then it was just that they should be treated in a similar manner themselves and that they would deserve such a fate. During those exciting and inspiring days the burden of his addresses was more like John the Baptist's call to repentance than anything else. The reiteration would have been monotonous had not his own earnestness and enthusiasm taken away any sense of it. It was quite noticeable how as time went on he mentioned less the shortcomings

of the British and reiterated the wrongs done by his own people.
Indeed, many of his followers remonstrated with him about this. But
he refused to pay any attention. During the struggle he never
wavered either to the right or to the left, but went straight forward
against this deep-rooted evil. The most common sentence of all that
he kept repeating in the vernacular was this: "If 'untouchability'
belongs to the Hindu religion, then I am not a Hindu."

The most scathing of all his speeches were delivered in the Madras
Presidency, where "untouchability" has remained in the past rampant
and aggressive. In Malabar and Travancore there are not only outcaste
people who cannot be touched, but others who can never even be
approached, or looked on, without defilement. The Nayadis, for
instance, have to keep more than two hundred yards distant from the
main road, in order that even the sight of them shall not pollute.
They place a wretched rag on the ground and stand afar off, thus
begging for alms.

It is a fact to be mentioned with great shame and inward reproach
by those of us who are members of the Christian Church that in
Travancore the Church itself is not free from these very evils, and
therefore it has hitherto failed. It has even in the past been an interested partner, and has countenanced "untouchability" in practice.
This Church was established in the south-west of India over fifteen
hundred years ago by Syrian Christians. It has gradually become a
silent sanctioner and approver of "untouchability." To my own great
shame and confusion of face, during a visit to Kottayam, a place
which had long been the centre of this ancient form of Christianity,
I tried to obtain a gathering of Christians to meet with the pariahs
at a simple meal in the so-called "untouchable" quarter. But only
three persons of my own Christian faith joined with me, although I
had met many hundreds during the day, and this simple meal with
the pariahs had been made widely known. One of those who joined
me was the Principal of the Mar Thoma Seminary; another was a
young Roman Catholic padre; and a third was a devoted young
enthusiast of the Syrian Christian Church who was a follower of
Mahatma Gandhi. There were also with me two who were Hindus.

Things are better now. The Union College at Alwaye, where

members of the Syrian Church are conducting liberal higher education, and other Christian institutions are rapidly taking away this shame and reproach from the younger generation. The same might also be written concerning many noble Hindu educational establishments; but alike among Hindus and Christians, along that Malabar coast, the evil is still terribly prevalent, and sights may still be seen even today that would shock human hearts.

Mahatma Gandhi's Madras speeches echo this note of horror which I have been obliged to strike in my comments concerning both Hindu and Christian practice above. He writes as follows:

Nowhere is the "untouchable" so cruelly treated as in the Madras Presidency. His very shadow defiles the Brahmins. He may not even pass through Brahmin streets. Non-Brahmins treat him no better. Between the two the Panchama, as he is called in these parts, is ground to atoms. Yet Madras is a land of mighty temples and religious devotion. The people with big Caste marks on their foreheads, with their long locks and their bare, clean bodies, look like *rishis.** But their religion seems almost to be exhausted in these outward observances.

In spite of this Satanic treatment of our own kith and kin by the Caste people in this part of India, I retain my faith in these Southern people. I have told them at all their huge meetings, in no uncertain terms, that there can be no Swaraj without the removal of the curse from our midst. I have told them that our being treated as social lepers in practically the whole world is due to our having treated a fifth of our own race as such. Non-Co-operation is a plea for a change of heart, not merely in the English, but equally in ourselves. Indeed, I expect the change first in us, and then as a matter of course in the English. A nation that can throw away an agelong curse in a year; that can shed the drink-habit as we shed our garments; that can return to its original industry and suddenly utilize its spare hours to manufacture sixty crores' worth of cloth, will be a transformed nation. Its transformation must react upon the world. If this can

* Saintly sages.

be accomplished, as I have faith it may, it must constitute even
for the scoffer a convincing demonstration of God's grace. And
so I say that, if India can become transformed in this wise, no
power on earth can deny India's right to establish Swaraj.

In spite of all the clouds that are thickening on the Indian
horizon, I make bold to prophesy that the moment India has
repented of her treatment of the "untouchables" and has boy-
cotted foreign cloth, that moment India will be hailed by the
very English officials who seem to have hardened their hearts
as a free and brave nation. This transformation cannot take place
by any elaborately planned mechanical action; but it can take place
if God's grace is with us. Who can deny that God is working a
wonderful change in the hearts of every one of us?

He was not, however, content with a single onslaught in the South
of India, but returned to the attack again and again. He had himself
suffered terribly in South Africa, along with the whole Indian community, many of whom were High-Caste Hindus, owing to the
treatment meted out to them by Christian people. Though in India
he refers very seldom to this in detail, yet it is not possible for me to
forget the things which I have seen out there.

How can I ever forget, for instance, the shock of horror and dismay
which I had on first landing in South Africa in 1913? The
Archdeacon kindly met me on the wharf and asked me to preach in
his church. It was the First Sunday after Christmas, and I preached a
Christmas sermon of "peace and good will to all mankind." I had no
idea whatever that anything had happened while I was preaching
that sermon; but Mr. Gandhi had expressed to my friend and companion, Mr. W. W. Pearson, of Manchester, that he himself would like
to hear me preach. Mr. Pearson had taken him to the church door,
and he had been refused an entrance even after all the circumstances
of the request had been courteously explained and it was known
who was being refused. Mr. Gandhi was thus a pariah in South Africa
to that European Christian congregation. Therefore I would again
explain that the title "Our Shame and Theirs" has been used by me
in this special sense; for we in the West must feel that the shame has

to be shared by Christians as well as Hindus.

Let me recall in conclusion the noble struggle undertaken at Vykom, in Travancore, under Mr. Gandhi's direction, while he was lying on a bed of sickness far away at Juhu, near Bombay. It represented the turning-point in the campaign against "untouchability." I was present during the Vykom struggle and can write of it as an eye-witness.

Vykom is a little village with a large temple at its centre. The main highway through the village, an important thoroughfare, passes on either side of this temple, which divides the road itself at that point. There are very many "untouchables" among the village population in this low-lying part of the country, but since the Brahmins' houses are close to the temple these crowds of "untouchables," from time immemorial, have been refused the right to pass through the Brahmins' quarters by the side of the temple along the main road. They have been obliged instead to make a long circuit. A young Syrian Christian, a follower of Mr. Gandhi, who was by profession a barrister, named George Joseph, had first determined to offer passive resistance against this inhuman prohibition. He took with him along the forbidden road an "untouchable." They were both beaten by the Brahmins for polluting the road. Then the police intervened. When George Joseph again made the attempt in company with a pariah he was arrested by the State police.

Immediately, in accordance with the plan of campaign, the whole company, who were with their leader, offered passive resistance in the same manner and were arrested also, until the State prisons were unable to bear the burden. Then the second phase in the struggle began. The police were instructed to make a cordon across the road. They were to allow only High-Caste people to pass, but to stop all "untouchables." Thereupon the passive resisters stood before the barrier in an attitude of prayer along with the "untouchables" day after day for many weeks. All the while the moral conscience of the Brahmins and of the State officials was being appealed to in various ways. The whole struggle was carried on without a single act of violence and in a deeply religious manner.

The crisis came when this part of the country became flooded with water during the monsoon. The water on the road reached as high as the waists of the passive resisters. The military police were allowed by the State to moor boats across the road, and to stand in them while on guard. The plight of the passive resisters became more and more pitiable; but they endured these hardships bravely and never gave way for a single hour. In the end, after many months of such endurance, the State was able at last, with the consent of the Brahmins, to open the road. The Vykom struggle was won, not for that one road only, but for the Brahmin quarters elsewhere. Since that time many similar Passive Resistance campaigns have shown the effectiveness of this method of overcoming one evil without stirring up fresh evils of bitterness in their turn. [See Appendix 6.]

Part II

THE HISTORICAL SETTING

Satyagrahis with Gandhi seated in the middle

10

A Confession of Faith, 1909

A document of exceptional interest has been published in a volume of Mahatma Gandhi's writings by my friend, the Hon. G. A. Natesan, Madras, to which he had asked me to contribute the preface many years ago. The document is called *A Confession of Faith*, 1909. It represents Mr. Gandhi's leading ideas during the period of his life when the influence of Tolstoy was peculiarly strong upon him. It was the epoch of his correspondence with Tolstoy [see Chapter 11] and also of his own distribution to the world, with Tolstoy's permission, of a very remarkable letter by Tolstoy to a Hindu correspondent. He asked specially for this permission because Tolstoy's religious writings for years had come to him as a great light in the midst of his own personal religious problems. He called the agricultural settlement for Europeans and Indians, which he himself founded as a Tolstoyan at Lawley, near to Johannesburg, "Tolstoy Farm." His own account of it will be given later. [See Chapter 12.]

While the *Confession of Faith* as a document thus represented his own views almost exactly twenty years ago, it must not be imagined that he has stood still ever since. His personality is far too dynamic for that. At the same time, it is clear that the economic side of his programme had already, under Tolstoy's influence, assumed a very distinct character, with certain marks of permanence. On the two issues of Ahimsa (Non-Violence) and Khaddar (home-spun and home-woven cloth) he had already established his own position.

Perhaps the greatest change in his attitude towards big issues since has been that taken in the year 1920, when he at last reluctantly came to the conclusion that, for the time being, he must non-co-operate with the British Empire, because it had begun to symbolize for him the spirit of Violence. But even in this matter he has always refused to join with the party representing complete and final severance, regarding an inner change of heart among the British as still possible.

With regard to the place of machinery in human life, it would appear to me—from some of his more recent utterances—that he might be ready in certain directions to modify some of the things that he put down in 1909. Again, in opening ten years ago the Tibbia Medical School and Hospital at Delhi, he clearly showed that there is a side of modern Western medical science with which he would be in sympathy. This was also symbolized by his entire willingness to undergo an operation for appendicitis at Colonel Maddock's hands in the Sassoon Hospital, Poona, in 1924. I was with him at that time, and his praise and gratitude for the skill and loving-kindness of both his nurse and his doctor came from the depth of his heart.

Therefore, while every word of this *Confession of Faith* in 1909 must not be taken as still holding good for his actual belief in 1929, yet it shows the germinal thought twenty years ago, out of which practically all his more recent activities have sprung. Thus it has become an historical record of great value to the biographer. It should be observed that what Mr. Gandhi has given with such brevity and conciseness in this *Confession of Faith,* 1909, can be found expanded at far greater length in his pamphlet called *Indian Home Rule,* which was written at the same period. He still allows that book to be published, as an expression of his own views during that creative period of his life when he was in the midst of his South African struggle.

His revolt against "modern civilization" was probably at its height during this year 1909. He was prepared to follow Count Tolstoy to the extreme point in practice. It is right also to state that he has never altered his own radical opposition to our modern ways since he wrote this *Confession;* nor has he modified his own personal habits of life or accommodated them to the new age. He still whole-heartedly believes in a rural civilization as the one ideal for mankind, and enjoins upon his followers the obligation of sticking closely to the soil, and thus labouring to earn their daily bread.

When the greatest crisis of all came in his life, during the Non-Co-operation Movement, and he was brought up for trial before the judge, he affirmed his own trade and occupation to be that of "a farmer and a weaver." In this manner, and in his daily dress and daily manual toil, he still deliberately regards the peasant's life as the most wholesome occupation for mankind. He still rejects the city life with all its mechanical contrivances and artificial ways of living as essentially immoral.

Looking at all that has happened in the interval since 1909, his words quoted in his *Confession of Faith* concerning Germany and England as "living in the Hall of Death" are remarkable. They should give us pause, and make us put the searching question to ourselves whether we are not in Europe still "living in the Hall of Death" in the year 1929.

His *Confession of Faith,* 1909, runs as follows:

1. There is no impassable barrier between East and West.
2. There is no such thing as Western or European Civilization; but there is a modern form of Civilization which is purely material.
3. The people of Europe, before they were touched with modern civilization, had much in common with the people of the East.
4. It is not the British people who rule India, but modern civilization rules India through its railways, telegraph, telephone, etc.
5. Bombay, Calcutta, and other chief cities are the real plague-spots of Modern India.
6. If British rule were replaced tomorrow by Indian rule based on modern methods, India would be none the better, except that she would be able then to retain some of the money that is drained away to England.
7. East and West can only really meet when the West has thrown overboard modern civilization almost in its entirety. They can also seemingly meet when the East has also adopted modern civilization. But that meeting would be an armed truce; even as it is between Germany and England, both of which nations are living in the "Hall of Death," in order to avoid being devoured the one by the other.

8. It is simply impertinence for any man, or any body of men, to begin, or to contemplate, reform of the whole world. To attempt to do so by means of highly artificial and speedy locomotion, is to attempt the impossible.

9. Increase of material comforts, it may be generally laid down, does not in any way whatsoever conduce to moral growth.

10. Medical science is the concentrated essence of black magic. Quackery is infinitely preferable to what passes for high medical skill.

11. Hospitals are the instruments that the Devil has been using for his own purpose, in order to keep his hold on his kingdom. They perpetuate vice, misery, degradation, and real slavery. I was entirely off the track when I considered that I should receive a medical training. It would be sinful for me in any way whatsoever to take part in the abominations that go on in the hospitals.* If there were no hospitals for venereal diseases, or even for consumptives, we should have less consumption and less sexual vice amongst us.

12. India's salvation consists in unlearning what she has learnt during the past fifty years. The railways, telegraphs, hospitals, lawyers, doctors, and such like have all to go, and the so-called upper classes have to learn to live consciously, religiously, and deliberately the simple peasant life, knowing it to be a life giving true happiness.

13. India should wear no machine-made clothing, whether it comes out of European mills or Indian mills.

14. England can help India to do this, and then she will have justified her hold on India. There seem to be many in England today who think likewise.

15. There was true wisdom in the sages of old having so regulated society as to limit the material conditions of the people: the rude plough of perhaps five thousand years ago is the plough of the husbandman today. Therein lies salvation. People live long under such conditions, in comparative

---

* He refers here especially to vivisection.

peace, much greater than Europe has enjoyed after having taken up modern activity; and I feel that every enlightened man, certainly every Englishman, may, if he chooses, learn this truth and act according to it.

It is the true spirit of passive resistance that has brought me to the above almost definite conclusions. As a passive resister I am unconcerned whether such a gigantic reformation (shall I call it?) can be brought about among people who find their satisfaction from the present mad rush. If I realize the truth of it I should rejoice in following it, and therefore I could not wait until the whole body of people had commenced.

All of us who think likewise have to take the necessary step; and the rest, if we are in the right, must follow. The theory is there; our practice will have to approach it as much as possible. Living in the midst of the rush, we may not be able to shake ourselves free from all taint. Every time I get into a railway car, or use a motor-bus, I know that I am doing violence to my sense of what is right.

I do not fear the logical result on that basis. When there was no rapid locomotion, teachers and preachers went on foot, braving all dangers, not for recruiting their health, but for the sake of humanity. Then were Benares and other places of pilgrimage holy cities; whereas today they are an abomination.

11

PASSIVE RESISTANCE IN SOUTH AFRICA

The one thing which is likely to cause the name of Mahatma Gandhi to stand out distinct in the history of South Africa is the weapon of Passive Resistance. This singular weapon, by the sheer force of his own genius, he first forged and hammered until he had made it fit for his own use, and then afterwards employed it for moral warfare with marvellous effect. Throughout his prolonged struggle on behalf of his own countrymen in South Africa, when General Smuts was his opponent, he used this weapon and none other. When he began the struggle he found the name of India so sunk in public estimation that he himself and all his companions were commonly called "coolies" even by men of education like General Botha. Within twenty-three years he raised this name of India to such a moral height that he left South Africa amid the generous farewells of Europeans, who expressed their deep respect for him and his compatriots.

Many had engaged in Passive Resistance before Mr. Gandhi, but those who had done so had been too isolated in their methods to reap fruitful results. They had only made a personal impression. The secret of Gandhi was this: he was the first to organize corporate moral resistance, and to obtain at last in South Africa, through rigid discipline, a firmly united community ready to go to any lengths of suffering as a body for the sake of conscience. Perhaps it would be true to say that since the days of the early Christian Church no such effective acts of Passive Resistance have been organized as those which Mahatma Gandhi inspired.

Already the unique importance of this Passive Resistance struggle is being recognized, and the name of Gandhi as the leader of that struggle is rising in public estimation. Professor Gilbert Murray, in a very striking article called "The Life of the Soul," which was first published in the *Hibbert Journal,* has called attention to him as a modern genius of world significance. Since that article was written, in every part of the civilized world his name has become almost a household word, and oppressed nationalities in every continent have begun to look to him as their champion.

Therefore it is obviously of great importance to understand, as far as possible from Mahatma Gandhi's own lips, the main motives that have urged him forward in this unique moral direction with such singular spiritual power. These had been published in a small and comparatively unknown volume by the Rev. J. J. Doke, Baptist minister in Johannesburg, who was one of Mr. Gandhi's closest friends. The record is given of a conversation concerning the way in which Passive Resistance, or Soul-Force, became a living inspiration to Mr. Gandhi himself. Mr. Doke writes as follows:

One day I questioned Mr. Gandhi concerning the source from whence he derived his original idea.

"I remember," he told me, "how one verse of a Gujarati poem, which I learned at school as a child, clung to me. In substance it was this:

If a man gives you a drink of water and you give him a
    drink in return, that is nothing.
Real beauty consists in doing good against evil.

"Even as a child this verse had a powerful influence over me and I tried to carry it out in practice. Then came the Sermon on the Mount."

"But," said I, "surely the Bhagavad Gita came first?"

"No," he replied. "Of course I knew the Bhagavad Gita in Sanskrit tolerably well; but I had not made its teaching in that particular a study. It was the New Testament which really awakened me to the rightness and value of Passive Resistance.

"When I read in the Sermon on the Mount such passages as 'Resist not him that is evil; but whosoever smiteth thee on thy right cheek, turn to him the other also,' and 'Love your enemies; pray for them that persecute you, that ye may be sons of your

Father which is in heaven,' I was simply overjoyed, and found my own opinion confirmed where I least expected it. The Bhagavad Gita deepened the impression, and Tolstoy's *The Kingdom of God Is Within You* gave it a permanent form.

"I do not like the term 'Passive Resistance.' It fails to convey all I mean. It describes a method, but gives no hint of the system of which it is only a part. Real beauty—and that is my aim—is in doing good against evil.

"Still I adopt the phrase because it is well known and easily understood, and because at the present time the great majority of my people can only grasp that idea. Indeed, to me the ideas that underlie the Gujarati hymn I have quoted and the Sermon on the Mount should in time revolutionize the whole of life.

"Passive Resistance is an all-sided sword: it can be used anyhow: it blesses him who uses it, and also him against whom it is used, without drawing a drop of blood. It produces far-reaching results. It never rusts and cannot be stolen. The sword of Passive Resistance does not require a scabbard, and one cannot be forcibly dispossessed of it.

"Some years ago, when I began to take an active part in the public life of Natal, the adoption of this method occurred to me as the best course to pursue if petitions should ultimately fail; but in the unorganized condition of our Indian community at that time the attempt to practise it seemed useless.

"In Johannesburg, however, when the Asiatic Registration Act was introduced, the Indian community was so deeply stirred and so knit together in a common determination to resist it that the moment seemed opportune. Some action they were determined to take, and it seemed best for the Colony, and also right in itself, that their action should not take a riotous form but that of Passive Resistance. They had no vote in Parliament, no hope of obtaining redress. No one would listen to their complaints. The Christian Churches were indifferent.

"So I proposed this pathway of suffering, and after much discussion it was adopted. In September, 1906, there was a large gathering of Indians in the Old Empire Theatre, when the position was thoroughly faced. Then, under the inspiration of deep feeling and on the proposal of one of our leading men, they swore a solemn oath committing themselves to Passive Resistance.

"As I have said, Passive Resistance was from the first a misnomer. But the expression had been accepted as it was popular. The idea was more completely and better expressed by the term 'Soul-Force.' As such it was as old as the human race.

"Jesus Christ, Daniel, and Socrates represented the purest form of Passive Resistance, or Soul-Force. All these teachers counted their bodies as nothing in comparison with their souls.

"Tolstoy was the best and brightest modern exponent of the doctrine. He not only expounded it but lived according to it. In India the doctrine was understood and commonly practised long before it came into vogue in Europe. It is easy to see that Soul-Force is infinitely superior to body-force. If people, in order to secure redress of wrongs, resort only to Soul-Force, much of the present suffering would be avoided. There is no such thing as failure in the use of this kind of force.

"'Resist not evil' means that evil is not to be repelled by evil but by good; in other words, physical force is to be opposed not by its like but by Soul-Force. The same idea was expressed in Indian philosophy by the expression, 'freedom from injury to every living thing.' It is quite plain that Passive Resistance thus understood is infinitely superior to physical force, and that it requires greater courage than the latter.

"The only condition for a successful use of this force is a recognition of the existence of the soul as apart from the body, and its permanent and superior nature; and this recognition must amount to a living faith and not to a mere intellectual grasp.

"The struggle in the Transvaal is not without its interest for India. We are engaged in raising men who will give a good account of themselves in any part of the world. We have undertaken the struggle on the following assumptions:

"(a) Passive Resistance is always infinitely superior to physical force.

"(b) There is no inherent barrier between Europeans and Indians anywhere.

"(c) Whatever may have been the motives of the British rulers in India there is a desire on the part of the British Nation at large to see that justice is done. It would be a calamity to break the connection between the British people and the people of India. If we are treated as free men, whether in India or elsewhere, the connection between the British people and the people of India will not only be mutually beneficial, but is calculated to be of enormous advantage to the world religiously, and therefore socially and politically. In my opinion each nation is the complement of the other.

"The methods adopted in order to secure relief are equally pure and simple. Violence in any shape or form is entirely eschewed. Self-suffering is the only true and effective means of securing lasting reforms. The Passive Resisters endeavour to meet and conquer hatred by love. They oppose the brute or physical force by Soul-Force. They hold that loyalty to an earthly sovereign or an earthly constitution is subordinate to loyalty to God and His constitution.

"In interpreting God's constitution through their conscience they admit that they may possibly be wrong. If they are wrong they alone suffer and the established order of things continues.

"In the process 2,500 Indians, or nearly one-half of the resident Indian population, or one-fifth of the possible Indian population of the Transvaal, have suffered imprisonment, carrying with it terrible hardships. Some of them have gone to gaol again and again. Many families have been impoverished."

It was at the time when this conversation with the Rev. J. J. Doke occurred that Mr. Gandhi received a letter from Count Tolstoy in Russia which encouraged him in his own singular struggle and cheered him in times of spiritual loneliness. So important is this letter, that I shall not abbreviate it; and I would specially ask that it should be read with care by those who wish to understand Mr. Gandhi; for he regarded himself at this time as Tolstoy's disciple, and tried literally to follow the method of life that he recommended. Tolstoy wrote to Mr. Gandhi this letter:

I received your journal and was pleased to learn all contained therein concerning the passive resisters; and I felt like telling you all the thoughts which that reading called up to me.

The longer I live, and especially now, when I vividly feel the nearness of death, I want to tell others what I feel so particularly clearly and what to my mind is of great importance, namely, that which is called "Passive Resistance," but which is in reality nothing else than the teaching of love uncorrupted by false interpretations. That love, which is the striving for the union of human souls and the activity derived from it, is the highest and only law of human life; and in the depth of his soul every human being (as we most clearly see in children) feels and knows this; he knows this until he is entangled by the false teachings of the world. This law was proclaimed by all—by the Indian as by the Chinese, Hebrew, Greek, and Roman sages of the world. I think this law was most clearly expressed by Christ, who plainly said, "In love alone is all the law and the prophets."

But, foreseeing the corruption to which this law of love may be subject, he straightway pointed out the danger of its corruption, which is natural to people who live in worldly interests—the danger, namely, which justifies the defence of these interests by the use of force, or, as he said, "with blows to answer blows, by force to take back things usurped," etc. He knew, as every sensible man must know, that the use of force is incompatible with love as the fundamental law of life; that as soon as violence is permitted, in whichever case it may be, the insufficiency of the law of love is acknowledged, and by this the very law of love is denied. The whole Christian civilization, so brilliant outwardly, grew up on this self-evident and strange misunderstanding and contradiction, sometimes conscious but mostly unconscious.

In reality, as soon as force was admitted into love, there was no more love; there could be no love as the law of life; and as there was no law of love there was no law at all except violence, i.e. the power of the strongest. So lived Christian humanity for nineteen centuries. It is true that in all times people were guided by violence in arranging their lives.

The difference between the Christian nations and all other nations is only that in the Christian world the law of love was expressed clearly and definitely, whereas it was not so expressed in any other religious teaching, and that the people of the Christian world have solemnly accepted this law, whilst at the same time they have permitted violence and built their lives on violence; and that is why the whole life of the Christian peoples is a continuous contradiction between that which they profess and the principles on which they order their lives—a contradiction between love which has been accepted as the law of life and violence which is recognized and praised, being acknowledged even as a necessity in different phases of life, such as the power of rulers, courts, and armies. This contradiction always grew with the development of the people of the Christian world, and lately it reached the ultimate stage.

The question now evidently stands thus: either to admit that we do not recognize any Christian teaching at all, arranging our lives only by power of the stronger, or that all our compulsory taxes, court and police establishments, but mainly our armies, must be abolished.

This year, in spring, at a Scripture examination in a girls' high school at Moscow, the teacher and the bishop present asked the girls questions on the Commandments, and especially on the Sixth, "Thou shalt not kill." After a correct answer the bishop generally put another question, whether killing was always in all cases forbidden by God's law, and the unhappy young ladies were forced by previous instruction to answer, "Not always"— that killing was permitted in war and in execution of criminals. Still, when one of these unfortunate young ladies (what I am telling is not an invention, but a fact told me by an eye-witness), after her first examination was asked the usual question, if killing were always sinful, she became agitated, and, blushing, decisively answered, "Always"; and to all the usual sophisms of the bishop she answered with decided conviction that killing was always forbidden in the Old Testament and not only killing was forbidden by Christ but even every wrong against a brother. Notwithstanding all his grandeur and art of speech, the bishop became silent and the girl remained victorious.

Yes, we can talk in our newspapers of the progress of aviation, of complicated diplomatic relations, of different clubs and conventions, of unions of different kinds, of so-called productions of art, and keep silent about what the young lady said. But it cannot be passed over in silence, because it is felt, more or less dimly, but always felt, by every man in the Christian world, Socialism, Communism, Anarchism, Salvation Army, increasing crime, unemployment, the growing insane luxury of the rich and misery of the poor, the alarmingly increasing number of suicides—all these are the signs of that internal contradiction which must be solved and cannot remain unsolved. And they must be solved in the sense of acknowledging the law of love and denying violence.

Therefore your activity in the Transvaal, as it seems to us at this end of the world, is the most essential work, the most important of all the work now being done in the world, wherein not only the nations of the Christian, but of all the world, will unavoidably take part.

It will easily be understood how these words from the aged Russian prophet and seer encouraged Mr. Gandhi in his undertakings. He pressed forward in Natal also after the Passive Resistance in the Transvaal (to which Tolstoy refers) was ended. Just before his departure from South Africa he addressed the following words of encouragement to his old Passive Resistance companions and helpers in Natal:

I shall soon be far from Phoenix, if not actually in the Motherland, and I would leave behind me my innermost thoughts.

The term "Passive Resistance" does not fit the activity of the Indian Community during the past eight years. Its equivalent in the vernacular, rendered into English, means Truth-Force. I think

Tolstoy called it also Soul-Force, or Love-Force, and so it is. Carried out to its utmost limit this force is independent of pecuniary or other material assistance. Violence is the negation of this great spiritual force, which can only be cultivated or wielded by those who will entirely eschew violence. It is a force that may be used by individuals as well as by communities. It may be used as well in political as in domestic affairs. Its universal applicability is a demonstration of its permanence and invincibility. It can be used alike by men, women, and children.

It is impossible for those who consider themselves to be weak to apply this force. Only those who realize that there is something in man which is superior to the brute nature in him, and that the latter always yields to it, can effectively be passive resisters. This force is to violence what light is to darkness.

In politics its use is based upon the immutable maxim that government of the people is possible only so long as they consent either consciously or unconsciously to be governed. We did not want to be governed by the Asiatic Act of 1907 of the Transvaal, and it had to yield before this mighty force. Two courses were open to us: (i) to use violence when we were called upon to submit to the Act; or (ii) to suffer the penalties prescribed under the Act, and thus to draw out and exhibit the force of the soul within us, for a period long enough to appeal to the sympathetic chord in the governors or the law-makers. We have taken long to achieve what we set about striving for. That was because our Passive Resistance was not of the most complete type. All passive resisters do not understand the full value of the force, nor have we men who always from soul-conviction refrain from violence.

The use of this force requires the adoption of poverty, in the sense that we must be indifferent whether we have the wherewithal to feed or clothe ourselves. During the past struggle all passive resisters were not prepared to go that length. Some again were only passive resisters so-called. They came without any conviction, often with mixed motives, less often with impure motives. Some even, while engaged in the struggle, would have resorted to violence except for most vigilant supervision. Thus it was that the struggle became prolonged; for the exercise of the purest Soul-Force in its perfect form brings about instantaneous relief. For this, prolonged training of the individual soul is an absolute necessity, so that a perfect passive resister has to be almost, if not entirely, a perfect man.

We cannot all suddenly become such men, but the greater the spirit of Passive Resistance in us the better men we shall become. Its use, therefore, is indisputable, and it is a force which, if it became universal, would revolutionize social ideals, do away with despotisms, and destroy the ever-growing militarism under which the nations of the West are groaning and are being almost crushed to death, and which promises to overwhelm even the nations of the East.

If the past struggle has produced even a few Indians who would dedicate themselves to the task of becoming passive resisters as nearly perfect as possible, they would not only have served themselves in the truest sense of the term, but they would also have served humanity at large.

Thus viewed, Passive Resistance is the noblest and the best education. It should come, not after the ordinary literary education of children; it should precede it. It will not be denied that a child, before it begins to write its alphabet and to gain worldly knowledge, should know what the soul is, what truth is, what love is, what powers are latent in the soul. It should be an essential of real education that a child should learn that, in the struggle of life, it can easily conquer hate by love, untruth by truth, violence by self-suffering. It was because I felt the force of this truth that I endeavoured to train the children at Tolstoy Farm, and then at Phoenix, along these lines, and one of the reasons for my departure to India is still further to realize, as I already do in part, my own imperfection as a passive resister, and then to try to perfect myself; for I believe that it is in India that the nearest approach to perfection is most possible.

Most of the later passages quoted in this chapter may be found in the "Golden Number" of *Indian Opinion,* which was published at Phoenix in 1914, at the end of the Passive Resistance struggle, and was edited by Mr. H. S. L. Polak. He had come out from England in 1903, and had joined Mr. Gandhi a year later at Johannesburg, coming gradually to hold his ideals. Mr. Polak threw himself heart and soul into the Indian cause, and shared with his wife a high moral enthusiasm for humanity, which has never grown dim. He lived from time to time at Phoenix Ashram, and took his part in the discipline of the place. He twice toured India to explain to the Government and the people the grievances under which the South African Indians laboured and their methods of Passive Resistance to secure redress. Under the guidance of the late Mr. G. K. Gokhale, the President-Founder of the Servants of India Society, he had helped to arouse nation-wide interest in the welfare of Indians overseas, a later symptom of which was the abolition of the system of indentured labour emigration. [See Chapter 8.]

Mr. Polak went to prison with Mr. Gandhi in 1913, during the final stage of the Passive Resistance struggle. Though he had arranged to return to England with his family after the struggle had terminated with the Gandhi-Smuts Agreement of 1914, he stayed on in South Africa, at Mr. Gandhi's request, to watch, on behalf of the Indian community, the operation of the Agreement and to consolidate the Indian position, for more than two years after Mr. Gandhi's return to India, thus performing a difficult and invaluable service.

Throughout the whole of Mahatma Gandhi's later career in India itself the ideas which are here set down may be shown to be the moving and compelling thoughts in all his actions. His mind had become rough-hewn during the South African struggle, until it had acquired a courageous outlook upon every human situation, which made him always choose the heroic path. Two lines of a Gujarati poem became very dear to him, and he would frequently sing them at his morning and evening prayers:

> The pathway of the Lord can only be trodden by heroic souls:
> The cowards shrink from it.

12

TOLSTOY FARM

In order to understand in a practical manner the spiritual forces which lay beneath the Passive Resistance campaign in South Africa it is necessary to study the history of the two Ashrams which Mahatma Gandhi himself founded at different times while he was living in that country. The former was called Phoenix, and was situated fourteen miles away from Durban; the second was named Tolstoy Farm, at Lawley, near Johannesburg. These two centres of discipline in hardihood and fearlessness played an increasingly important part during the different Passive Resistance struggles in South Africa.

The chief weakness of the later Non-Co-operation Movement in India was this—that it had not been prepared for on a scale commensurate with its very widely extended range over the whole of India. The Indian people were unused to such moral discipline as Mahatma Gandhi demanded. The Ashram at Sabarmati, near Ahmedabad, which he had founded on his return to India from South Africa, was not sufficient to supply leaders for every part of the vast area of the struggle. This lack of adequate leadership more than anything else led to the final outbreak of violence in Bombay and Chauri Chaura which will be described later.

We have from Mr. Gandhi's own pen a deeply interesting description of his attempt to found his Ashram at Lawley, called Tolstoy Farm, in collaboration with an architect, Mr. H. Kallenbach, who had become his follower. The account which follows has historical interest because it shows to what length Mr. Gandhi was prepared to go in the doctrine of Ahimsa, or Non-Violence. For at Tolstoy Farm he allowed snakes infesting human habitations to be killed.

This logical weakness, that he has always recognized between theory and practice, and has referred to again and again in the columns of

Tolstoy Farm

Young India, has never been wholly circumvented. It has distressed him more than anything else, as the chapter on Ahimsa in this volume will have shown. [See Chapter 7.]

It will be seen from his own account of the founding of Tolstoy Farm that his intention was to provide a home of religious discipline and moral training from whence he would be able to carry on the Passive Resistance struggle.

He writes thus about it:

> My ideas about Satyagraha or Soul-Force had now matured, and I had realized its universality as well as its excellence; I was therefore perfectly at ease. The book *Indian Home Rule* was written in order to demonstrate the sublimity of Satyagraha, and that book is a true measure of my faith in its efficacy. I was perfectly indifferent to the numerical strength of the fighters on our side.
>
> But I was not free from anxiety on the score of finance. It was, indeed, hard to prosecute a long-protracted struggle without funds. I did not realize then as clearly as I do now that a struggle can be carried on without funds, that money very often spoils a righteous fight, and that God never gives a Satyagrahi, or passive resister, anything beyond his strict needs. But I had faith in God, who did not even then desert me, but raised me from the slough of despondency. For as I set my foot in Cape Town I received a cable from England that Sir Ratanji Jamshedji Tata had given £4,000 to the Satyagraha funds. This sum amply sufficed for our immediate needs and we forged ahead.
>
> But this, or even the largest possible gift of money, could not by itself help forward a Satyagraha struggle—a fight on behalf of Truth consisting chiefly in self-purification and self-reliance. A Satyagraha struggle is impossible without capital in the shape of character. As a splendid palace deserted by its inmates looks a ruin, so does a man without character. No one could tell how long the struggle would last. On the one hand, there were the Boer Generals determined not to yield even one inch of ground, and, on the other hand, there was a handful of Satyagrahis pledged to fight unto death or victory. It was like a

war between ants and the elephant, who could crush thousands of them under each one of his feet. Fighting meant imprisonment or deportation for them. But what about their families in the meanwhile? There was only one solution for this difficulty, namely, that all the families should be kept at one place, and should become members of a sort of co-operative commonwealth. Thus there would be no scope for fraud, nor would there be injustice to any. Public funds would be largely saved, and the families of Satyagrahis would be trained to live a new and simple life in harmony with one another. Indians belonging to various provinces and professing divers faiths would have an opportunity of living together.

But where was the place suitable for a settlement of this nature? To live in a city would have been like straining at a gnat and swallowing a camel. The house-rent alone would perhaps amount to the same sum as the food bill, and it would not be easy to live a simple life amidst the varied distractions of a city. It was therefore clear that the place selected should be neither too far from nor too near a city.

The place required, then, must be in the Transvaal, and that not too near Johannesburg. Mr. Kallenbach bought a farm of about 1,100 acres, and gave the use of it to Satyagrahis free of any rent or charge. Upon the farm there were nearly one thousand fruit-bearing trees and a small house at the foot of a hill with accommodation for half a dozen persons. Water was supplied from two wells as well as a spring. The nearest railway station, Lawley, was about a mile from the farm and Johannesburg twenty-one miles. We decided to build houses upon this farm and to invite the families of Satyagrahis to settle there.

The settlers hailed from Gujarat, South India and North India, and there were Hindus, Mussalmans, Parsees, and Christians among them. About forty of them were young men, two or three old men, five women, and twenty to thirty children, of whom four or five were girls.

The Christian and other women were meat-eaters. Mr. Kallenbach and I thought it desirable to exclude meat from the farm. But how would we ask people who had no scruples in the matter, and who were coming over here in their days of adversity, to give up meat even temporarily? I did not take long clearly to visualize my duty in these circumstances. If the Christians and Mussalmans asked for beef, that too must be provided for them. To refuse them admission to the farm was absolutely out of the question.

But where love is, there God is also. The Mussalman friends had already granted me permission to have a purely vegetarian kitchen. I had now to approach Christian sisters whose husbands or sons were in jail. I had often come in such intimate contact with the Christian friends who were now in jail, and who had on like occasions consented to having a vegetarian dietary; but this was the first time that I had to deal at close quarters with their families in their absence. I represented to the sisters the difficulty of housing accommodation as well as of finance, and my own deep-rooted sentiment in the matter. At the same time I assured them that even beef would be provided for them if they wanted. The sisters kindly consented not to have meat, and the cooking department was placed in their charge. With another man I was detailed to assist them. My presence acted as a check upon petty bickerings. The food was to be the simplest possible. The time as well as the number of meals was fixed up. There was to be one single kitchen and all were to dine in a single row. Every one was to see to the cleaning of his own dish and other things. Satyagrahis lived on Tolstoy Farm for a long time, but neither the women nor the men ever asked for meat. Drink, smoking, etc., were, of course, totally prohibited.

A school was indispensable for the youngsters and the children. This was the most difficult of our tasks, and we never achieved complete success in this matter till the very last. The burden of the teaching work was largely borne by Mr. Kallenbach and myself. The school could be held only after noon, when both of us were thoroughly exhausted by our morning labour, and so were our pupils. The teachers therefore would often be dozing as well as the taught. We would sprinkle water on the eyes, and by playing with the children try to pull them up and to pull up ourselves, but sometimes in vain. The body peremptorily demanded rest and would not take a denial. But this was only one and the least of our many difficulties; for the classes were conducted in spite of these dozings.

But this teaching experiment was not fruitless. The children were saved from the infection of intolerance, and learnt to view one another's religions and customs with a large-hearted charity. They learnt how to live together like blood-brothers. They imbibed the lessons of mutual service, courtesy, and industry. And from what little I know about the later activities of some of the children on Tolstoy Farm I am certain that the education which they received there has not been in vain. Even if imperfect it was a thoughtful and religious experiment, and among the sweetest reminiscences of Tolstoy Farm the reminiscences of this teaching experiment are no less sweet than the rest.

The fast of Ramzan arrived. There were Mussalman young- sters among us, and we felt we must encourage them to keep the fast. We arranged for them to have meals in the evening. There was no meat, of course, nor did anyone ask for it. To keep the Mussalman friends company the rest of us had only one meal a day, in the evening. As a rule we finished our evening meal before sunset; so the only difference was that the others finished their supper about when the Mussalman boys com- menced theirs. These boys were so courteous that they did not put anyone to extra trouble, although they were observing fasts, and the fact that the non-Muslim children supported them in the matter of fasting left a good impression on all. I do not remember that there ever was a quarrel, much less a split, between the Hindu and the Mussalman boys on the score of religion. On the other hand, I know that, although staunch in their own beliefs, they all treated one another with respect and assisted one another in their respective religious observances.

Gokhale arrived in South Africa while we were still living on the farm. I will place here on record a half-sweet, half-bitter reminiscence.

There was no cot on the farm, but we borrowed one for Gokhale. There was no room where he could enjoy full privacy. For sitting accommodation we had nothing beyond the benches in our school. Even so, how could we resist the temptation of bringing Gokhale in spite of his delicate health to the farm? And how could he help seeing it, either?

I was foolish enough to imagine that Gokhale would be able to put up with a night's discomfort, and to walk about a mile and a half from the station to the farm. I had asked him before-hand, and he had agreed to everything without bestowing any thought upon it, thanks to his simplicity and overwhelming confidence in me. It rained that day, as Fate would have it, and I was not in a position suddenly to make any special arrangement. I have never forgotten the trouble to which I put Gokhale that day in my ignorant affection. The hardship was too much for him to bear and he caught a chill. We could not take him to the kitchen and dining-hall. He had been put up in Mr. Kallenbach's room. His dinner would get cold while we brought it from the kitchen to his room. I prepared special soup, and Kotwal prepared special bread for him; but these could not be taken to him hot. We managed as best we could.

Gokhale uttered not a syllable, but I understood from his face what a folly I had committed. When he came to know that all of us slept on the floor, he removed the cot which had been brought for him, and had his own bed also spread on the floor. That whole night was a night of repentance for me.

As the reminiscences of Tolstoy Farm would be incomplete without an account of Gokhale's visit thereto, so would they be if I omitted to say something about the character and conduct of Mr. Kallenbach. It was really a wonder how he lived on Tolstoy Farm among our people as if he were one of us. Gokhale was not the man to be attracted by ordinary things. But even he felt strongly drawn to the revolutionary change in Kallenbach's life. Kallenbach had been brought up in the lap of luxury, and had never known what privation was. In fact, indul-gence had been his religion. He had had his fill of all the pleasures of life, and he had never hesitated to secure for his comfort everything that money could buy.

It was no commonplace for such a man to live, move, and have his being on Tolstoy Farm, and to become one with the Indian settlers. This was an agreeable surprise for the Indians. Some Europeans classed Kallenbach as either a fool or a lunatic, while others honoured him for his spirit of renunciation. Kallenbach never felt his renunciation to be painful; in fact, he enjoyed it even more than he had enjoyed the pleasures of life before. He would be transported with rapture while describing the bliss of a simple life; and for a moment his hearers would be tempted to go in for it. He mixed so lovingly with the young as well as the old that separation from him even for a short time left a clearly felt void in their lives.

Mr. Kallenbach and I had frequent talks on religion, which usually centred on fundamentals like non-violence or love, truth, and the like. When I said that it was a sin to kill snakes and such other animals, Mr. Kallenbach, too, was shocked to hear it, as well as my numerous other European friends. But in the end he admitted the truth of that principle in the abstract. At the very beginning of my intercourse with him Mr. Kallenbach had seen the propriety of carrying out in practice every principle of which he was convinced intellectually, and therefore he had been able to effect momentous changes in his life without a moment's hesitation. Now, if it was improper to kill serpents, we must cultivate their friendship, thought Mr. Kallenbach. He therefore first collected books on snakes, with a view to identify different species of reptiles. He there read that not all snakes are poisonous, and some of them actually serve as protectors of field crops. He taught us all to recognize different kinds of snakes, and at last tried to tame a huge cobra which was found on the farm.

Mr. Kallenbach fed it every day with his own hands in its cage. I gently argued with him. "Although you do all this," I said, "in a friendly spirit, your friendliness may not be quite clear to the cobra, especially as your kindness is not unalloyed with fear. Neither you nor I have the courage to play with it, if it was free; and what we should really cultivate is courage of *that* stamp. Therefore, though there is friendliness, there is not love in this act of taming the cobra. Our behaviour should be such that the cobra can see through it. We see every day that all animals grasp at once whether the other party loves or fears them. Again, you do not think the cobra to be venomous, and yet have imprisoned it in order to study its ways and habits. This is a kind of self-indulgence for which there should be no room in the case of real friendship."

My argument appealed to Mr. Kallenbach, but he could not bring himself all at once to release the cobra. I did not exercise any pressure upon him. I too was taking interest in the life of the cobra; and the children, of course, enjoyed it immensely. No one was allowed to harass the cobra, which, however, was casting about for some means of escape. Whether the door of the cage was inadvertently left open, or whether the cobra managed to open it, in a couple of days Mr. Kallenbach found the cage empty as one morning he proceeded to call upon his friend. Mr. Kallenbach was glad of it, and so was I.

As a result of these experiments we did not fear snakes as much as we otherwise might have done; but it must not be supposed that no one on the farm feared serpents, or that there was a total prohibition against killing them. To have a conviction that there is violence or sin in a certain course of conduct is one thing; to have the power of acting up to that conviction is quite another. A person who fears snakes and who is not ready to resign his own life cannot avoid killing snakes in cases of emergency. One day a snake was found in Mr. Kallenbach's own room at such a place that it seemed impossible either to drive it away or to catch it. One of the students saw it, and, calling me there, asked me what was to be done. He wanted my permission to kill it. He could have killed it without such permission, but the settlers would not take such a step without consulting me. I saw that it was my duty to permit the student to kill the snake. Even as I am writing this I do not feel that I did anything wrong in

granting the permission. I had not the courage to seize the ser-
pent with the hand, or otherwise to remove the danger to the
settlers; and I have not cultivated such courage to this day.

Such dangerous experiments could have their places only in
a struggle of which self-purification was the very essence.
Tolstoy Farm proved to be a centre of spiritual purification and
penance for the final campaign. I have serious doubts as to
whether the struggle could have been prosecuted for eight
years, whether we could have secured larger funds, and whether
the thousands of men who participated in the last phase of the
struggle would have borne their share in it, if there had been no
Tolstoy Farm. It was never placed in the limelight, yet it attracted public sympathy to itself. The Indians saw that the Tolstoy
Farmers were doing what they themselves were not prepared to
do, and what they looked upon in the light of hardship. The
public confidence was a great asset to the movement when it
was organized afresh on a large scale in 1913.

With regard to the Ashram at Phoenix, which is still being used
today for the weekly publication of *Indian Opinion,* and also for fur-
nishing a quiet retreat to any one who desires to lead a retired life in
the country, I have recent personal recollections. Of all the places
that I have visited in South Africa it was the one that reminded me
most of all of Santiniketan Ashram in India. There is the same peaceful atmosphere, which has a spiritual background behind it. Just as
Santiniketan was the house of prayer for Maharshi, the father of
Rabindranath Tagore, and also for the poet himself, so Phoenix has
been the scene of the spiritual strivings of Mahatma Gandhi at times
when he went through some of the severest of all his struggles and
disappointments in South Africa. Far beyond any other moments the
times that I spent with him at Phoenix Ashram were precious to me
for his sake.

In the passage from his writings that follows we are brought into
the very midst of the greatest of all the Passive Resistance struggles
in South Africa on behalf of the Indian indentured labourers on the
Natal sugar plantations. It represents a crisis in the struggle when he

was prepared to throw himself and every available resource at his command into the front of the battle. About this last struggle before he returned to India I can write from my own knowledge, because Mr. Gokhale, who was very ill in India while it was proceeding, asked me to go over to Natal along with Mr. W. W. Pearson in order to take part in it. Therefore I was able to watch day by day the spirit in which it was carried on. When we arrived, Mr. Gandhi, Mr. Kallenbach, Mr. Polak, and all the leaders had already been arrested and imprisoned, along with many of the Indian ladies. The three whom I have mentioned by name had, however, been subsequently released in order to carry on negotiations. Never at any time in the whole of my experience have I seen nobler men and women, suffering every hardship joyfully, than I did then. Specially I can remember the sight of the Indian ladies who had been to prison and had endured every kind of suffering. What impressed me most of all was the gentleness with which they bore everything and the kindliness with which they spoke of their prison warders. It was impossible for me after that wonderful experience ever to doubt the spiritual power of Passive Resistance as a means of enabling moral character to develop. The only parallel that I could think of in past history—and it was a very close one—was the joy of the Early Christians when they suffered persecution for righteousness' sake.

Mr. Gandhi writes as follows:

We now decided to take a step which we had reserved till the last, and which in the event fully answered our expectations. I had contemplated sacrificing all the settlers in Phoenix at a critical period. That was to be my final offering to the God of Truth. The settlers at Phoenix were mostly my close co-workers and relations. The idea was to send all of them to jail with the exception of a few who would be required for the conduct of *Indian Opinion* and of children below sixteen. This was the maximum of sacrifice open to me in the circumstances.

I went to Phoenix and talked to the settlers about my plans. First of all I held a consultation with the sisters living there. I knew that the step of sending women to jail was fraught with serious risk. Most of the sisters in Phoenix spoke Gujarati. They had not had the training or experience of the Transvaal sisters. Moreover, most of them were related to me, and might think of going to jail only on account of my influence with them. If afterwards they flinched at the time of actual trial or could not stand the jail, they might be led to apologize, thus not only giving me a deep shock, but also causing serious damage to the movement. I decided not to broach the subject to my wife, as she could not say "No" to any proposal I made, and if she said "Yes," I would not know what value to attach to her assent, and also because I knew that in a serious matter like this the husband should leave the wife to take what step she liked on her own initiative, and should not be offended at all even if she did not take any step whatever.

I talked to the other sisters, who readily fell in with my proposal, and expressed their readiness to go to jail. They assured me that they would complete their term in jail, come what might. My wife overheard my conversation with the sisters, and, addressing me, said:

"I am sorry that you are not telling me about this. What defect is there in me which disqualifies me for jail? I also wish to take the path to which you are inviting the others."

"You know I am the last person to cause you pain," I replied. "There is no question of my distrust in you. I would be only too glad if you went to jail, but it should not appear at all as if you went at my instance. In matters like this everyone should act relying solely upon one's own strength and courage. If I asked you, you might be inclined to go just for the sake of complying with my request. And then, if you began to tremble in the law-court or were terrified by hardships in jail, I could not find fault with you, but how would it stand with me? How could I then harbour you or look the world in the face? It is fears like these which have prevented me from asking you, too, to court jail."

"You may have nothing to do with me," she said, "if, being unable to stand jail, I secure my release by an apology. If you can endure hardships and so can my boys, why cannot I? I am bound to join the struggle."

"Then I am bound to admit you to it," said I. "You know my conditions and you know my temperament. Even now reconsider the matter, if you like; and if after mature thought you deliberately come to the conclusion not to join the movement, you are free to withdraw. And you must understand that there is nothing to be ashamed of in changing your decision even now."

"I have nothing to think about," said she; "I am fully determined."

I suggested to the other settlers also that each should take his or her decision independently of all others. Again and again, and in a variety of ways, I pressed this condition on their attention, that none should fall away whether the struggle was short or long, whether the Phoenix settlement flourished or faded, and whether he or she kept good health or fell ill in jail. All were ready.

It is one thing, however, to read words like those in cold print, and another thing to see these ladies, as I actually did, when they returned from prison with their health in many cases utterly broken down in the hard prison life which they had been obliged to endure. Mrs. Gandhi suffered most of all, and when I saw her for the first time after her release it seemed to me that she would be unable to get strong again, owing to her shattered health.

Yet there can be no doubt whatever that it was the bravery of these frail, gentle women, who had been trained to endurance in Phoenix Ashram, and had gained from thence the religious devotion needed to carry them through such hardships without shrinking, that did more than anything else to bring this last and greatest Passive Resistance struggle in Natal to a successful end.*

---

* In this struggle it was reckoned that nearly four thousand Indians courted imprisonment, including many women. Among Europeans who were with Mr. Gandhi, Mr. Kallenbach and Mr. Polak both suffered the severe hardships of jail in the Transvaal and took their part in every indignity side by side with their Indian fellow-prisoners.

13

Satyagraha in India

As soon as the South African struggle was over Mr. Gandhi sailed for Southampton, intending after a short stay in England to return to India. But on the very day when he landed in England war against Germany had been declared. He made up his mind with his usual promptness, and on that very day offered to enlist unconditionally for the whole duration of the War, in order to undertake ambulance work at the Front. He had gained distinction for this work in the Boer War, when he had carried the only son of Lord Roberts out of action at Spion Kop, under fire, and had been publicly mentioned in dispatches. [See Appendix 7.]

His offer was accepted. He was placed in a responsible post with an Indian unit; but owing to over-exposure while on duty he was taken seriously ill with pleurisy and his life was in danger. When he had recovered he was ordered by the doctors to leave the cold North at once for the sunshine and warmth of India.

Soon after his arrival he was asked at a public dinner in Madras to propose the toast of "The British Empire"; he gladly did so. The Hon. Mr. Corbet, Attorney-General of Madras, introduced him as one who had "laboured strenuously with absolute self-devotion for the consolidation of the British Empire." Mr. Gandhi spoke as follows:

> During my three months' tour in India, as also in South Africa,
> I have been so often questioned how I, a determined opponent
> of modern civilization and an avowed patriot, could reconcile
> myself to loyalty for the British Empire, of which India was
> such a large part; how it was possible for me to find it consistent
> that India and England could work together for mutual benefit.
> It gives me the greatest pleasure this evening, at this great and

important gathering, to re-declare my loyalty to this British Empire, and my loyalty is based upon very selfish grounds. As a passive resister I discovered that a passive resister has to make good his claim to Passive Resistance, no matter under what circumstances he finds himself, and I discovered that the British Empire had certain ideals with which I have fallen in love, and one of those ideals is that every subject of the British Empire has the freest scope possible for his energies and honour, and whatever he thinks is due to his conscience. I think that this is true of the British Empire as it is not true of any other Government. (Applause.) I feel, as you here perhaps know, that I am no lover of any Government, and I have more than once said that that Government is best which governs least; and I have found that it is possible for me to be governed least under the British Empire. Hence my loyalty to the British Empire. (Loud applause.)

On many different occasions Mr. Gandhi declared himself in public as "a lover of the British Empire" because it stood for racial equality and gave freedom for the exercise of the rights of private conscience.

During the next three years of the War he offered the Government of India again and again to organize ambulance work for Mesopotamia and lead out there a picked body of Indian volunteers. But the Viceroy, while warmly thanking him, explained that his presence in India was of more importance than any help he could render at the Front. It should be noted that at this time he received the Kaiser-i-Hind Gold Medal for distinguished humanitarian service in the cause of the Empire. From time to time the Viceroy consulted him on vital questions during the War, and he gave the authorities his own unstinted support. Especially valued were his outspoken words against secret revolutionary conspiracies leading to assassination. As an absolute believer in Non-Violence his words in condemnation of such forms of violence carried great weight, because his own patriotism and service to his country could not be questioned.

But in such a vast country as India, with its countless millions of people, the evils connected with a highly centralized and bureaucratic administration soon became apparent. Mahatma Gandhi is a saint in politics, a rare combination. He could never bear to countenance injustice.

At first he regarded these evils as merely local. He was prepared to meet them with his own much cherished weapon of Passive Resistance. In this way he believed that he was performing a public duty to the British Empire of which he was an active member. He carried through each of these struggles with such cheerful good will and friendly candour that he soon won over his opponents. Above all, he "played the game," and never took an unfair advantage. On more than one occasion the Government officials, impressed by his utter sincerity, met him half-way. Thus certain very serious troubles were set right without any bad feeling being engendered. It is noticeable that he offered Passive Resistance to Indian mill-owners no less than to British officials. He never appealed to racial bitterness.

Towards the end of the War he took one step on behalf of the British Empire, in his zeal and enthusiasm, which bewildered even his best friends. For he went recruiting among the villagers in order to enlist them to go and fight against the Turks and Germans. He defended his action by saying that it was better to fight than to shrink back as a coward; that it was mere cowardice which kept the villagers back and not moral principle at all. Moral courage, he added, was far higher than physical courage: but physical courage was to be preferred to cowardice.

This recruiting campaign nearly cost him his life, for he became badly infected with dysentery, and at one time was on the point of death.

In the light of all this uncompromising and devoted service in India during the War his revolt against the whole system of Indian government in 1920 becomes all the more significant. In his letters to Englishmen quoted below [see Chapter 14] he explains all this in detail. Here it is only necessary to add that even at the height of the Non-Co-operation Movement he endeavoured personally to the utmost to maintain good will with the British people, and to explain that it was not the British people he was attacking but the system of British Administration. He still eagerly looked forward to the time when that system should be changed so that he might again be able to co-operate as he had done before. I can personally bear witness that never even the remotest trace of bitterness against Englishmen as such ever entered his mind. On the contrary, his experience in South Africa, both with the British and the Dutch, made him quite positive in his own mind that they would respect his utter frankness of opposition, and also his good-humour, in the drastic struggle that he was carrying on against what he held to be the rottenness of their administration. When he called their Government "Satanic" many Englishmen smiled, and the word was quoted against him as a joke; but he was in deadly earnest in his condemnation. He did not merely talk: he acted.

We have in a concise form an interesting account given by Mahatma Gandhi of the different earlier Passive Resistance struggles in India which led up to all the All-Indian Non-Co-operation Movement. This passage is well worth studying in order to understand his mind. I have enclosed in parentheses some notes explaining in my own words what each struggle was about whatever Mr. Gandhi's words do not make the matter clear. He writes as follows:

It was through the instrumentality of Bhai Motilal, the public-spirited and good tailor of Wadhwan, that I first became interested in the Viramgam question. I had just arrived from England and was proceeding to Kathiawar in the year 1915. I was travelling third class. At Wadhwan station Motilal came up to me with a small party. He gave me some account of the hardships inflicted on the people at Viramgam, and said:

"Please do something to end this trouble (i.e., the establishment of a new customs barrier between British India and the Kathiawar States). It will be doing an immense service to Kathiawar, the land of your birth."

There was an expression of both compassion and firmness in his eyes.

"Are you ready to go to jail?" I asked.

"We are ready to march to the gallows," was the quick reply.

"Jail will do for me," I said. "But see that you do not leave me in the lurch."

"That only time can show," said Motilal.

I reached Rajkot, obtained detailed information, and commenced correspondence with Government. In speeches at different places I dropped a hint that the people should be ready to offer passive resistance at Viramgam if necessary. These speeches were brought to the notice of Government. In this they served Government and, unintentionally, served the people also. Finally I had a talk with Lord Chelmsford on the matter. He promised abolition of the customs barrier, and was as good as his word. I know others also tried for this. But I am strongly of opinion that the imminent possibility of Passive Resistance was the chief factor in obtaining the desired redress.

Then came the anti-Indenture struggle (to prevent indentured Indian labour being recruited for the British Colonies). Great efforts were put forth to get indenture repealed. There was a considerable public agitation. The Bombay meeting fixed May 31, 1917, as the date from which onwards indentured labour should be stopped. A deputation of ladies first waited upon the Viceroy in connection with this. I cannot help mentioning here the name of the high-souled sister, Mrs. Jaiji Petit. It was she who may be said to have organized this deputation. Here, too, success came merely through preparedness for Satyagraha, or Passive Resistance. But it is important to remember the distinction—that in this case public agitation was also necessary. The stopping of indentured labour was very much more important than the abolition of the Viramgam customs barrier. Lord Chelmsford committed a series of blunders, beginning with the passing of the Rowlatt Act. Still, I think he was a wise ruler. But what Viceroy can escape for long the influence of the permanent officials of the Civil Service?

The third in order came the Champaran struggle (undertaken in order to remedy the evils that had grown up connected with the indigo plantations). Here Satyagraha had actually to be offered. Mere preparedness for it did not suffice, as powerful vested interests were arrayed in opposition. The peace maintained by the people of Champaran deserves to be placed on record. I can bear witness to the perfect non-violence of the leaders in thought, word, and deed. Hence it was that this agelong abuse came to an end in six months.

The fourth struggle was that of the mill-hands of Ahmedabad against the mill-owners. Gujarat is perfectly familiar with its history. How peaceful the labourers were! As for the leaders, there can hardly be anything for me to say. Still I hold the victory in this case was not quite pure because the fast I had to observe* in order to sustain the labours in their determination exercised indirect pressure upon the mill-owners. The fast was bound to influence them, as I enjoyed friendly relations with them. Still, the moral is clear.

The fifth was the Khaira struggle (concerning the over-assessment of the land revenue by the Government in a time of scarcity). I cannot say that in this case all the local leaders of Satyagraha adhered to the pure truth. Peace was certainly maintained. The non-violence of the peasantry, however, was only superficial, like that of the mill-hands. So we came out of the struggle with bare honour. However, there was a great awakening among the people. But Khaira had not fully grasped the lesson of Non-Violence; the mill-hands had not understood the true meaning of peace. The people had, therefore, to suffer.

The sixth was in connection with the Rowlatt Act. (This Act involved persons who might be innocent being kept in prison without open trial.) Therein our inherent shortcomings came to the surface. But the original foundation was well and truly laid. We admitted all our shortcomings. I had to confess my Himalayan blunder.** I had also to undertake a fast myself and invite others to do so. The Rowlatt Act was a dead-letter, even when it was promulgated, and that Black Act was finally repealed. This struggle taught us a great lesson.

---

* When he saw that the mill-labourers were breaking their word and preparing to go back to work without effecting their object, Mr. Gandhi declared that he would go on fasting until the object of the strike was obtained.

** He refers to his ignorance that the masses were certain to become violent if left to themselves.

The seventh was the Non-Co-operation struggle in order to right the Khilafat and the Punjab wrongs and to win Swaraj. It is still going on. And my confidence is unshaken that, if a single Satyagrahi holds out to the end, victory is absolutely certain.

This is the beauty of Satyagraha. It comes up to us; we have not to go out in search for it. There is a virtue inherent in the principle itself. A Dharmayudda (war of righteousness) in which there are no secrets to be guarded, no scope for cunning, and no place for untruth, comes unsought; and a man of religion is ever ready for it. A struggle which has to be previously planned is not a righteous struggle. In a righteous struggle God Himself plans the campaigns and conducts the battles. A war of righteousness can be waged only in the name of God; and it is only when the Satyagrahi feels quite helpless, when he is apparently on his last legs, and finds utter darkness all around him, that God comes to the rescue. God helps us when we feel ourselves humbler than the very dust under our feet. Only to the weak and helpless is divine succour vouchsafed.

In order to understand the drastic manner in which he carried on these "wars of righteousness" the instance of the Khaira struggle may be more fully explained. Mr. Gandhi asked me at that time to act as peacemaker and mediator, and therefore its facts are well known to me.

Under the land system of India the Government is the landlord over a great part of the country. The tenants are villagers holding tiny portions of land for which they pay rent to the Government. This rent is called "land revenue." The year 1917–18 had been an exceptionally bad one for the villagers, and they asked for "suspension of revenue" until the ensuing year, when it was hoped a better harvest might be reaped. Government granted "full suspension" for one village and "half suspension" for one hundred and three villages, but that was not regarded as sufficient. They asked for a fresh inquiry which would prove the justice of their own demand. The Bombay Government remained adamant, and the peasants were threatened with immediate eviction unless they paid the rent. Mr. Gandhi called the peasants together, and the following vow of Passive Resistance was taken:

Knowing that the crops of our villages are less than four annas (i.e. 25 percent), we had requested the Government to suspend the revenue collection till the ensuing year. As, however, Government has not acceded to our prayer, we, the under-signed, hereby solemnly declare that we shall not pay the full or remaining revenue, but we will let the Government take such legal steps as they may think fit to collect the same, and we shall gladly suffer all the consequences of our refusal to pay. We shall allow our lands to be confiscated, but we shall not of our own accord pay anything and thereby lose our self-respect and prove ourselves wrong. If Government decide to suspend the second instalment of revenue throughout the district, those amongst us who are in a position to pay will pay the whole or the balance of the revenue as may be due. The reason why those of us who have the money to pay still do not, is that if they do the poorer might in panic sell their things or borrow to pay and thereby suffer.

Under the circumstances we believe it is the duty of those who are able to pay to protect the poor.

In the end a compromise was reached without a fresh inquiry. It is noticeable, however, that the Joint Parliamentary Committee on Indian Reform in 1919 reported that there was a flaw at this very point in the land-revenue system of India, and asserted that some constitutional method of revision of these land-revenue assessments was badly needed. Yet even as late as last year, in spite of incessant demands from the different Legislative Councils in India for such constitutional revision procedure to be formulated, no action had yet been taken. The result has been that Mr. Gandhi was obliged to lead another Passive Resistance movement in Bardoli in the year 1928, in order to obtain a revision of the land assessment in that district. This Bardoli struggle was also carried through with non-violence, and it has recently ended in a revision being granted.

It is not necessary to enter into details concerning the events in the Punjab under Martial Law in 1919. The "war mind" was still predominant, and the things that were done under Martial Law betrayed the war mentality. The shock to Mahatma Gandhi was overwhelming. I was with him in the Punjab in October of that year. He was so weak in health, after his prolonged dysentery, that he was obliged to lie down for the greater part of the day owing to physical exhaustion. Yet he carried on his inquiries into what had happened on the spot and came to know the worst. He was one of the authors of the *Congress Inquiry Report on the Punjab Disturbances.*

In spite of the deep humiliation and distress that the findings of this Inquiry caused him, he yet was able to recommend to the All-India National Congress at Amritsar in December, 1919, that the Reforms should be accepted and worked in a constitutional manner. Only the magic of his own personality obtained a peaceful National Congress decision at such an embittered time as that.

But the final blow came in 1920. When the House of Lords passed a resolution refusing to condemn General Dyer, and the Hunter Commission Report wavered in its own condemnation of official action; when at the same time the Treaty of Sèvres was signed which shattered every hope of a generous treatment of Turkey at the conclusion of the War: then at last his cup of humiliation was full, and he made the great decision of his life to refuse to co-operate any longer with the British Government in India until both these wrongs were righted and Swaraj was obtained. This decision was carried, with his weight behind it, at a special meeting of the All-India National Congress which met at Calcutta in September, 1920. The one added clause which his influence made unanimous was this— that the struggle should be carried on in a strictly non-violent manner.

It was called by the clumsy title Non-Violent Non-Co-operation.

14

"To Every Englishman"

No one can understand Mahatma Gandhi's attitude towards Great Britain and the British Empire unless he has come to realize that "Amritsar" was the critical event which changed Mahatma Gandhi from a whole-hearted supporter into a pronounced opponent. Of his attitude before that event took place he has written as follows:

> Hardly ever have I known anybody to cherish such loyalty as I did to the British Constitution. I can see now that my love of truth was at the root of this loyalty. It has never been possible for me to simulate loyalty, or, for that matter, any other virtue. The National Anthem used to be sung at every meeting that I attended in Natal. I then felt that I must also join in the singing. Not that I was unaware of the defects in the British rule, but I thought that it was on the whole acceptable. In those days I believed that the British rule was on the whole beneficial to the ruled. Never in my life did I exploit this loyalty, never did I seek to gain a selfish end by its means. It was for me more in the nature of an obligation, and I rendered it without expecting a reward.
>
> I likewise taught the National Anthem to the children of my family. Later on the text began to jar on me. As my conception of Ahimsa went on maturing I became more vigilant about my thought and speech. The lines in the National Anthem, "Scatter her enemies" and "Frustrate their knavish tricks," particularly jarred upon me. I shared my feelings with Dr. Booth,* who

---

* Dr. Booth was the very kindly medical officer on the sugar plantations in Natal, who afterwards became ordained. He became Vicar of St. Barnabas, Cape Town, and was greatly loved by the Indian Community in South Africa.

agreed that it ill became a believer in Ahimsa to sing those lines. How could we assume that the so-called "enemies" were "knavish"? And because they were enemies, were they bound to be in the wrong? From God we could only ask for justice. Dr. Booth entirely endorsed my sentiments, and he composed a new anthem for his congregation.

In South Africa, over a period of more than twenty years, Mr. Gandhi had received such racial treatment as would have turned anyone except a saint into a mood of bitterness leading to revolt; for inhuman wrongs had to be suffered every day under the cruelty of the colour bar with all its hateful implications.

Yet in South Africa, as I well know from personal experience, he never for a moment lost heart or despaired of justice in the end. He had constant struggles with General Smuts. He went willingly and even joyfully to prison. But he never attacked the British Constitution, because he believed at that time that it was founded upon justice. His faith always won its own reward in the end, and he came victorious out of every moral struggle. At each step he gained a slight advance both in social and political freedom for his fellow-countrymen. Indeed, these moral victories at last assumed a world-wide importance. At the close of the last and greatest Passive Resistance struggle in South Africa he explained his own standpoint at Johannesburg in his farewell words as follows:

> It is my knowledge, right or wrong, of the British Constitution which has bound me to the British Empire. Tear that Constitution to shreds and my loyalty will also be torn to shreds. On the other hand, keep it intact and you hold me bound unreservedly in this service. The choice has lain before us, who are Indians in South Africa, either to sunder ourselves from the British Empire or to struggle by means of Passive Resistance in order that the ideals of the British Constitution may be preserved— but only those ideals. The theory of racial equality in the eyes of the law, once recognized, can never be departed from; and its principle must at all costs be maintained—the principle, that is to say, that in all the legal codes which bind the Empire

together there shall be no racial taint, no racial distinction, no colour disability.

Even in India, as we have seen, after his return from South Africa, he led many moral struggles, of a character similar to those fought in the Transvaal and in Natal, with marked success—each campaign ending in a fresh victory for truth and justice, and also in increasing good will. He had been able to set free the poor villagers of Champaran from long-established oppression, and also to wage a successful moral war against the system of indentured labour by which Indians were recruited for the colonial sugar plantations. He also fought with the same moral weapons against his own countrymen, the mill-owners of Ahmedabad, when they were the oppressors of the Indian labourers.

All this while, both in South Africa and in India, I have heard Mahatma Gandhi declare: "If I did not believe whole-heartedly that racial equality was a man's birthright within the British Empire I should be a rebel."

I do not think that he has ever departed for a moment from that position. If today, after being imprisoned afresh in India by those who have charge of Indian affairs, he were convinced that a change of heart had come about, and that racial equality was assured, he would be a "rebel" no longer. According to his own opinion the principles of the British Constitution still stand, but those who have administered them have acted unjustly.

If I interpret him rightly his own position at that time was this. He had lost faith in the British Administration in India—it was a Satanic Government. But he had not lost faith in the British Constitution itself. He still believed that India could remain within the British Commonwealth on the basis of racial equality, and that the principle of racial equality would come out triumphantly vindicated by the Indian struggle. He held himself to be the champion of that theory, and in this sense the upholder of the British Constitution. For that reason he has repeatedly maintained that the British connection with India should still be accepted, provided only that the full Dominion status granted to Canada, South Africa, and the Irish Free State should not be withheld from India itself.

But the patience of "Young India" had become nearly exhausted, and at the last All-India National Congress Mr. Gandhi agreed to a compromise resolution whereby Passive Resistance should be reopened on January 1, 1930, if the British Government did not grant self-government to India before that date.

I have gone through all the words he employed at his trial, and on other solemn public occasions, in regard to this supreme issue on which so much depends. In spite of their terrible severity I do not think he has actually departed as yet from the position he had always adopted in his earlier speeches with regard to the rightness of the *theory* of the British Constitution. It is against the *practice* that he has continually rebelled; and his "rebellion" against "Amritsar," when there seemed to him to be no true sense of repentance in the British administration for what had been done, was the strongest of all.

How strong this feeling about "Amritsar" was may perhaps be understood by a brief quotation from the poet Rabindranath Tagore. In the year 1920, at Bombay, when he was too ill to be present at a meeting of protest, he sent me with a message to deliver in his name. It contained the following passages, which I have very slightly abbreviated:

> A great crime has been done in the name of the law in the Punjab. Such terrible eruptions of evil leave their legacy of the wreckage of ideals behind them. What happened in Jallianwalla Bagh was itself a monstrous progeny of a monstrous war, which for four years had been defiling God's world with fire and poison, physical and moral. The immensity of the sin has bred callousness in the minds of those who have power in their hands, with no check of sympathy within or fear of resistance without. The cowardliness of the powerful, who owned no shame in using their machines of frightfulness upon the unarmed and unwarned villagers, and inflicting humiliations upon their fellow-beings behind the screen of an indecent mockery of justice, has become only possible through the opportunity which the late War has given to man for constantly outraging his own higher nature, trampling truth and honour underfoot. The disruption of the basis of civilization

will continue to produce a series of moral earthquakes, and men will have to be ready for still further sufferings. That the balance will take a long time to be restored is clearly seen by the vengefulness ominously tinging red the atmosphere of the peace deliberations.

But we have no place in these orgies of triumphant powers rending to pieces the world according to their own purposes. What most concerns us is to know that moral degradation not only pursues those inflicting indignities upon the helpless, but also their victims. The dastardliness of cruel injustice confident of its impunity is ugly and mean; but the fear and impotent anger which they are apt to breed upon the minds of the weak are no less abject. Brothers, when physical force in its arrogant faith in itself tries to crush the spirit of man, then comes the time for him to assert that his soul is indomitable. We shall refuse to own moral defeat by cherishing in our hearts foul dreams of retaliation. The time has come for the victims to be the victors in the field of righteousness.

When brother spills the blood of his brother and exults in his sin, giving it a high-sounding name; when he tries to keep the blood-stains fresh on the soil as a memorial of his anger: then God in shame conceals it under the green grass and the sweet purity of His flowers. Let us take our lesson from His hand, even when the smart of the pain and insult is still fresh— the lesson that all meanness, cruelty, and untruth are for the obscurity of oblivion, and only the Noble and True are for eternity.

It was in the midst of a moral struggle, starting with such indignation as this and eschewing all appeals to violence, that Mr. Gandhi wrote his famous letter to the Viceroy which opened the Passive Resistance campaign among Hindus and Mussalmans alike called "Non-Violent Non-Co-operation." For to the "Punjab" wrong had more recently been added a further indictment called the "Khilafat wrong," which I have briefly explained in another chapter. [See Chapter 2.]

The letter to the Viceroy runs as follows:

It is not without a pang that I return the Kaisar-i-Hind Gold Medal granted to me by your predecessor for my humanitarian work in South Africa, for my services as officer-in-charge of the Indian Volunteer Ambulance Corps in 1906, and the Boer War Medal for my services as assistant superintendent of the Indian Volunteer Stretcher-bearer Corps during the Boer War of 1899–1900. I venture to return these medals in pursuance of the scheme of Non-Co-operation inaugurated today in connection with the Khilafat movement. Valuable as these honours have been to me, I cannot wear them with an easy conscience so long as my Mussalman countrymen have to labour under a wrong done to their religious sentiment. Events that have happened during the past month have confirmed me in the opinion that the Imperial Government has acted in the Khilafat matter in an unscrupulous, immoral, and unjust manner, and have been moving from wrong to wrong in order to defend their immorality. I can retain neither respect nor affection for such a Government.

The attitude of the Imperial and Your Excellency's Governments on the Punjab question has given me additional cause for grave dissatisfaction. I had the honour, as Your Excellency is aware, as one of the Congress commissioners to investigate the causes of the disorders in the Punjab during April of 1919. And it is my deliberate conviction that Sir Michael O'Dwyer was totally unfit to hold the office of Lieutenant-Governor of Punjab, and that his policy was primarily responsible for infuriating the mob at Amritsar. No doubt the mob excesses were unpardonable: incendiarism, the murder of five innocent Englishmen, and the cowardly assault on Miss Sherwood were most deplorable and uncalled for. But the punitive measures taken by General Dyer, Colonel Frank Johnson, Colonel O'Brien, Mr. Bosworth Smith, Rai Shri Ram Sud, Mr. Mallik Khan, and other officers were out of all proportion to the crime of the people, and amounted to wanton cruelty and inhumanity almost unparalleled in modern times. Your Excellency's light-hearted treatment of the official crime, your exoneration of Sir Michael O'Dwyer, Mr. Montagu's dispatch, and, above all, the shameful ignorance of the Punjab events and callous disregard of the feelings of Indians betrayed by the House of Lords, have filled me with the gravest misgivings regarding the future of the Empire, have estranged me completely from the present Government, and have disabled me from tendering, as I have hitherto whole-heartedly tendered, my loyal co-operation.

In my humble opinion the ordinary method of agitating by way of petitions, deputations, and the like is no remedy for moving to repentance a Government so hopelessly indifferent to the welfare of its charge as the Government of India has proved to be. In European countries condonation of such grievous wrongs as the Khilafat and the Punjab would have resulted in a bloody revolution by the people. They would have resisted at all cost national emasculation such as the said wrongs imply. But half of India is too weak to offer violent resistance, and the other half is unwilling to do so. I have, therefore, ventured to suggest the remedy of Non-Co-operation, which enables those who wish to do so to dissociate themselves from the Government, and which, if it is unattended by violence and undertaken in an orderly manner, must compel it to retrace its steps and undo the wrongs committed. But whilst I shall pursue the policy of Non-Co-operation in so far as I can carry the people with me, I shall not lose hope that you will yet see your way to do justice. I therefore respectfully ask Your Excellency to summon a Conference of the recognized leaders of the people, and in consultation with them find a way that would placate the Mussalmans and do reparation to the unhappy Punjab.

When the appeal thus presented to the Viceroy had been made in vain, and Non-Co-operation with the Indian Government had been widely established, Mr. Gandhi wrote on different occasions letters to the Englishmen residing in India, explaining the character of the movement and the reasons why he was unable to co-operate with a system which he regarded as evil. His first letter ran thus:

Dear Friend,

I wish that every Englishman may see this appeal, and give thoughtful attention to it.

Let me introduce myself to you. In my humble opinion no Indian has co-operated with the British Government more than I have for an unbroken period of twenty-nine years of public life in the face of circumstances that might well have turned any other man into a rebel. I ask you to believe me when I tell you that my co-operation was not based upon the fear of the punishments provided by your laws or any other selfish motives. It was free and voluntary co-operation, based on the belief that the sum-total of the British Government was for the benefit of India. I put my life in peril four times for the sake of the Empire: at the time of the Boer War, when I was in charge of the Ambulance Corps whose work was mentioned in General Buller's dispatches; at the time of the Zulu Revolt in Natal, when I was in charge of a similar corps; at the time of the commencement of the late War, when I raised an ambulance corps, and as a result of the strenuous training had a severe attack of pleurisy; and, lastly, in fulfilment of my promise to Lord Chelmsford at the War Conference in Delhi, I threw myself in such an active recruiting campaign in Khaira District, involving long and trying marches, that I had an attack of dysentery which proved almost fatal. I did all this in the full belief that acts such as mine must gain for my country an equal status in the Empire. So last December I pleaded hard for a trustful co-operation. I fully believed that Mr. Lloyd George would redeem his promise to the Mussalmans, and that the revelations of the official atrocities in the Punjab would secure full reparation for the Punjabis. But the treachery of Mr. Lloyd George and its appreciation by you, and the condonation of the Punjab atrocities, have completely shattered my faith in the good intentions of the Government and the nation which is supporting it.

But, though my faith in your good intentions is gone, I recognize your bravery; and I know that what you will not yield to justice and reason you will gladly yield to bravery.

See what the British Empire means to India:

1. Exploitation of India's resources for the benefit of Great Britain.
2. An ever-increasing military expenditure and a Civil Service the most expensive in the world.
3. Extravagant working of every Department in utter disregard of India's poverty.
4. Disarmament and therefore emasculation of a whole nation lest an armed nation might imperil the lives of a handful of you in our midst.
5. Traffic in intoxicating drugs and liquors for the purpose of maintaining a top-heavy administration.
6. Progressively repressive legislation in order to suppress an ever-growing agitation seeking to express a nation's agony.
7. Degrading treatment of Indians residing in British Dominions.
8. Total disregard of our feelings by glorifying the Punjab Administration and flouting the Muhammadan sentiment.

I know you would not mind if we could fight and wrest the sceptre from your hands. You know we are powerless to do that; for you have ensured our incapacity to fight in open and honourable battle. Bravery on the battlefield is thus impossible for us. Bravery of the soul still remains open to us.

His second letter begins in a somewhat similar manner. In it, however, he advanced an offer, which he repeated on several occasions as the struggle proceeded, that if only the British Administration would deal faithfully with the awful poverty of India by working towards the building up of home industries in the villages and abandoning the revenue they received from the drink and drugs traffic, then he on his part would look upon these two acts as opening up a pathway for the renewal of cooperation. He wrote thus:

Dear Friend,

I cannot prove my honesty to you if you do not feel it. Some of my Indian friends charge me with camouflage when I say that we need *not* hate Englishmen while we *may* hate the system that they have established. I am trying to show them that one may detest the wickedness of a brother without hating him. Jesus denounced the wickedness of the Scribes and Pharisees, but he did not hate them. He did not enunciate this law of love for the man and hate for the evil in man for himself only, but he taught the doctrines for universal practice. Indeed, I find it in all the Scriptures of the world.

I claim to be a fairly accurate student of human nature and vivisector of my own failings. I have discovered that man is superior to the system he propounds. And so I feel that you as an individual are infinitely better than the system you have evolved as a corporation. Each one of my countrymen in Amritsar on that fateful April 10th was better than the crowd of which he was a member. He as a man would have declined to kill those innocent bank-managers. But in that crowd many a man forgot himself. Hence it is that an Englishman in office is different from an Englishman outside. Similarly an Englishman in India is different from an Englishman in England. Here in India you belong to a system that is vile beyond description. It is possible, therefore, for me to condemn the system in the strongest terms, without considering you to be bad and without imputing bad motives to every Englishman. You are as much slaves of the system as we are. I want you, therefore, to reciprocate, and not to impute to me motives which you cannot read in the written word. I give you the whole of my motive when I tell you that I am impatient to mend or end a system which has made India subservient to a handful of you, and which has made Englishmen feel secure only in the shadow of the forts and the guns that obtrude themselves on one's notice in India. It is a degrading spectacle for you and for us. Our corporate life is based on mutual distrust and fear. This, you will admit, is unmanly. A system that is responsible for such a state of things is necessarily Satanic. You should be able to live in India as an integral part of its people, and not always as foreign exploiters. One thousand Indian lives against one English life is a doctrine of dark despair, and yet, believe me, it was enunciated in 1919 by the highest of you in the land.

I almost feel tempted to invite you to join me in destroying a system that has dragged both you and us down. But I feel that I cannot as yet do so. We have not shown ourselves earnest, self-sacrificing, and self-restrained enough for that consummation.

But I do ask you to help us in the boycott of foreign cloth and in the anti-drink campaign.

The Lancashire cloth, as English historians have shown, was forced upon India, and her own world-famed manufactures were deliberately and systematically ruined. India is therefore at the mercy, not only of Lancashire, but also of Japan, France, and America. Just see what this has meant to India. We send out of India every year sixty crores (more or less) of rupees for cloth. We grow enough cotton for our own cloth. Is it not madness to send cotton outside India, and have it manufactured into cloth there and shipped to us? Was it right to reduce India to such a helpless state?

A hundred and fifty years ago we manufactured all our cloth. Our women spun fine yarn in their own cottages, and supplemented the earnings of their husbands. The village weavers wove that yarn. It was an indispensable part of national economy in a vast agricultural country like ours. It enabled us in a most natural manner to utilize our leisure. Today our women have lost the cunning of their hands, and the enforced idleness of millions has impoverished the land. Many weavers have become sweepers. Some have taken to the profession of hired soldiers. Half the race of artistic weavers has died out, and the other half is weaving imported foreign yarn for want of finer hand-spun yarn.

You will perhaps now understand what boycott of foreign cloth means to India. It is not devised as a punishment. If the

Government were today to redress the Khilafat and the Punjab wrongs, and consent to India attaining immediate Swaraj, the boycott movement must still continue. Swaraj means at the least the power to conserve Indian industries that are vital to the economic existence of the nation, and to prohibit such imports as may interfere with such existence. Agriculture and hand-spinning are the two lungs of the national body. They must be protected against consumption at any cost.

This matter does not admit of any waiting. The interests of the foreign manufacturers and the Indian importers cannot be considered, when the whole nation is starving for want of a large productive occupation ancillary to agriculture.

You will not mistake this for a movement of general boycott of foreign goods. India does not wish to shut herself out of international commerce. Things other than cloth which can be made better outside India, she must gratefully receive upon terms advantageous to the contracting parties. Nothing can be forced upon her. But I do not wish to peep into the future. I am certainly hoping that before long it will be possible for England to cooperate with India on equal terms. Then will be the time for examining trade relations. For the time being I bespeak your help in bringing about a boycott of foreign cloth.

Of similar and equal importance is the campaign against drink. The liquor shops are an insufferable curse imposed on society. There was never so much awakening among the people as now upon this question. I admit that here, the Indian ministers can help more than you can. But I would like you to speak out your mind clearly on that question. Under every system of Government, as far as I can see, prohibition will be insisted on by the Nation. You can assist the growth of the ever-rising agitation by throwing the weight of your influence on the side of the Nation.

Mr. Gandhi made a third appeal, through an interview, which he afterwards published:

My attitude towards the English is one of utter friendliness and respect. I claim to be their friend, because it is contrary to my nature to distrust a single human being or to believe that any nation on earth is incapable of redemption. I have respect for Englishmen, because I recognize their bravery, their spirit of sacrifice for what they believe to be good for themselves, their cohesion, and their powers of vast organization. My hope about them is that they will at no distant date retrace their steps, revise their policy of exploitation of undisciplined and ill-organized races, and give tangible proof that India is an equal friend and partner in the British Commonwealth to come.

Whether such an event will ever come to pass will largely depend upon our own conduct. That is to say, I have hope of England because I have hope of India. We will not for ever remain disorganized and imitative. Beneath the present disorganization, demoralization, and lack of initiative I can discover organization, moral strength, and initiative forming themselves. A time is coming when England will be glad of India's friendship, and India will disdain to reject the proffered hand because it has once despoiled her. I know that I have nothing to offer in proof of my hope. It is based on an immutable faith. And it is a poor faith that is based on proof commonly so-called.

Mr. Gandhi made his last appeal of all, before his imprisonment, in an article entitled, "Do I Hate Englishmen?" to which question he emphatically answered, "No." The article ends thus:

By a long course of prayerful discipline I have ceased for over forty years to hate anybody. I know that this is a big claim. Nevertheless I make it in all humility. But I can and I do hate evil wherever it exists. I hate the system of Government that the British people have set up in India. I hate the ruthless exploitation of India even as I hate from the bottom of my heart the hideous system of untouchability for which millions of Hindus have made themselves responsible.

But I do *not* hate the domineering Englishmen, as I refuse to hate the domineering Hindus. I seek to reform them in all the loving ways that are open to us. My non-co-operation has its root not in hatred but in love. My personal religion peremptorily

forbids me to hate anybody. I learnt this simple yet grand doctrine when I was twelve years old through a school-book, and
the conviction has persisted up to now. It is daily growing on
me; I beg, therefore, to assure every Englishman who might
have misunderstood me that I shall never be guilty of hating
Englishmen though I might have to fight them fiercely, even as
I did in 1921. It will be a Non-Violent fight, it will be clean, it
will be truthful.

Mine is not an exclusive love. I cannot love Mussalmans or
Hindus and hate Englishmen. For if I merely love Hindus and
Mussalmans because their ways are on the whole pleasing to
me, I shall soon begin to hate them when their ways displease
me, as they may well do any moment. A love that is based on
the goodness of those you love is a mercenary affair; whereas,
true love is self-effacing and demands no consideration. It is like
that of a model Hindu wife, Sita, for instance, who loved her
Rama even whilst he bid her pass through a raging fire. It was
well with Sita, for she knew what she was doing. She sacrificed
herself out of her strength, not out of her weakness. Love is the
strongest force in the world which the world possesses, and yet
it is the humblest imaginable.

One mistaken impression which led to altogether unwarranted
bitterness in England was the refusal of Mr. Gandhi, at the height of
the Non-Co-operation Movement, to take any part in the official
welcome to the Prince of Wales, who had been invited to come out
to India by the Viceroy, Lord Reading.

This unwise step of inviting the Prince to India, at such an unpro-
pitious time, was taken against the advice of the best and wisest
counsellors. But when it was done, Mr. Gandhi immediately called
for a boycott. The explanation that he publicly offered was not widely
known in England. It runs as follows:

I draw a sharp and fundamental distinction between boycotting
the Prince and boycotting any welcome arranged for him.
Personally I would extend the heartiest welcome to His Royal
Highness, if he came without official patronage and the protecting

wings of the Government of the day. Being the heir to a constitutional monarch, the Prince's movements are regulated and dictated by the ministers, no matter how much the dictation may be concealed beneath diplomatically polite language. In suggesting the boycott, therefore, the promoters have suggested boycott of an insolent bureaucracy and dishonest ministers of His Majesty.

You cannot have it both ways. It is true that under a constitutional monarchy, royalty is above politics; but you cannot send the Prince on a political visit for the purpose of making political capital out of him, and then complain against those who will not play your game. With the knowledge that India was bleeding at heart, the Government of India should have told His Majesty's Ministers that the moment was inopportune for sending the Prince. I venture to submit that it is adding insult to injury to bring the Prince, and through his visit steal honours for a Government that deserves to be dismissed with disgrace. I claim that I prove my loyalty by saying that India is too deeply in mourning to take part in and to welcome His Royal Highness, and that the Ministers and the Indian Government show their disloyalty by making the Prince a cat's-paw of their deep political game. If they persist, it is the clear duty of India to have nothing to do with the visit.

Even if Englishmen might doubt the expediency of the step taken by Mr. Gandhi in boycotting the visit, no one can deny that he has fairly stated his case; and at this interval of time very few Englishmen would resent his action, when thus made clear as to its motive by one whose truthfulness is beyond question.

Mr. Gandhi has lived with Englishmen, both in England and South Africa, for nearly thirty years of his life. He had also been in touch with them in India. They have respected him, and he has respected them. Mutual regard has thus led on to close friendships, which have now become an intimate part of his own life. Thus he has become an altogether friendly and sympathetic judge of English character, and in his own estimates of individual Englishmen he is rarely mistaken. He has a fine way of making lifelong friends, and he has always proved himself as loyal and devoted to them as they have been to him.

As one of Nature's gentlemen, in his manners and habits of life, he never offends by saying or doing anything that would be out of taste. The outlook of the average Englishman, with its strong insularity, must often appear crude to him; but he tolerates with good-humour what is said and done, when the lack of manners is due to bad taste. He upholds in his own character Cardinal Newman's great phrase: "Hence it is that it is almost a definition of a gentleman, to say that he is one who never inflicts pain." For his courtesy, in every little act, is as unobtrusive as it is all-embracing.

Of one thing he is certain, and he has often spoken to me about it, sometimes putting it in a very homely manner. "An Englishman," he said once to me, "never respects you till you stand up to him. Then he begins to like you. He is afraid of nothing physical; but he is very mortally afraid of his own conscience, if ever you appeal to it and show him to be in the wrong. He does not like to be rebuked for wrong-doing at first; but he will think over it, and it will get hold of him and hurt him till he does something to put it right."

It will be seen that the ultimate success in any Satyagraha Movement lies in just such an appeal to conscience. If the average Englishman were *not* open to such an appeal, then it is possible that the whole programme of a Satyagraha struggle would have to be modified, and the moral attack made from another angle.

It must be clear to anyone who has studied the record of Mr. Gandhi's different struggles that his estimate of the effectiveness of the appeal to an Englishman's moral conscience has proved singularly correct. In practically every instance where the moral cause was just, and where no violence occurred, he has won the battle. Probably no single man living can point to such great victories won in the cause of truth and justice as he can today. He places the credit of this very largely with the Englishman himself. It may even be questioned whether the simple fact of the humiliation and suffering he himself has undergone, owing to the repeated failure on the part of his followers to remain non-violent, has not done more to endear him to the hearts of English men and women who have heard the story than any further outward success would have done. This has been my own experience when lecturing in England on his work and personality.

The time has come to consider very carefully whether in the light of all that has happened in recent years more cannot be done to meet Mahatma Gandhi on his own moral grounds. Many times over he has repeated that if the British Government in India would seriously take up the cause of the poor villagers, by prohibiting alcohol and drugs on the one hand and encouraging the "Khaddar" Movement on the other, he would be prepared to reconsider the question of co-operation. It should not be impossible to find a way to come to terms with such an offer as that. Above all, from first to last, it must be remembered he has at heart the burden of the poor.

15

"THE GREAT SENTINEL"

The Satyagraha campaign of 1919, after the passing of the Rowlatt Act, together with Mr. Gandhi's noble withdrawal when violence broke out, won Rabindranath Tagore's heartfelt admiration from Santiniketan. He had himself been through the same inner struggle, and had been sickened at the news which came "trickling through" from the Punjab under the Martial-Law regime, which had assumed its most ruthless form at Amritsar.

In a moment of supreme indignation, which brought his tortured spirit some relief, the Poet had given up his knighthood, and had written a memorable letter to the Viceroy explaining the reasons which compelled him to take such a step. This was his own personal act of non-co-operation with a Government which he was convinced had committed unpardonable wrongs. The news of this gesture of the Poet ran quickly through the world, and cleared the air as nothing else could possibly have done at that critical time. For very few who lived outside India knew what had been really taking place under the cover of Martial Law; and these things came as a great shock later, when General Dyer gave his evidence before the Commission, and defended his own actions at Amritsar on the ground of creating a "moral effect" in the Punjab.

Up to the this point there had been hardly any divergence between the two spiritual leaders. Gandhi's noble appeal of soul-force against brute-force had won Tagore's entire approval. When, in earlier years at Santiniketan, I had gone out with W. W. Pearson to help in the Passive Resistance struggle in South Africa, we had carried the Poet's blessing with us. He had taken thus from his retirement, as far as he possibly could, his own part in the struggle. At one point, indeed, the Poet had diverged from Mahatma Gandhi, in the year 1918. He did not like him assuming an active part in the World War by recruiting Indian soldiers in the Khaira district who should fight with weapons of violence. He felt that Mr. Gandhi in this action was compromising his own principles. Whatever others might do, it seemed to the Poet wrong that *he* should thus recruit for war purposes; but so very great was his admiration of his character as an heroic champion of soul-force that at one time in 1919, and also 1920, he was fully prepared to follow him and throw in his lot with him if he gave the word. In one of his letters written to me from abroad, he speaks of this in the clearest possible manner; and the Poet's fearless temperament, which had been evident when he surrendered his knighthood, as well as on other occasions, made such an offer as this immensely significant.

There is a letter written to Mahatma Gandhi at the beginning of the Passive Resistance struggle in April 1919 which makes the Poet's own position abundantly clear. It shows his whole-hearted sympathy with the principle of soul-force, and also with its practical application by a moral genius like Mahatma Gandhi. It contains the following passages:

> Power in all its forms is irrational; it is like the horse that drags the carriage blindfolded. The moral element in it is only repre-sented in the man who drives the horse. Passive Resistance is a force which is not necessarily moral in itself; it can be used against truth as well as for it. The danger inherent in all force grows stronger when it is likely to gain success, for then it becomes temptation.

> I know your teaching is to fight against evil by the help of good, but such a fight is for heroes and not for men led by impulses of the moment. Evil on one side naturally begets evil on the other, injustice leading to violence and insult to vengefulness.

> In this crisis you, as a great leader of men, have stood among us to proclaim your faith in the ideal which you know to be that of India, the ideal which is both against the cowardliness of hidden revenge and the cowed submissiveness of the terror-stricken. You have said, as Lord Buddha has done in his time and for all time to come:

"Overcome anger by the power of non-anger, and evil by the power of good."

We must know that moral conquest does not insist on success, that failure does not deprive it of its own dignity and worth. Those who believe in the spiritual life know that to stand against wrong, which has overwhelming material power behind it, guarantees a victory of active faith in the idea in the teeth of evident defeat.

I have always felt, and said accordingly, that the great gift of freedom can never come to a people through charity. We must win it before we can own it. And India's opportunity for winning it will come to her when she can prove that she is morally superior to the people who rule her by their right of conquest. She must willingly accept her penance of suffering, which is the crown of the great. Armed with her utter faith in goodness, she must stand unabashed before the arrogance that scoffs at the power of spirit.

And you come to your motherland in the time of her need to remind her of her mission, to lead her in the true path of conquest, to purge her present-day politics of that feebleness which imagines that it has gained its purpose when it struts in the borrowed feathers of diplomatic dishonesty.

This is why I pray most fervently that nothing which tends to weaken our spiritual freedom may intrude into our marching line; that martyrdom for the cause of truth may never degenerate into fanaticism for mere verbal forms, descending into the self-deception that hides itself behind sacred names.

The Poet attached to the letter two of his own Bengal poems, which he had himself translated into English:

Let me hold my head high in this faith, that Thou art our
    shelter, that all fear is mean distrust of Thee.
Fear of man? But what man is there in this world, what king,
    O King of Kings, that is Thy rival, who holdest me for all
    time and in all truth?

What power is there in this world to rob me of freedom? For
do not Thy arms reach the captive through the dungeon
walls, bringing unfettered release to the soul?

And must I cling to this body in fear of death, as a miser to
his barren treasure? Has not this spirit of mine the eternal
call to the feast of everlasting life?

Let me know that all pain and death are shadows of the
moment; that the dark force which sweeps between me and
Thy truth is but the mist before the sunrise; that Thou
alone art mine for ever and greater than all pride of
strength that dares to mock my manhood with its menace.

Give me the supreme courage of love, this is my prayer, the
courage to speak, to do, to suffer at Thy will, to leave all or
be left alone.

Give me the supreme faith of love, this is my prayer, the faith
of the life in death, of the victory in defeat, of the power
hidden in the frailness of beauty, of the dignity of pain that
accepts hurt, but disdains to return it.

It was necessary for Rabindranath Tagore to go to Europe and
America during the year 1920 and the earlier part of the year 1921.
He was therefore unable to be present in person at the beginning of
the Non-Co-operation Movement. He did not witness, as I did, the
amazing way in which vast multitudes of people—ordinary men and
women, who had not been drilled, or disciplined, or strictly
trained—learnt by instinct from Mahatma Gandhi the ethics of Passive
Resistance, and offered themselves for prison joyfully without any
violence at first. The authorities, on their side, at this early stage acted
with some consideration. Though women offered themselves for
arrest and were arrested, there were singularly few imprisonments
among them. But among the men and youths, the imprisonments
soon mounted up to many thousands, and the brutal exercise of official
power soon began to make its appearance. The heroism of those
days, especially among the students, can never be forgotten by those
who witnessed it personally.

Then a violent spirit began to enter the Movement from the side of the people, while at the same time violence increased against them. There were also acts of social tyranny against those who refused to participate in the Movement. Just as Non-Co-operation gathered power from numbers, so it gathered excitement. Where it swept the country—as I witnessed in East Bengal—this excitement broke all bounds. I had been with Mahatma Gandhi during the Passive Resistance days in Natal in 1913–14. But this appeared to me to be something entirely new and less spiritual.

When the Poet returned from Europe, at the very height of the vast Non-Co-operation Movement, and watched its effect upon the people of his own province Bengal, he was profoundly disappointed with what he saw in that part of India. He felt that the popular attitude had become one of wild excitement rather than of deep moral conviction. As he expressed it, in a remarkable phrase, it "shouted to him: it did not 'sing.'" What was still more evident to him in Bengal was a mere blind following rather than a spiritual leadership. There was a strong outburst of long pent-up feelings, leading to violence of speech and action, rather than the sustained power of patient soul-force, ready to suffer in silence without striking a single blow, about which he had so often heard from us when we had returned from South Africa.

A further divergence, which in course of time became more serious still, was the Poet's inability to take any active part in the Khaddar Movement along with Mahatma Gandhi, because it appeared to be put forward as a universal panacea for India's poverty, while the Poet regarded it only as an accessory method of rendering help. He could not understand Mr. Gandhi's entire stress upon the manufacture of Khaddar alone, as though all other things were unimportant.

These were real differences of opinion, and whenever an opportunity offered, the two friends met together, and very long discussions took place at which I was privileged to be present. What seemed most evident on each of these occasions was a difference of temperament so wide that it was extremely difficult to arrive at a common intellectual understanding, though the moral ties of friendship remained entirely unbroken. Let me repeat, the Poet's belief in soul-force has always been fundamental. It colours all his own poems and his own personal outlook upon human life. But whenever the popular methods appeared to him to diverge from that high standard, he became pained and immediately expressed himself in writing. Mahatma Gandhi's description of him as "The Great Sentinel" was a masterly title, which once for all described his exact position in an admirably chosen phrase at that crisis.

A time came, a little later, when I was drawn, much against my own will, into the same controversy with regard to violent methods of action. For it seemed to me that Mahatma Gandhi was going much too far, and literally "playing with fire," when he himself took the lead in burning huge heaps of foreign clothes. Not only did it appear to me to carry with it a certain racial bitterness, which was foreign to his own pure nature, but also inevitably to lead on to further violence. Both in the public press and also by outward action, I felt bound to put forward my protest against this.

Therefore, as the Non-Co-operation Movement proceeded, the inherent defects in it became more pronounced. Its very popularity became its greatest hindrance. Mahatma Gandhi himself saw the dangers, and gave the warning again and again. But it was already too late. The excitement had gone too deep. The great masses of India had awakened to the sense of their own power without having received sufficient spiritual training to keep that power under control. There was nothing except his own personality, intense enough in its own inner quality, to retain a magnetic hold over the minds of the masses in their sudden awakening to their new acquisition of explosive freedom. He himself was able, for a time, amazingly to hold violence at bay. Along with his lieutenants he worked with superhuman energy in order to maintain control. But the excitement of the times, and the excessive strain caused by daily overwork, made the leaders themselves unaware of the pace at which the current was driving the frail boat of their national endeavour towards the rapids. There were two or three premonitory warnings, and then the crash came at Bombay, when violence raged day after day in the city almost unchecked, in spite of heroic efforts to prevent it.

During all these last tumultuous days I had been called away from India to Kenya and South Africa, and had come back into the midst of the confusion at the end of the Bombay Riots. Mahatma Gandhi had gone through his act of penance and self-purification. His high courage had not left him, but he looked haggard and emaciated, as one who had just passed through the valley of the shadow of death. Indeed, to die would have been to him, at such a time as this, an infinite release. But it was not to happen. [See Appendix 8.]

During the months that followed, his efforts toward creating Non-Violence in the atmosphere of Non-Co-operation were ever more incessant. He wore himself out with tireless activity by day and with sleepless watch and prayer by night. Only a spirit like the finest tempered steel could have stood such a test of endurance. Then the second outbreak of violence came, at Chauri Chaura. His own tragic description of these things is given in the next chapter.

At that hour of outward failure Mahatma Gandhi rose to the greatest spiritual height which he had ever reached in his whole career. With a mighty effort, amid the angry cries and bitter words of his own followers, he called off the struggle. He had declared in the first instance for Non-Violence as its essential feature, and he had kept his word. Politically, it spelt desperate failure. Morally, it was the greatest triumph he had ever won—the victory of the soul.

The different phases of this moral issue can be clearly traced. The answer to the Poet's objections, and to my own, which follows, is a very noble appeal. The cry of the souls of the countless millions of India's poor, in their unrelieved misery and stark want, runs through every word of it.

In the subsequent chapter, which relates his trial and imprisonment, it is noticeable that this cry of the poor people rings louder in his ears than the Punjab and Khilafat wrongs. These have gradually sunk into the background. The perpetual misery of a starving peasantry forms the gravest part of his indictment of the Administration.

The following is his first answer to the Poet:

> The Bard of Santiniketan has contributed to the *Modern Review* a brilliant essay on the present movement. It is a series

of word-pictures such as he alone can paint. It is an eloquent protest against authority, slave mentality, or whatever description one gives of blind acceptances of a passing mania, whether out of fear or hope. It is a welcome and wholesome reminder to all workers that we must not be impatient; we must not impose authority, no matter how great.

The Poet tells us summarily to reject anything and everything that does not appeal to our reason or heart. If we would gain Swaraj, we must stand for Truth as we know it at any cost. A reformer who is enraged because his message is not accepted must retire to the forest to learn how to watch, wait, and pray.

With all this we must heartily agree, and the Poet deserves the thanks of his countrymen for standing up for Truth and Reason. There is no doubt that our last state will be worse than our first, if we surrender our reason into somebody's keeping. And I would feel extremely sorry to discover that the country had unthinkingly and blindly followed all I had said or done. I am quite conscious of the fact that blind surrender to love is often more mischievous than a forced surrender to the lash of the tyrant....

It is good, therefore, that the Poet has invited all who are slavishly mimicking the call of the spinning-wheel boldly to declare their revolt. His essay serves as a warning to us all who in our impatience are betrayed into intolerance, or even violence, against those who differ from us. I regard the Poet as a Sentinel warning us against the approach of enemies called Bigotry, Lethargy, Intolerance, Ignorance, and other members of that brood.

But whilst I agree with all that the Poet has said as to the necessity of watchfulness lest we cease to think, I must not be understood to endorse the proposition that there is any such blind obedience on a large scale in the country today. I have again and again appealed to reason, and let me assure him that if happily the country has come to believe in the spinning-wheel as the giver of plenty, it has done so after laborious thinking. I am not sure that even now educated India has assimilated the truth underlying the spinning-wheel. He must not mistake the surface dirt for the substance underneath. Let him go deeper and see for himself whether it has been accepted from blind faith or from reasoned necessity.

I do, indeed, ask the poet and sage to spin the wheel as a sacrament. When there is war, the poet lays down the lyre, and the lawyer his law reports. The poet will sing the true note after the war is over; the lawyer will have occasion to go to his books when people have time to fight among themselves. When a house is on fire, all the inmates go out, and each one takes up a bucket to quench the fire. When all about me are dying for want of food, the only occupation permissible for me is to feed the hungry.

It is my conviction that India is a house on fire, because its manhood is being daily scorched; it is dying of hunger because it has no work to buy food with. Khulna is starving, not because the people cannot work, but because they have no work. The ceded districts are passing successively through a fourth famine. Orissa is a land suffering from chronic famines.

Our cities are not India. India lives in her seven hundred and fifty thousand villages. The cities live upon the villages. They do not bring their wealth from other countries. The city people are brokers and commission agents for the big houses of Europe, America, and Japan. The cities have co-operated with the latter in the bleeding process that has gone on for the past two hundred years. It is my belief, based on experience, that India is daily growing poorer. The circulation about her feet and legs has almost stopped. And if we do not take care, she will collapse altogether.

To a people famishing and idle the only acceptable form in which God can dare to appear is Work, and promise of food as wages. God created man to work for his food. Is it any wonder if India has become one vast prison? Hunger is the argument that is driving India to the spinning-wheel. The call of the spinning-wheel is the noblest of all because it is the call of love. And love is Swaraj. We must think of the millions who are today less than animals, who are almost in a dying state. The spinning-wheel is the reviving draught for millions of our dying countrymen and countrywomen.

"Why should I, who have no need to work for food, spin?" This may be the question asked. Because I am eating what does not belong to me. I am living on the spoliation of my countrymen. Trace the course of every coin that finds its way into your pocket, and you will realize the truth that I write.

Swaraj has no meaning for the millions, if they do not know how to employ their enforced idleness. The attainment of this Swaraj is possible within a short time, but it is so possible only by the revival of the spinning-wheel.

I claim that in losing the spinning-wheel we lost our left lung. We are therefore suffering from galloping consumption. The restoration of the wheel arrests the progress of the fell disease. There are certain things which all must do in all climes. The spinning-wheel is the thing which all must turn in the Indian climate, for the transition stage at any rate, and the vast majority must for all time.

It was our love of foreign cloth that ousted the wheel from its position of dignity. Therefore I consider it a sin to wear foreign cloth. I must confess that I do not draw a sharp distinction between economics and ethics. Economics that hurt the moral well-being of an individual or a nation are immoral, and therefore sinful. Thus the economics that permit one country to prey upon another are immoral. It is sinful to eat American wheat and let my neighbour, the grain-dealer, starve for want of custom. It is sinful to buy and use articles made by sweated labour. Similarly, it is sinful for me to wear the latest finery of Regent Street when I know that if I had but worn the things woven by the neighbouring spinners and weavers, that would have clothed me, and fed and clothed them at the same time. On the knowledge of my sin bursting upon me, I must consign the foreign garments to the flames and thus purify myself, and thenceforth rest content with the rough homespun cloth made by my neighbours. On knowing that my neighbours may not, having given up the occupation, take kindly to the spinning-wheel, I must take it up myself and thus make it popular.

In burning my foreign clothes I burn my shame. I must refuse to insult the naked by giving them clothes they do not need, instead of giving them work which they sorely need. I will not commit the sin of becoming their patron.

Nor is the scheme of Non-Co-operation or Swadeshi an exclusive doctrine. My modesty has prevented me from declaring from the house-top that the message of Non-Co-operation, Non-Violence and Swadeshi is a message to the world. It must fall flat if it does not bear fruit in the soil where it has been delivered.

At the present moment, India has nothing to share with the world, save her degradation, pauperism, and plagues. Is it her ancient Scriptures that we should send to the world? Well, they are printed in many editions, and an incredulous and idolatrous world refuses to look at them, because we, the heirs and custodians, do not like them. Before, therefore, I can think of sharing with the world, I must possess. Our Non-Co-operation is neither with the English nor with the West. It is with the system which the English have established, with the material civilization and its attendant greed and exploitation of the weak. Our Non-Co-operation is a retirement within ourselves, a refusal to co-operate with the English administrators on their own terms. We say to them, "Come and co-operate with us on our terms, and it will be well for us, for you, and the world."

We must refuse to be lifted off our feet. A drowning man cannot save others. In order to be fit to save others, we must try to save ourselves. Indian nationalism is not exclusive, nor aggressive, nor destructive. It is health-giving, religious, and therefore humanitarian. India must learn to live before she can aspire to die for humanity. The mice which helplessly find themselves between the cat's teeth acquire no merit from their enforced sacrifice.

True to his poetical instinct, the Poet lives for the morrow, and would have us do likewise. He presents to our admiring gaze the beautiful picture of the birds early in the morning singing hymns of praise as they soar into the sky. These birds had their day's food, and soared with rested wings in whose veins new blood had circulated during the previous night. But I have had the pain of watching birds, who for want of strength could not be coaxed even into a flutter of their wings. The human bird under the Indian sky gets up weaker than when he pretended to retire. For millions, it is an eternal vigil or an eternal trance. It is an indescribably painful state which has to be experienced to be realized. I have found it impossible to soothe suffering patients with a song from Kabir. The hungry millions ask for one poem, invigorating food. They cannot be given it. They must earn it. And they can earn only by the sweat of their brow.

Mr. Gandhi's next article in answer to the Poet's own misgivings concerning the Non-Co-operative Movement runs thus:

The Poet of Asia is fast becoming the poet of the world. Increasing prestige has brought to him increasing responsibility. His greatest service to India must be his poetic interpretation of India's message to the world. The Poet is therefore sincerely anxious that India should deliver no false or feeble message in her own name. He is naturally jealous of his country's reputation. He says he has striven hard to find himself in tune with the present movement. He confesses that he is baffled. He can find nothing for his lyre in the din and the bustle of Non-Co-operation.

In three forceful letters he has endeavoured to give expression to his misgivings, and he has come to the conclusion that Non-Co-operation is not dignified enough for the India of his vision, that it is a doctrine of negation and despair. He fears that it is a doctrine of separation, exclusiveness, narrowness, and negation.

No Indian can feel anything but pride in the Poet's exquisite jealousy of India's honour. It is good that he should have sent to us his misgivings in language at once beautiful and clear.

No Indian can feel anything but pride in the Poet's doubts. I may fail to convince him or the reader who may have been touched by his eloquence, but I would like to assure him and India that Non-Co-operation in conception is not any of the things he fears, and he need have no cause to be ashamed of his country for having adopted Non-Co-operation. If in actual application it appears in the end to have failed, it will be no more the fault of the doctrine than it would be of Truth if those who claim to apply it in practice do not appear to succeed. Non-Co-operation may have come in advance of its time. India and the world must then wait; but there is no choice for India, save between violence and Non-Co-operation.

Nor need the Poet fear that Non-Co-operation is intended to erect a Chinese wall between India and the West. On the contrary, Non-Co-operation is intended to pave the way to real honourable and voluntary cooperation based on mutual respect and trust. The present struggle is being waged against compulsory co-operation, against one-sided combination, against the armed imposition of modern methods of exploitation masquerading under the name of civilization.

Non-Co-operation is a protest against an unwitting and unwilling participation in evil.

The Poet's concern is largely about the students. He is of opinion that they should not have been called upon to give up Government schools before they had other schools to go to. Here I must differ from him. I have never been able to make a fetish of literary training. My experience has proved that by itself it adds not an inch to one's moral height. I am firmly of opinion that the Government schools have unmanned us, rendered us helpless and Godless. They have filled us with discontent, have made us despondent. They have made us what we were intended to become—clerks and interpreters.

A Government builds its prestige upon the apparently voluntary association of the governed. And if it was wrong to co-operate with the Government in keeping us slaves, we were bound to begin with those institutions in which our association appeared to be most voluntary. The youths of a nation are its hope. I hold that, as soon as we discovered that the system of Government was wholly or mainly evil, it became sinful for us to associate our children with it.

But the Poet's protest against the calling out of the boys is really a corollary to his objection to the very doctrine of Non-Co-operation. He had a horror of everything Negative. His whole soul seems to rebel against the negative commandments of religion. I must give his objection in his own inimitable language. He writes:

"R———, in support of the present movement, has often said to me that passion for rejection is a stronger power in the beginning than the acceptance of an ideal. Though I know it to be a fact, I cannot take it as a truth. Brahmavidya in India has for its objects Mukti (emancipation), while Buddhism has Nirvana (extinction). Mukti draws our attention to the positive, and Nirvana to the negative side of truth. Therefore Buddha emphasized the fact of Dukkha (misery), which had to be avoided; and Brahmavidya emphasized the fact of Ananda (joy), which had to be attained."

In these and kindred passages the reader will find the key to the Poet's mentality. In my humble opinion, rejection is as much an ideal as the acceptance of a thing. All great religions teach that two opposite forces act upon us and that the human endeavour consists in a series of eternal rejections and acceptances. Non-Co-operation with evil is as much a duty as co-operation with good. I venture to suggest that the Poet has done an unconscious injustice to Buddhism in describing Nirvana as merely a negative state. I make bold to say that Mukti, emancipation, is as much a negative state as Nirvana. Emancipation from, or extinction of, the bondage of the flesh leads to Ananda (eternal bliss).

I therefore think that the Poet has been unnecessarily alarmed at the negative aspect of Non-Co-operation. We had lost the power of saying "no." It had become disloyal, almost sacrilegious, to say "no" to the Government. This deliberate refusal to co-operate is like the necessary weeding process that a cultivator has to resort to before he sows. Weeding is as necessary to agriculture as sowing. Indeed, even whilst the crops are growing, the weeding fork, as every husbandman knows, is an instrument of almost daily use.

The nation's Non-Co-operation is an invitation to the
Government to co-operate with it on its own terms, as is every
nation's right and every good Government's duty. Non-Co-
operation is the nation's notice that it is no longer satisfied to be
in tutelage. The nation has taken to the harmless (for it) natural
and religious doctrine of Non-Co-operation in the place of the
unnatural and irreligious doctrine of violence. And if India is
ever to attain the Swaraj of the Poet's dream, she will do so only
by Non-Violent Non-Co-operation. Let him deliver his message
of peace to the world, and feel confident that India, through her
Non-Co-operation, if she remains true to her pledge, will have
exemplified his message. Non-Co-operation is intended to give
the very meaning to patriotism that the Poet is yearning after.
An India prostrate at the feet of Europe can give no hope to
humanity. An India awakened and free has a message of peace
and good will to give to a groaning world.

After thus explaining in full, with quotations from either side, this
difference of opinion between the two greatest spiritual leaders of
India, wherein the larger issues of the whole Non-Co-operation
Movement were discussed and matters of world-wide moment were
debated, it is with considerable hesitation that I have decided to
complete the present chapter with the incident of the "Burning of
Foreign Cloth," wherein I was all too painfully involved. But it seems
absolutely necessary to do so, because the excited encouragement of
repeated actions of this kind by Mr. Gandhi himself in all parts of the
country, and especially in Bombay, soon led on to further violence.
For instance, the crowd which gathered to the Burning of Foreign
Cloth on one occasion, in Bombay, was so great that it was estimated
at over a hundred thousand, and a wave of rowdyism from that time
forward began to run through the city. Minor acts of assault against
those who were wearing foreign dress frequently occurred.

In other ways also a conflagration of human passion was kindled.
Personally, I had taken an active part at the outset in Non-Violent
Non-Co-operation, believing that it was a righteous cause in face of
the crying evils done in the Punjab. Thus I was forced into the position

of publicly protesting against what appeared to me a breach of the spirit of Non-Violence when it became vividly apparent.

But the Burning of Foreign Cloth went on unchecked until the events at Bombay and Chauri Chaura, which will be mentioned in the next chapter, brought to a sudden and disastrous conclusion this phase of the struggle.

In answer to my own protest and to almost innumerable private letters, Mahatma Gandhi wrote the following article in *Young India:*

> The reader will, I am sure, appreciate my sharing with him the following beautiful and pathetic letter from Mr. Andrews. He writes to me:
>
> "I know that your Burning of Foreign Cloth is with the idea of helping the poor, but I feel that you have gone wrong. There is a subtle appeal to racial feeling in that word 'foreign' which day by day appears to need checking and not fomenting. The picture of your lighting that great pile, including delicate fabrics, shocked me intensely. We seem to be losing sight of the great outside world to which we belong and concentrating selfishly on India; and this must (I fear) lead back to the old, bad, selfish nationalism. If so, we get into the vicious circle from which Europe is trying so desperately to escape. But I cannot argue it out. I can only say again that it shocked me, and seemed to me a form of violence; and yet I know how violence is abhorrent to you. I do not at all like this question of foreign cloth being made into a religion.
>
> "I was supremely happy when you were dealing giant blows at the fundamental moral evils—drunkenness, drug-taking, untouchability, race arrogance, etc., and when you were, with such wonderful and beautiful tenderness, dealing with the hideous vice of prostitution. But lighting bonfires of foreign cloth and telling people that it is a religious sin to wear it; destroying in the fire the noble handiwork of one's own fellow men and women, of one's brothers and sisters abroad, saying it would be 'defiling' to use it—I cannot tell you how different all this appears to me! Do you know I almost fear now to wear the

Khaddar that you have given me, lest I should appear to be judging other people, as a Pharisee would, saying, 'I am holier than thou!' I never felt like this before.

"You know how, when anything that you do hurts me, I must cry out to you, and this has hurt me."

This is his letter.

It is so like him. Whenever he feels hurt over anything I have done—and this is by no means the first of such occasions—he deluges me with letters without waiting for an answer. For it is love speaking to love, not arguing. And so it has been over the burning of foreign clothes.

I remain just as convinced as ever of the necessity of burning. There is no emphasis, in the process, of race feeling. I would have done precisely the same thing in sacred and select family or friendly circles. In all I do or advise, the infallible test I apply is, whether the particular action will hold good in regard to the dearest and the nearest. The teaching of the faith I hold dear is unmistakable and unequivocal in the matter. I must be the same to friend and foe. And it is this conviction which makes me so sure of so many of my acts which often puzzle friends.

I remember having thrown into the sea a pair of beautiful field-glasses, because they were a constant bone of contention between a dear friend and myself. He felt the hesitation at first, but he saw the right of the destruction of a beautiful and costly thing, a present withal from a friend. Experience shows that the richest gifts must be destroyed without compensation and hesitation if they hinder one's moral progress. Will it not be held a sacred duty to consign to the flames most precious heirlooms, if they are plague infected? I can remember having broken to bits, when a young man, the loved bangles of my own dear wife, because they were a matter of difference between us. And if I remember aright, they were a gift from her mother. I did it, not out of hate, but out of love—ignorant, I now see in my ripe age. The destruction helped us and brought us nearer.

If the emphasis were on all foreign *things,* it would be racial, parochial, and wicked. The emphasis is on all foreign *cloth*. The restriction makes all the difference in the world. I do not want to shut out English lever watches or the beautiful Japanese lacquer work. But I must destroy all the choicest wines of Europe, even though they might have been prepared and preserved with all the most exquisite care and attention. Satan's snares are most subtly laid, and they are the most tempting, when the dividing line between right and wrong is so thin as to be imperceptible. But the line is there all the same, rigid and inflexible. Any crossing of it may mean certain death.

India is racial today. It is with the utmost effort that I find it possible to keep under check the evil passions of the people. The general body of the people are filled with ill will because they are weak and hopelessly ignorant of the way to shed their weakness. I am transferring the ill will from men to things. Love of foreign cloth has brought foreign domination, pauperism, and what is worst, shame to many a home. The reader may not know, that not long ago hundreds of "untouchable" weavers of Kathiawar, having found their calling gone, became sweepers for the Bombay municipality. And the life of these men has become so difficult that many lose their children and become physical and moral wrecks; some are helpless witnesses of the shame of their daughters and even their wives. The reader may not know that many women of this class in Gujarat, for want of domestic occupation having taken to work on public roads, under pressure of one sort or another, are obliged to sell their honour. The reader may not know that the proud weavers of the Punjab, for want of occupation, not many years ago, took to the sword, and were instrumental in killing the proud and innocent Arabs at the bidding of their officers, not for the sake of their country, but for the sake of their livelihood. It is difficult to make a successful appeal to those deluded hirelings and wean them from their murderous profession.

Is it now any wonder if I consider it a sin to touch foreign cloth? Will it not be a sin for a man with a very delicate digestive apparatus to eat rich foods? Must he not destroy them or give them away? I know what I would do with rich foods, if I had

a son lying in bed who must not eat them, but would still gladly
have them. In order to wean him from the hankering, I would,
though able to digest them myself, refrain from eating them and
destroy them in his presence, so that the sin of eating may be
borne home to him.

If destruction of foreign cloth be a sound proposition from
the highest moral standpoint, the possibility of a rise in the
price of Swadeshi cloth need not frighten us. Destruction is the
quickest method of stimulating production. By one supreme
effort and swift destruction, India has to be awakened from her
torpor and enforced idleness. Here is what Mr. Allen, the author
of the *Assam Gazetteer,* wrote in 1905 of Kamrup:

"Of recent years, the use of imported clothing has been
coming into favour, an innovation which has little to recommend it, as the time formerly spent at the loom is not, as a rule,
assigned to any other useful occupation."

The Assamese, to whom I have spoken, realize the truth of
these words to their cost. Foreign cloth to India is like foreign
matter to the body. The destruction of the former is as necessary
for the health of India as the latter for the health of the body.

Nor need we be afraid, by evolving the fullest Swadeshi
spirit, of developing a spirit of narrowness and exclusiveness. We
must protect our own bodies from disruption through indulgence, before we would protect the sanctity of others. India is
today nothing but a dead mass movable at the will of another.
Let her become alive by self-purification, and she will be a
boon to herself and mankind. Let her be carelessly self-indulgent,
aggressive, grasping; and if she rises, she will do so only to
destroy and be a curse to herself and mankind.

And for a firm believer in Swadeshi there need be no
Pharisaical self-satisfaction in wearing home-spun. A Pharisee is
a patron of virtue. The wearer of home-spun, from a Swadeshi
standpoint, is like a man making use of his lungs. A natural and
obligatory act has got to be performed, whether others do it
out of impure motives or refrain altogether.

16

THE BOMBAY RIOTS

Probably no greater shock has ever come in recent years to any national leader, in the midst of an heroic struggle, than that from which Mahatma Gandhi suffered at Bombay in 1921. For, contrary to all his confidence and almost triumphant expectation of a peaceful boycott, the Bombay labourers suddenly broke out into madness, in the mill area, at the time of the Prince of Wales's visit, and thus ruined at one blow the non-violent aspect of the Non-Co-operation Movement.

The shock of this untoward event was all the more intense for Mr. Gandhi himself, because he was actually present on the spot in Bombay, impotent and helpless. Even the magic of his personality, which had wrought such wonders at other times, could not assuage the violence of the crowds. He had arranged beforehand on the day of the Prince's arrival a bonfire of foreign clothes, expecting thereby to be able to attract the crowd to another centre. But the masses of the labouring people, down in the mill area, were so entirely out of hand and impatient of all control in the general excitement of those days, that they left the bonfire on one side, and started an orgy of inflamed and maddening rioting instead, killing innocent passers-by and burning liquor shops to the ground. This violence raged for some days before it was stopped. It ended at last chiefly owing to the vow of Mr. Gandhi to fast until it ceased. This fast inspired the magnificently courageous efforts of his followers as they worked with desperate earnestness to prevent the riots from spreading still farther.

But while now, on looking back, it is not so hard to understand the course of events which led up to the outbreak, yet at the time it seemed impossible for Mahatma Gandhi himself to get knowledge beforehand of the heat of passion that was smouldering beneath the surface ready to break out into a blaze.

The spiritual exaltation of those days—when he was almost hourly expecting the crisis to happen whereby Swaraj would be obtained—had lifted him above these lower mists of human passion. The enthusiasm of his followers, whereby he was surrounded, was quite unique. Things of great moment were being put right in a day, such as in ordinary times would have taken generations to accomplish. For instance, a single visit of Mahatma Gandhi to Assam, at the height of the Non-Co-operation Movement, had carried the sensitive and patriotic Assamese people forward on a wave of public enthusiasm, which had swept away bad opium habits of half a century of addiction. Still more wonderful was the fact that, after this wave of enthusiasm subsided, the old vicious opium addiction did not return. The same might have been recorded about liquor evils, and prostitution, and untouchability, and other vices elsewhere. Thus it seemed literally true, in those wonderful and inspiring days, that the age of miracles had returned. Old abuses were being swept away, not by the advent of a military power, but by the gentle dictatorship of a saint.

Therefore the sudden and unexpected blow was bitter indeed, when the whole fabric of this peaceful moral reform was shattered, owing to the mad events of mob violence, first at Bombay and afterwards at Chauri Chaura.

But if the shock to Mahatma Gandhi was terrible in its intensity, and almost paralysing at first in its sudden onset, his recovery from it was noble. For his act of repentance and self-humiliation was full of moral courage and atoning sacrifice. Such a public repentance as he insisted on in prison was not made easy for him by some of the most ardent of his own followers, who had come to him from a distance. They pressed him not to acknowledge such abasement, and despised him for his weakness. But they had not been able to visualize the power of evil let loose, as Mahatma Gandhi had done, and they had but little spiritual insight.

But God had been merciful—so Mr. Gandhi wrote in pathetic words of deepest contrition. The Divine Providence had brought him face to face with the evil that was still deep-seated in his own heart, rendering him powerless. For the mob had not ceased from its violence, even when he had gone out into its very midst. He had been brushed aside. Thus he had been rendered defenceless by his own people, and his cause had been betrayed from within. But out of his very helplessness he had called unto God for deliverance and the divine answer had come to his cry.

Greater, therefore, in the spiritual world had been this moral victory over himself than could have been wrought by any outward success of Non-Co-operation.

As the Poet, Rabindranath Tagore, on another occasion, had said:

My Master has bidden me sit by the wayside,
And sing the Song of the Defeated.
For she is the Bride whom He woos in secret.

At no moment in his whole career did Mahatma Gandhi rise higher than during those days before his final imprisonment. He had to meet the angry reproaches of his own followers, and to be told to his face that he was wrecking the whole Non-Co-operation Movement at the climax of its greatest power. From the purely political aspect, that was probably true. But in the spiritual realm there is a transvaluation of all such values.

While Mahatma Gandhi himself rose high to meet a great occasion, the same could not be said of the British Administration in India. For it seized this exact moment, when the Movement was in confusion, for striking a blow at the leader. From a worldly point of view, it was a diplomatic stroke, but it had no chivalry in it.

That note of chivalry, however, was truly given from the official side, even in those dark days when human passions were running very high, by the action of the presiding judge at the trial. The whole account was related to me by some of Mahatma Gandhi's most intimate followers, who were present in the court. Just at the point when the closing scene had become almost too tragically painful to endure, the judge with dignity of tone and perfectly chosen words gave his verdict acknowledging the saintly nobility of the prisoner. Mahatma Gandhi's courteous thanks in return brought the whole trial to an end.

It is a true and genuine pleasure to me to be able to go on to record from my own personal experience, as well as that of others, how at a still later critical moment Colonel Maddock, the good physician, performed with delicate skill, amid great difficulties, the surgical operation which saved Mahatma Gandhi's life. The tender care of the matron and nurse of the Sassoon Hospital, Poona, where the operation was performed, can also never be forgotten. Such deeds of love helped to take away much of the bitterness of those days; and the whole of India rejoiced, along with multitudes in other lands, when the prisoner was released in 1924, after two years' imprisonment, instead of six.

The present chapter will record his writings after the Bombay riots, and also after those at Chauri Chaura. The former runs thus:

> The reputation of Bombay, the hope of my dreams, was being stained yesterday even whilst in my simplicity I was congratulating the citizens upon their Non-Violence in the face of provocation. The Prince's visit itself and the circumstances attending the ceremonials arranged, and public money wasted for the manufacture of a welcome to His Royal Highness, constituted an unbearable provocation. And yet Bombay had remained self-restrained. This, I thought, was a matter for congratulation. The burning of the pile of foreign cloth was an eloquent counter-demonstration to the interested official demonstration.
>
> Little did I know that, at the very time when the Prince was passing through the decorated route and the pile of foreign cloth was burning, in another part of the city the mill-hands were in criminal disobedience, forcibly depriving those that were wearing foreign caps of their head-dresses and pelting inoffensive Europeans. As the day went up, the fury of the mob, now intoxicated with its initial success, rose also. They burnt tramcars and a motor, smashed liquor shops and burnt two.
>
> I heard of the outbreak at about one o'clock, and motored with some friends to the area of disturbance, and heard the most painful and humiliating story of molestation of Parsee sisters. No one from among a crowd of over fifteen hundred who had

surrounded my car denied the charge, as a Parsee with hot rage and quivering lips was with the greatest deliberation relating the story. An elderly Parsee gentleman said, "Please save us from this mob-rule." This news of the rough handling of Parsee sisters pierced me like a dart. Yes, some Parsees had joined the welcome. They had a right to hold their own view, free of molestation. There can be no coercion in Swaraj. The Moplah fanatic, who forcibly converts a Hindu, believes that he is acquiring religious merit. A Non-Co-operator, or his associate, who uses coercion has no apology whatsoever for his criminality.

As I reached the Two Tanks, I found a liquor shop smashed, two policeman badly wounded and lying unconscious on cots without anybody caring for them. I alighted. Immediately the crowd surrounded me and yelled, "Mahatma Gandhi ki jai."* That sound usually grates on my ears, but it had never grated so much as it did yesterday when the crowd, unmindful of the two sick brethren, choked me with the shout at the top of their voices. I rebuked them and they were silent. Water was brought for the two wounded men. I requested two of my companions and some of the crowd to take the dying policemen to the hospital. Then I proceeded to the scene a little farther up, where I saw a fire rising. There were two tramcars which were burnt by the crowd. On returning, I witnessed a burning motor-car. I appealed to the crowd to disperse, told them that they had damaged the cause of the Khilafat, the Punjab, and Swaraj. I returned sick at heart and in a chastened mood.

At about five, a few brave Sindhi young men came to report that in Bindhi Bazaar the crowd was molesting every passer-by who had a foreign cap, and even seriously beating him if he refused to give up his cap. A brave old Parsee who defied the crowd, and would not give up his hat, was badly handled. Maulana Azad Sobhani and I went to Bindhi Bazaar and reasoned with the crowd, telling them that they were denying their religion by hurting innocent men. The crowd made a show of dispersing.

---

* Victory to Mahatma Gandhi.

The police were there, but they were exceedingly restrained. We went farther. On retracing our steps, we found to our horror a liquor-shop on fire. Even the fire brigade was obstructed in its work. Thanks to the efforts of Pandit Nekiram Sharma and others, the inmates of the shop were able to come out.

The crowd did not consist of hooligans only, or boys. It was not an unintelligent crowd. They were not all mill-hands. It was essentially a mixed crowd, unprepared and unwilling to listen to anybody. For the moment it had lost its head. And it was not a single crowd, but several crowds, numbering not less than twenty thousand. It was bent upon mischief and destruction.

I heard that there was firing resulting in deaths, and that in Anglo-Indian quarters every one of the volunteers came in for hard beating, if he did not put off his homespun cap or shirt. I heard that many were seriously injured. I am writing this in the midst of six Hindu and Mussalman workers, who have just come in with broken heads and bleeding, and one with a broken nasal bone and other lacerated wounds. They went to Parel, led by Maulanas Azad Sobhani and Moazzam Ali, to pacify the mill-hands, who, it was reported, were holding up tramcars there. The workers, however, were unable to proceed to their destination. They returned with their bleeding wounds to speak for themselves.

Non-Co-operators cannot escape liability. It is true that Non-Co-operators were ceaselessly remonstrating everywhere with the people at considerable risk to themselves, to arrest or stop the mischief; but that is not enough for launching out on Civil Disobedience, or to discharge us from liability for the violence that has taken place. We claim to have established a peaceful atmosphere, to have attained by our Non-Violence sufficient control over the people to keep their violence under check. We have failed when we ought to have succeeded. For yesterday was a day of our trial. We were, under our pledge, bound to protect the person of the Prince from any harm or insult. And we broke that pledge, inasmuch as any one of us insulted or injured a single European or any other who took part in the welcome to the Prince. They were as much entitled to take part in the welcome as we were to refrain. Nor can I shirk from my own personal responsibility. I am more instrumental than any other in bringing into being the spirit of revolt. I find myself not fully capable of controlling and disciplining that spirit. I must do penance for it. For me the struggle is essentially religious. I believe in fasting and prayer, and I propose henceforth to observe, every Monday, a twenty-four hours' fast till Swaraj is attained.

Within less than four months from the date of the Bombay riots the second great act of violence took place at Chauri Chaura. The mob, led by those who shouted aloud the name of Mahatma Gandhi, hacked to death a number of policemen, and burnt them along with the police station. The tragedy came just when Mahatma Gandhi had sent an ultimatum to the Viceroy threatening civil disobedience in Bardoli. When the news about Chauri Chaura reached him, he called off immediately the civil disobedience in Bardoli and faced his enraged followers. He wrote thus:

God had been abundantly kind to me. He had warned me the third time that there is not as yet in India that truthful and Non-Violent atmosphere which alone can justify mass disobedience described as civil, gentle, truthful, humble, knowing, wilful yet loving, never criminal and hateful.

God warned me in 1919, when the Rowlatt Act agitation was started. I retraced my steps, called it a Himalayan miscalculation, humbled myself before God and man, and stopped not merely mass Civil Disobedience, but even my own, which I know was intended to be civil and Non-Violent.

The next time it was through the events of Bombay that God gave a terrific warning. He made me eye-witness of the deeds of the Bombay mob on November 17th. The humiliation was greater than in 1919. But it did me good. I am sure that the nation gained by the stopping of Civil Disobedience. India stood for Truth and Non-Violence by the suspension.

But the bitterest humiliation was still to come. Madras *did* give the warning, yet I heeded it not. But God spoke clearly through

Chauri Chaura. I understand that the constables who were so brutally hacked to death had given much provocation. They had even gone back upon the word, just given by the Inspector, that they would not be molested; but when the procession had passed, the stragglers were interfered with and abused by the constables. The former cried out for help. The mob returned. The constables opened fire. The little ammunition they had was exhausted, and they retired to the police station for safety. The mob, my informant tells me, therefore set fire to the station. The self-imprisoned constables had to come out for dear life, and as they did so they were hacked to pieces and the mangled remains were thrown into the raging flames.

It is claimed that no Non-Co-operation volunteer had a hand in the brutality, and that the mob had not only the immediate provocation, but also general knowledge of the high-handed tyranny of the police in that district. No provocation can possibly justify the brutal murder of men who had been rendered defenceless and had virtually thrown themselves on the mercy of the mob. And when India claims to be Non-Violent, and hopes to mount the throne of Liberty through Non-Violent means, mob-violence even in answer to grave provocation is a bad augury.

Chauri Chaura is after all an aggravated symptom. I have never imagined that there has been no violence, mental or physical, in the places where repression is going on. Only I have believed that the repression is out of all proportion to the insignificant popular violence in the areas of repression. The determined holding of meetings in prohibited areas I do not call violence. The violence I am referring to is the throwing of brickbats or intimidation and coercion practised in stray cases. As a matter of fact, in Civil Disobedience there should be no excitement. Civil Disobedience is a preparation for mute suffering. Its effect is marvellous, though unperceived and gentle. But I regarded a certain amount of excitement as inevitable, a certain amount of unintended violence even pardonable, i.e. I did not consider Civil Disobedience impossible in somewhat imperfect conditions. Under perfect conditions, disobedience when civil is hardly felt. But the present movement is admittedly a dangerous experiment under fairly adverse conditions.

The tragedy of Chauri Chaura is really the index-finger. It shows the way India may easily go if drastic precautions be not taken. We dare not enter the Kingdom of Liberty with mere lip homage to Truth and Non-Violence.

Suspension of mass Civil Disobedience and subsidence of excitement are necessary for further progress; indeed, indispensable to prevent further retrogression. I hope, therefore, that by suspension every Congressman or woman will not only not feel disappointed, but he or she will feel relieved of the burden of unreality and of national sin.

Let the opponent glory in our humiliation, or so-called defeat. It is better to be charged with cowardice and weakness than to be guilty of denial of our oath and sin against God. It is a million times better to appear untrue before the world than to be untrue to ourselves.

And so, for me, the suspension of mass Civil Disobedience and other minor activities that were calculated to keep up excitement is not enough penance for my having been the instrument, howsoever involuntary, of the brutal violence by the people at Chauri Chaura.

I must undergo personal cleansing. I must become a fitter instrument, able to register the slightest variation in the moral atmosphere about me. My prayers must have much deeper truth and humility about them than they evidence. And for me there is nothing so helpful and cleansing as a fast accompanied by the necessary mental co-operation.

I know that the mental attitude is everything. Just as a prayer may be merely a mechanical intonation as of a bird, so a fast may be a mere mechanical torture of the flesh. Such mechanical contrivances are valueless for the purpose intended.

But a fast undertaken for fuller self-expression, for attainment of the spirit's supremacy over the flesh, is a most powerful factor in one's evolution. After deep consideration, therefore, I am imposing on myself a five days' continuous fast, permitting myself water. It commenced on Sunday evening, it ends on Friday evening. This is the least I must do.

I have taken into consideration the All-India Congress Committee meeting in front of me. I have in mind the anxious pain which even the five days' fast will cause many friends; but I can no longer postpone the penance, nor lessen it.

I urge co-workers not to copy my example. The motive in their case will be lacking. They are not the originators of Civil Disobedience. I am in the unhappy position of a surgeon proved skilless to deal with an admittedly dangerous case. I must either abdicate or acquire greater skill.

I hope that the workers will leave no stone unturned to find out the evil-doers, and urge them to deliver themselves into custody. But whether the murderers accept my advice or not, I would like them to know that they have seriously interfered with Swaraj operations. I would like them to know, too, that this Movement is not a cloak or a preparation for violence. I would, at any rate, suffer every humiliation, every torture, absolute ostracism, and death itself, to prevent the Movement from becoming violent or a precursor of violence. I make my penance public, also, because I am now denying myself the opportunity of sharing their lot with the prisoners.

Non-Violent Non-Co-operators can only succeed when they have succeeded in attaining control over the hooligans of India, in other words, when the latter also have learnt patriotically or religiously to refrain from their violent activities, at least whilst the campaign of Non-Co-operation is going on. The tragedy at Chauri Chaura, therefore, roused me thoroughly.

"But what about your manifesto to the Viceroy and your rejoinder to his reply!" spoke the voice of Satan. (It was the bitterest cup of humiliation to drink.) "Surely it is cowardly to withdraw the next day after pompous threats to the Government and promises to the people of Bardoli." Thus Satan's invitation was to deny Truth and therefore Religion; to deny God Himself. I put my doubts and troubles before the

Working Committee and other associates whom I found near me. They did not all agree with me at first. Some of them probably do not even now agree with me. But never has a man been blessed, perhaps, with colleagues as considerate and forgiving as I have. They understood my difficulty, and patiently followed my argument. The result is before the public in the shape of the resolutions of the Working Committee. The drastic reversal of practically the whole of the aggressive programme may be politically unsound and unwise, but there is no doubt that it is religiously sound; and I venture to assure the doubters that the country will have gained by my humiliation and confession of error.

The only virtue I want to claim is Truth and Non-Violence. I lay no claim to superhuman powers. I want none. I wear the same corrupt flesh that the weakest of my fellow-beings wears, and am therefore as liable to err as any. My services have many limitations, but God has up to now blessed them in spite of the imperfections.

For confession of error is like a broom that sweeps away dirt and leaves the surface cleaner than before. I feel stronger for my confession. And the cause must prosper for the retracing. Never has man reached his destination by persistence in deviation from the straight path.

The immediate consequence of this act of Mahatma Gandhi was profound dismay, except among his closest followers, who knew his mind most nearly. There was a depression all over the country which could everywhere be felt. When I went in and out of the villages at this time, I found that the discouragement had penetrated the country as well as the cities. It was at this moment, as I have related, that the Government of India struck its blow. On the charge that certain articles published in *Young India* had caused disaffection, Mahatma Gandhi was arrested.

17

TRIAL AND IMPRISONMENT

The Trial

All that Mahatma Gandhi had tried to say so often in such a simple manner is borne out by the words uttered at his trial, when he was arrested and charged with causing "disaffection."

He pleaded guilty, because he believed that an Administration which had done such harm was no longer worthy of affection. In his statement, the most noticeable thing is this, that in the course of the two years during which the Non-Co-operation Movement had been in progress the gravamen of his charge against the Administration had shifted from the two wrongs done in the Punjab and towards the Mussalmans to the one indictment of the oppression of the poor.

At one time, in 1921, when the Non-Co-operation Movement was at its height and its success was by no means unlikely, Mr. Gandhi declared publicly that if the Administration would honestly take up the "poverty" question and put its heart into the spread of home-spinning and home-weaving, while at the same time bringing to an end the scandalous drink and drugs traffic, he would regard this as a sign of a change of heart. Again and again this was brought to the notice of the administrators, but nothing came of it.

The trial itself was noteworthy, both for the dignity of the prisoner at the bar and also for the noble utterance of the judge who delivered the sentence. Much of the bitterness at the time was taken away from men's minds owing to the judge's speech. Each day, during the arrest and trial, I was living with the railway workmen who had gone on strike at Tundla. It was impossible for me to attend the trial in the midst of public duties. Mahatma Gandhi wrote to me telling me on his account not to neglect my work, and that he himself was as happy as a bird. [See Appendix 9.] In his long written instructions to Hakim Ajmal Khan before he was shut up in a prison, he referred mainly to his own heart-longing for Hindu-Muslim Unity. [See Appendix 10.] After his release in 1924 it was the outbreak of violence between these two religions that caused him the acutest suffering of all, and led to his prolonged fast at Delhi. His words at the Trial were these:

> Before I read this statement, I would like to state that I entirely endorse the learned Advocate-General's remarks in connection with my humble self. It is the most painful duty with me, but I have to discharge that duty knowing the responsibility that rests upon my shoulders, and I wish to endorse all the blame that the learned Advocate-General has thrown on my shoulders in connection with the Bombay, Madras, and Chauri Chaura occurrences. Thinking over these deeply and sleeping over them, night after night, it is impossible for me to dissociate myself from the diabolical crimes of Chauri Chaura, or the mad outrages of Bombay. He is quite right when he says that, as a man of responsibility, a man having received a fair share of education, having had a fair share of experience of this world, I should have known the consequences of every one of my acts. I know that I was playing with fire. I ran the risk, and if I was set free, I would still do the same. I have felt it this morning, that I would have failed in my duty if I did not say what I said here just now.
>
> I wanted to avoid violence; I want to avoid violence. Non-Violence is the first article of my faith. It is also the last article of my creed. But I had to make my choice. I had either to submit to a system which I considered had done an irreparable harm to my country, or incur the risk of the mad fury of my people bursting forth, when they understood the truth from my lips. I know that my people have sometimes gone mad. I am deeply sorry for it, and I am therefore here to submit, not to a light penalty, but to the highest penalty. I do not ask for mercy. I do

not plead any extenuating act. I am here, therefore, to invite and cheerfully submit to the highest penalty that can be inflicted upon me for what in law is a deliberate crime, and what appears to me to be the highest duty of a citizen. The only course open to you, the Judge, is, as I am just going to say in my statement, either to resign your post or inflict on me the severest penalty, if you believe that the system and law you are assisting to administer are good for the people. I do not expect that kind of conversion, but by the time I have finished with my statement, you will perhaps have a glimpse of what is raging within my breast to run this maddest risk which a sane man can run.

I owe it, perhaps, to the Indian public and to the public in England that I should explain why from a stanch Loyalist and Co-operator I have become an uncompromising disaffectionist and Non-Co-operator. To the Court, too, I should say why I plead guilty to the charge of promoting disaffection towards the Government established by law in India.

My public life began in 1893, in South Africa, in troubled weather. My first contact with British authority in that country was not of a happy character. I discovered that as a man and an Indian I had no rights. More correctly, I discovered that I had no rights as a man, because I was an Indian.

But I was not baffled. I thought that this treatment of Indians was an excrescence upon a system that was intrinsically and mainly good. I gave the Government my voluntary and hearty co-operation, criticizing it freely where I felt it was faulty, but never wishing its destruction.

Consequently, when the existence of the Empire was threatened in 1899 by the Boer challenge, I offered my services to it, raised a volunteer ambulance corps, and served at several actions that took place for the relief of Ladysmith. Similarly in 1906, at the time of the Zulu revolt, I raised a stretcher-bearing party and served till the end of the "rebellion." On both these occasions I received medals, and was even mentioned in dispatches. For my work in South Africa I was given by Lord Hardinge a Kaiser-i-Hind Gold Medal. When the War broke out in 1914 between England and Germany, I raised a volunteer ambulance corps in London consisting of the then resident Indians in London, chiefly students. Its work was acknowledged by the authorities to be valuable. Lastly, in India, when a special appeal was made at the War Conference in Delhi in 1918 by Lord Chelmsford for recruits, I struggled at the cost of my health to raise a corps in Khaira, and the response was being made when the hostilities ceased and orders were received that no more recruits were wanted. In all these efforts at service I was actuated by the belief that it was possible by such service to gain a status of full equality in the Empire for my countrymen.

The first shock came in the shape of the Rowlatt Act, a law designed to rob the people of all real freedom. I felt called upon to lead an intensive agitation against it. Then followed the Punjab horrors, beginning with the massacre at Jallianwala Bagh and culminating in crawling orders, public floggings, and other indescribable humiliations. I discovered, too, that the plighted word of the Prime Minister to the Mussalmans of India, regarding the integrity of Turkey and the holy places of Islam, was not likely to be fulfilled. But in spite of forebodings and the grave warnings of friends, at the Amritsar Congress in 1919 I fought for Co-operation and for working the Montagu-Chelmsford reforms, hoping that the Prime Minister would redeem his promise to the Indian Mussalmans, that the Punjab wound would be healed, and that the reforms, inadequate and unsatisfactory though they were, marked a new era of hope in the life of India.

But all that hope was shattered. The Khilafat promise was not to be redeemed. The Punjab crime was whitewashed; and most of the culprits went, not only unpunished, but remained in service, continued to draw pensions from the Indian revenues, and in some cases were even rewarded; I saw, too, that not only did the reforms not mark a change of heart, but they were only a method of further draining India of her wealth and of prolonging her servitude.

I came reluctantly to the conclusion that the British connection had made India more helpless than she ever was before, politically and economically. A disarmed India has no power of resistance against any aggressor if she wanted to engage in an armed conflict with him. So much is this the case that some of our best men consider that India must take generations before she can achieve the Dominion status. She has become so poor that she has little power of resisting famines.

Before the British advent, India spun and wove, in her millions of cottages, just the supplement she needed for adding to her meagre agricultural resources. This cottage industry, so vital for India's existence, has been ruined by incredibly heartless and inhuman processes, as described by English witnesses.

Little do town-dwellers know how the semi-starved masses of India are slowly sinking to lifelessness. Little do they know that their miserable comfort represents the brokerage they get for the work they do for the foreign exploiter, that the profits and the brokerage are sucked from the masses. Little do they realize that the Government established by law in British India is carried on for this exploitation of the masses. No sophistry, no jugglery in figures, can explain away the evidence that the skeletons in many villages present to the naked eye. I have no doubt whatsoever that both England and the town-dwellers of India will have to answer, if there is a God above, for this crime against humanity, which is perhaps unequalled in history.

The law itself in this country has been used to serve the foreign exploiter. My unbiased examination of the Punjab Martial Law cases has led me to believe that at least 95 percent. of convictions were wholly bad. My experience of political cases in India leads me to the conclusion that in nine out of every ten the condemned men were totally innocent. Their crime consisted in their love of their country. In ninety-nine cases out of a hundred, justice has been denied to Indians as against Europeans in the Courts of India.

This is not an exaggerated picture. It is the experience of almost every Indian who has had anything to do with such cases. In my opinion, the administration of the law is thus prostituted, consciously or unconsciously, for the benefit of the exploiter.

The greater misfortune is that the Englishmen and their Indian associates in the administration of the country do not know that they are engaged in the crime I have attempted to describe. I am satisfied that many Englishmen and Indian officials honestly believe that they are administering one of the best systems devised in the world, and that India is making steady, though slow, progress. They do not know that a subtle but effective system of terrorism, together with an organized display of force on the one hand, and the deprivation of all powers of retaliation or self-defence on the other, have emasculated the people and induced in them the habit of simulation. This awful habit has added to the ignorance and the self-deception of the administrators.

Section 124, A, under which I am happily charged, is perhaps the prince among the political sections of the Indian Penal Code designed to suppress the liberty of the citizen. Affection cannot be manufactured or regulated by law. If one has no affection for a person or system, one should be free to give the fullest expression to his disaffection, so long as he does not contemplate, promote, or incite to violence. But the section under which Mr. Banker and I are charged is one under which mere promotion of disaffection is a crime. I have studied some of the cases tried under it, and I know that some of the most loved of India's patriots have been convicted under it. I consider it a privilege, therefore, to be charged under that section.

I have endeavoured to give in their briefest outline the reasons for my disaffection. I have no personal ill will against any single administrator, much less can I have any disaffection towards the King's person. But I hold it to be a virtue to be disaffected towards a Government which in its totality has done more harm to India than any previous system. India is less manly under the British rule than she ever was before. Holding such a belief, I consider it to be a sin to have affection for the system. And it has been a precious privilege for me to be able to write what I have in various articles tendered in evidence against me.

In fact, I believe that I have rendered a service to India and England by showing in Non-Co-operation the way out of the unnatural state in which both are living. In my humble opinion, Non-Co-operation with evil is as much a duty as is Co-operation with good. But in the past, Non-Co-operation has been deliberately expressed in violence to the evildoer. I am endeavouring to show to my countrymen that violent Non-Co-operation only multiplies evil, and that as evil can only be sustained by violence, withdrawal of support of evil requires complete abstention from violence.

Non-Violence implies voluntary submission to the penalty for Non-Co-operation with evil. I am here, therefore, to invite and submit cheerfully to the highest penalty that can be inflicted upon me for what in law is a deliberate crime, and what appears to me to be the highest duty of a citizen. The only course open to you, the Judge, is either to resign your post and thus dissociate yourself from evil, if you feel that the law you are called upon to administer is an evil, and that in reality I am innocent; or to inflict on me the severest penalty, if you believe that the system and the law you are assisting to administer are good for the people of this country, and that my activity is therefore injurious to the common weal.

The Judge then gave his full judgment as follows:

Mr. Gandhi, you have made my task easy in one way by pleading guilty to the charge. Nevertheless, what remains, namely, the determination of a just sentence, is perhaps as difficult a proposition as a judge in this country could have to face. The law is no respecter of persons. Nevertheless, it will be impossible to ignore the fact that you are in a different category from any person I have ever tried or am likely to have to try. It would be impossible to ignore the fact that, in the eyes of millions of your countrymen, you are a great patriot and a great leader. Even those who differ from you in politics look upon you as a man of high ideals and of noble and of even saintly life.

I have to deal with you in one character only. It is not my duty and I do not presume to judge or criticize you in any other character. It is my duty to judge you as a man subject to the law, who by his own admission has broken the law and committed what to an ordinary man must be a grave offence against the State. I do not forget that you have constantly preached against violence and that you have on many occasions, as I am willing to believe, done much to prevent violence. But having regard to the nature of your political teaching, and the nature of many of those to whom it was addressed, how you could have continued to believe that violence would not be the inevitable consequence it passes my capacity to understand.

There are probably few people in India who do not sincerely regret that you should have made it impossible for any Government to leave you at liberty. But it is so. I am trying to balance what is due to you against what appears to me to be necessary to the interest of the public, and I propose in passing sentence to follow the precedent of a case in many respects similar to this case that was decided some twelve years ago, I mean the case against Bal Gangadhar Tilak under the same section. The sentence that was passed upon him as it finally stood was a sentence of simple imprisonment for six years. You will not consider it unreasonable, I think, that you should be classed with Mr. Tilak, i.e. a sentence of two years' simple imprisonment on each count of the charge, six years in all, which I feel it my duty to pass upon you. And I should like to say in doing so that if the course of events in India should make it possible for the Government to reduce the period and release you, no one will be better pleased than I.

Mr. Gandhi said in reply:

I would say one word. Since you have done me the honour of recalling the trial of the late Lokamanya Bal Gangadhar Tilak, I just want to say that I consider it to be the proudest privilege and honour to be associated with his name. So far as the sentence itself is concerned, I certainly consider that it is as light as any judge would inflict on me; and so far as the whole proceedings are concerned, I must say that I could not have expected greater courtesy.

It may be well to give some notes from my own personal experience before closing the chapter. Mahatma Gandhi, since his release
from his imprisonment, has won the heart of "every Englishman in
India," and, I would add, of every Englishwoman also, by his supreme
honesty and goodness. He has also won them by his good-humour,
which comes out almost unconsciously in everything he writes.
When he groans, for instance, beneath the weary weight of his
"Mahatmaship," and when he tries in vain to forbid the unruly
crowd of devotees touching his feet, or waking him up in the middle of the night to have a darshan,* he wins the sympathy at once of
every English layman. Again, in his absolutely fearless utterances
against child-marriage, child-widowhood, and untouchability, he
gains their whole-hearted respect. Still further is this the case when,
after receiving a laudatory illuminated address from the aldermen of
some municipal corporation, he himself suggests in reply that they
might go with him at once and spend the rest of the morning visiting
the municipal latrines, and inspecting the dwellings of the municipal
"untouchable" staff. His passion for sanitation and cleanliness, going
down to the smallest practical details, also wins him high approval. It
is noteworthy that even Miss Mayo, in her book *Mother India,* which
Mr. Gandhi humorously called a "drain inspector's report," has very
little to bring against him.

To turn to more general subjects, it is his usual custom on no
account to refuse any request made to him by the missionaries, or
officials, or English merchants, to meet them personally in order to
expound his views. Such requests are now very frequent when he
goes out on a tour, and his utter friendliness and courtesy break
down every reserve. He is the most perfect host to those who visit
him in his own Ashram, himself attending to them night and morning.
He is also an admirable guest, whenever he accepts an invitation to
visit others in his turn. Every missionary's heart in India is drawn
towards him, and he has some of his own dearest English friends
among them. Above all, everywhere and on every occasion, little
children are his favourite companions. At Sabarmati he never starts

---

* A religious gaze which is supposed to be propitious.

out walking without his own Ashram children going with him, holding his hands, and talking and laughing all the way. They are always a merry party. In every house he enters, it is the same thing. The children find him out at once, and never wish to leave him. He has shown, as few have done, that a saint can be absurdly human and amazingly practical in common life. He has absolutely no consciousness whatever of any dignity or prestige. The poorest and the lowliest are naturally at ease with him on all occasions, and the "untouchables" everywhere immediately claim him as their own.

One incident that Mahatma Gandhi tells in his *Autobiography* may well close this chapter. It refers to the time when he was well known throughout the British Army at the Front, during the Boer War, on account of his intrepidity in rescuing the wounded and his untiring self-sacrifice. He was coming with his Indian stretcher corps towards Chieveley Camp, where Lieutenant Roberts, the son of Lord Roberts, had been carried with a mortal wound. Mr. Gandhi's stretcher corps had brought the wounded officer from the field of action. He writes as follows:

> It was a sultry day, and everyone was thirsting for water. There was a tiny brook on the way where we could slake our thirst. But who was to drink first? We had proposed to come in after the British soldiers had finished. But they would not begin first, and urged us to do so; and for a while this kindly competition went on for giving precedence to one another.

18

THE FAST AT DELHI

Of all the acts in Mahatma Gandhi's eventful life perhaps the most revealing is the "Great Fast" at Delhi; for this is the name that has been often given to it by Indians themselves.

The fast began towards the end of September, 1924, and lasted for twenty-one days. It was undertaken at a time when he had only just recovered from a very serious illness and operation. With remarkable foresight, he had laid all stress in his letter to Hakim Ajmal Khan, just before his imprisonment, on Hindu-Muslim Unity. [See Appendix 10.] It was in order to uphold and sustain this unity that he undertook this fast.

For during the years 1922 to 1924 the storm-clouds gathered thick on the horizon, and the hurricane broke at last in all its fury of communal religious dissension during the summer of 1924. Acts of violence were committed almost every day, which showed that the masses of illiterate Hindus and Mussalmans had started irrational and fanatical disputes.

During the whole time of Mahatma Gandhi's convalescence at Juhu, after his operation, it was my own great privilege to be with him. [See Appendix 11.] His mind was bent on getting well enough to go to the north, where the trouble was most rapidly increasing, in order to relieve the tension before it became too late to do so.

But when at last he was able to go to the spot, the worst had already happened. In one place after another serious riots, accompanied with bloodshed, had broken out, and the most painful and humiliating news of all had come from Kohat, on the north-west frontier.

It was at this time, shortly after reaching Delhi, that the current of events seemed to have passed altogether beyond human control. The conflagration had been kindled, and the fires of religious hate were burning fiercely. Mahatma Gandhi spent night and day in sleepless watch and prayer, asking for Divine aid. At last he felt that he had received from God the clear guidance through the darkness that enabled him to go forward.

He determined, in spite of his weakness after very serious illness, to undertake a twenty-one days' fast as an act of penance on behalf of the sins and infirmities of his own people. He stated, in the letter which he published, that the fast was a matter between himself and God, for his own self-purification. Nevertheless, it could not possibly be kept from the public, and the simple news of it at once brought to an end the fatal riots which had been so frequent before. It also roused, as nothing else had done, the National leaders to deal with this one problem as a matter of life and death for India as a nation.

On the second day of the fast, when I reached Delhi from Santiniketan, Mahatma Gandhi told me personally the whole story of the origin of the fast as I have tried to explain it above. He declared fully to me that the mental agony which he had suffered, before the decision came about the fast, had been no longer bearable. The relief, on the other hand, after the light had broken in upon his mind, in the midst of prayer, had cleared away all doubts and hesitation, and he had received the assurance that the duty which had been given him to perform had come from God.

In answer to my earnest and anxious inquiries as to whether he intended to go on, even if the strain became too intense for his frail body to bear, he replied that his faith in God was so firmly rooted that he knew this would never happen. If he found that no further endurance was physically possible, he would agree to take food. With that promise we were obliged to be content.

On the twelfth day the crisis came. Both the doctors considered that his life was in immediate danger, and pressed him to take food. I was asked to accompany them, in order to persuade him to do so. It was his day of silence, and he wrote on a slate his reply to our anxious entreaty in these words: "Have faith in God." When we pressed him still further, he wrote again: "You have forgotten the power of prayer." We remained intensely anxious all that night, which was a night of storm and thunder at the close of the monsoon. But the next morning he showed no more signs of weakening, and he remained bright and radiant to the end, when the twenty-one days were completed. It is true that others have fasted for a longer period than this; but rarely has such a thing been done with a body so weak and emaciated with illness as his had been before the fast began.

He allowed me to edit his own weekly paper, *Young India,* during the whole of this period. The extracts which I am taking for this chapter are somewhat scattered, but together they may give to the Western reader something of the scene with its remarkable associations. Written as they were in the time of crisis itself, they carry with them their own atmosphere of vivid sentiment and emotion.

In the first place, Mr. Gandhi thus described his own attitude towards prayer and his reasons for keeping the fast:

> No act of mine is done without prayer. Man is a fallible being. He can never be sure of his steps. What he may regard as answer to prayer may be an echo of his pride. For infallible guidance man has to have a perfectly innocent heart, incapable of evil. I can lay no such claim. Mine is a struggling, striving, erring, imperfect soul. But I can rise only by experimenting upon myself and others. I believe in the absolute oneness of God, and therefore also of humanity. What though we have bodies? We have but one soul. The rays of the sun are many through refraction. But they have the same source. I cannot, therefore, detach myself from the wickedest soul, nor may I be denied identity with the most virtuous. Whether, therefore, I will or not, I must involve in my own experiment the whole of my kind. Nor can I do without experiment. Life is but an endless series of experiments.
>
> I knew that Non-Co-operation was a dangerous experiment. Non-Co-operation in itself is unnatural, vicious, and sinful. But Non-Violent Non-Co-operation, I am convinced, is a sacred duty at times. I have proved it in many cases. But there was every possibility of mistake in its application to large masses. But desperate diseases call for desperate remedies. Non-Violent Non-Co-operation was the only alternative to anarchy and worse.

Since it was to be Non-Violent, I had to put my life in the scales.

The fact that Hindus and Mussalmans, who were only two years ago apparently working together as friends, are now fighting like cats and dogs in some places, shows conclusively that the Non-Co-operation they offered was not Non-Violent. I saw the symptoms in Bombay, Chauri Chaura, and in a host of minor cases. I did penance then; it had its effect. But this Hindu-Muslim tension was unthinkable. It became unbearable on hearing of the Kohat tragedy. On the eve of my departure from Sabarmati for Delhi, Sarojini Devi* wrote to me that speeches and homilies on peace would not do. I must find out an effective remedy. She was in saddling the responsibility upon me. Had I not been instrumental in bringing into being the vast energy of the people? I must find the remedy if the energy proved self-destructive. I wrote to say that I should find it only by plodding. Empty prayer is as sounding brass or a tinkling cymbal. I little knew then that the remedy was to be this pro-longed fast. And yet I know that the fast is not prolonged enough for quenching the agony of my soul. Have I erred, have I been impatient, have I compromised with evil I may have done all these things or none of them. All I know is what I see before me. If real Non-Violence and Truth had been practised by the people who are now fighting, the gory duelling that is now going on would have been impossible. My responsibility is clearly somewhere.

I was violently shaken by the riots at Amethi, Sambhar, and Gulbarga. I had read the reports about Amethi and Sambhar prepared by Hindu and Mussalman friends. I had learnt the joint findings of Hindu and Mussalman friends who went to Gulbarga. I was writhing in deep pain, and yet I had no remedy. The news of Kohat set the smouldering mass aflame. Something had got to be done. I passed two nights in restlessness and pain. On Wednesday I knew the remedy—I must do penance. In the Ashram at the time of morning prayer we ask Shiva, God of

---

* The poetess, Sarojini Naidu.

Mercy, to forgive our sins knowingly or unknowingly committed. My penance is the prayer of a bleeding heart for forgiveness for sins unwittingly committed.

It is a warning to the Hindus and Mussalmans who have professed to love me. If they have loved me truly, and if I have been deserving of their love, they will do penance with me for the grave sin of denying God in their hearts. To revile one another's religion, to make reckless statements, to utter untruth, to break the heads of innocent men, to desecrate temples or mosques, is a denial of God. The world is watching—some with glee and some with sorrow—the dog-fight that is proceeding in our midst. We have listened to Satan. Religion—call it by what name you like—is made of sterner stuff. The penance of Hindus and Mussalmans is not fasting but retracing their steps. It is true penance for a Mussalman to harbour no ill for his Hindu brother, and an equally true penance for a Hindu to harbour none for his Mussalman brother.

I ask of no Hindu or Mussalman to surrender an iota of his religious principle. Only let him be sure that it is religion. But I do ask of every Hindu and Mussalman not to fight for an earthly gain. I should be deeply hurt if my fast made either community surrender on a matter of principle. My fast is a matter between God and myself.

During the fast itself I copied out for my own satisfaction the Gujarati hymns which seemed to give him most joy at such a time of spiritual strain combined with bodily weakness. These hymns are sung by simple village peasants in his own province. They are well known among the poor. The following translations will give some idea of their religious devotional setting:

I

The way of the Lord is for heroes; it is not meant for cowards.
Offer first your life and your all; then take the name of the Lord.
He only tastes of the Divine Cup who gives up his son, his
     wife, his wealth, and his own life.

For verily he who seeks for pearls must dive to the bottom of
the sea, endangering his very existence.

Death he regards as naught; he forgets all the miseries of mind
and body.

He who stands on the shore, fearing to take the plunge,
attains naught.

The pathway of love is the ordeal of fire. The shrinkers turn
away from it.

Those who take the plunge into the fire attain eternal bliss.

Those who stand afar off, looking on, are scorched by the flames.

Love is a priceless thing, only to be won at the cost of death.

Those who live to die, these attain; for they have shed all
thoughts of self.

Those heroic souls who are rapt in the love of the Lord, they
are the true lovers.

II

So long as the truth is not known by thee all thy austerities are
of no avail, even as untimely showers that serve no purpose.

Of what avail are ablution and ceremonial and almsgiving? Of
what avail are the Sadhu's equipments—his ashes smeared
all over his body and his matted locks?

Of what avail are penances and pilgrimages, the counting of
beads, the mark on the forehead, the drinking of Ganges
water?

Of what avail are the knowledge of the Vedas, the grammari-
an's rules, and all the arts? Of what avail are philosophic
erudition and a knowledge of letters?

All these things are devices which merely satisfy the outer
man. So long as the truth is not known by thee thy life is
fruitlessly thrown away, says Narasinha.

III

He is my captive; I have purchased Him. Oh! I have purchased Him!

Some say He is too light; others say He is too heavy. I have
  weighed Him well, and know that I have full Measure.
Some say He is too cheap; others say He is too dear. Some say
  He is priceless. Oh! I have paid my full price.
I paid my full price on the streets of Brindaban whilst He was
  at play with Radha.
No one knows how I have secured Him. He knows. For, says
  Mira, He has only kept the pledge. He gave me in my pre-
  vious birth.
He alone is mine, naught else. I have left my father and mother,
  my kith and kin; in company with Sadhus have I lost all
  sense of shame; for He alone is mine.
I fled and sought refuge with the saints and wept to see the
  world. I wept tears of love, and watered the Tree of
  Immortality. Now He alone is mine.
On the way I met two good men, who alike had gone mad
  after Him. I kept them over my head. Him I kept in my
  heart. Now He alone is mine.
I went to the root of things, and found nothing but Him
  alone. Now He alone is mine.
The news is abroad. Everyone knows that Mira is His bond-
  slave and He is her Lord. What was destined has come to
  pass. Now He alone is mine.

IV

God is the helper of the helpless and the strength of the weak.
  He stood by the side of the saints in their hour of trial.
So long as the Lord of Elephants trusted in his own strength
  he was defeated.
The moment he forgot his own strength, and in his weakness
  called upon the Lord, God was at hand to help him—even
  before His name was half-uttered.
Draupadi in her helplessness called upon the Lord.
Dushasana was worsted in his effort to unclothe her; for the
  Lord became her clothing. Try as one may the power of

asceticism, or physical or temporal might, a man is bound
to fail.

Verily the strength of the defeated is the name of the Lord.

V

Lord, forbid it that I should cast my eyes on things that bring
evil thoughts. Far better that I were blind.

Lord, forbid it that I should foul my lips with any words
stained with filth. Far better that they were sealed.

Lord, forbid it that I should hear any word of injury to
another, or listen to a word of contempt. Far better that I
were deaf.

Lord, forbid it that I should look with lust on those who
should be sisters to me. Far better that I were dead.

Lord, let Tuka flee from all this world of sense to find eternal
peace in Thee.

VI

It is devotion to the Lord that makes the world dear.

Not to be found in Paradise, the saints who went there covet
to be born again on this earth that they may fulfil their
devotion to the Lord.

God's men seek not freedom from birth and death; they ask
to be born again and again, that they may serve and pray
and praise and see the Lord face to face.

The house where Mahatma Gandhi was resting was outside the
city, at the foot of that famous Ridge which was used by the attacking
forces during the Siege of Delhi. The room where he lay faced this
Ridge, and there was a balcony on its southern side where he was
carried each day into the sunshine, when the weather was propitious.
The side of the Ridge on which the house was situated had become
a part of the club-life of Delhi; for a famous golf course formed the
great attraction. The Pillar of Asoka, with its beautiful edict of toleration
engraven on stone standing out against the sky, was ever present to

our eyes. It reminded us how 2,500 years ago, owing to the Buddhist teaching, mankind had been more tolerant in religion, and more humane to man and beast, than they had become in modern times. The edict itself was often quoted during the Unity Conference which was being held in sympathy with Mahatma Gandhi's own longings for peace and good will between Hindus and Mussalmans. The Metropolitan Bishop of Calcutta, Dr. Foss Westcott, had laid aside every other duty in order to be present at this Conference, and his visit had been a benediction.

In order to picture the scene as it passed before our eyes day by day during those deeply painful hours of watching and waiting, I have ventured to quote the editorial written towards the end of the fast. Owing to the absorbing interest of everything in those days that had to do with the fast it was very widely quoted at the time. It was as follows:

> At the foot of the Ridge at Delhi, on the farther side away from the city, is a house called *Dil-khush,* or Heart's Joy, where Mahatma Gandhi had been keeping his fast. Above the house stands out the historic Ridge itself with its crumbling ruins telling of many battles in days gone by. A "Mutiny Memorial" stands at its highest point.
>
> From the terrace on the upper story of Dil-khush there can be seen ruined buttresses and walls, and not far away from them Asoka's Pillar points in its finger to the sky. In the darkness of the night these landmarks stand out in the starlight and against the moon. Between the Ridge and the house below, where Mahatma Gandhi lies in silence day by day, suffering and exhausted, lines of motor-cars in the Delhi season block the road each afternoon, while the golfers play their rounds of golf.
>
> Mahatma Gandhi had called me to the terrace one after-noon. Some musicians had come, and he wished me to hear the music. It was one of his worst days; his weakness was extreme. A boy was singing softly at the far end of the terrace. As I passed in order to sit down and listen to the music, I could not but take note how drawn the face of the sufferer was with pain. The sight renewed my anxiety, and at first I hardly listened to the

music. The sun was setting in the west, and shafts of light were pouring from it, piercing the open glades where the golfers were busily playing their rounds of golf. The rocks and ruins on the hilltop were flushed with crimson and gold.

At last the beauty of the sky arrested me and soothed my inner fears; and then, as I looked towards the Ridge, there appeared to come before my imagination the whole story of the past. That Pillar, with its edict of toleration and non-violence, brought to my mind the Buddhist Age and the saintly King Asoka. The people of the land in those days were kindly and tolerant towards man and beast. It was an age of peace.

But those fortress ruins with the Mutiny Memorial told me of another chapter in human history, filled with bloodshed and bitter strife. On that evening the sun was setting peacefully in the west; but all through the previous night the Ridge had been lashed by rain and tempest, and the winds had fiercely raged. The thunder had rolled along its sides and echoed in its rocks and hollows, and the jagged lightning had played against its summit. Even so, in Indian history the calm beauty of those peaceful days of King Asoka had been followed by the storm-swept days of war. Last of all, in the Mutiny the Ridge had been stained with human blood and scarred by shot and shell.

Below the summit of the Ridge, in the open spaces where the modern golf links had been made, I watched the golfers come and go. The clubs were swung and the balls were hit; muscular men and women marched forward, while little boys carried their golf clubs behind. Physical activity was there in every limb—physical and temporal power.

Instinctively my gaze turned back to the frail, wasted, tortured spirit on the terrace by my side, bearing the sins and sorrows of his people. With a rush of emotion there came to memory the passage from the Book of Lamentations—"Is it nothing to you, all ye that pass by? Behold and see, if there is any sorrow like unto my sorrow." And in that hour of vision I knew more deeply, in my own personal life, the meaning of the Cross.

The last scene of all was full of deepest interest and moment in every detail. Here again I will quote the editorial which I wrote at the end of the fast, describing in order what happened:

In the evening of the day before the fast was broken Mahatma Gandhi was wonderfully bright and cheerful. Many of his most intimate friends came to see him as he lay upon his bed on the open roof of the house, which was flooded by the moonlight. It was only four days before the full moon.

The time came for evening prayers. As usual he called everyone who was in the house, including the Congress volunteers in attendance, to join him in the evening worship. The passage from the Bhagavad Gita, which is recited every night at Sabarmati Ashram, was said in unison. It tells about the complete conquest of the soul over the body's senses and appetites. At its close it speaks of the blessed peace in the heart of the one who conquers. As I looked at that bright face before me I could well understand the meaning of the words that were being recited.

After the Gita one of Kabir's hymns was sung by Balkrishna. Later on the same evening I asked for a translation, and I was told that Kabir in his hymn sings as a penitent to God, calling himself the chief of sinners. In God alone is his refuge. From experience I had learnt that hymns in this mood gave him most pleasure of all during his penance and fast. A very wonderful exposition of the Katha Upanishad followed by Vinoba, then a long silence. The friends parted one by one and he was left alone.

Before four o'clock in the morning of the next day we were called for the morning prayers. There was no moon and it was very dark. A chill breeze was blowing from the east. The morning star was shining in a clear open sky above the Ridge. The phantom shapes of trees that rustled in the wind could be seen from the open room where we were all seated. He was wrapped warm in a dark shawl, and I asked him whether he had slept well. He replied, "Yes, very well indeed!" It was a happiness to notice at once that his voice was stronger than the morning before, instead of weaker. It would be difficult to describe the emotion of that silence which followed on this last day of the long fast, as we sat there waiting for all the household to assemble. We were all remembering that the final day had come. All the windows of the room where he was resting were open, and I sat gazing now at the figure reclining darkly upon the bed and now out at the stars.

The hymn that was sung at this special morning worship was one that was a great favourite with Mahatmaji. It is in Gujarati. What it says is this: "The way to God is only meant for heroes: it is not meant for cowards. There must be self-abandonment to the full. Only those who are ready to give up all for His sake can attain. As the diver dives down into the sea for pearls, even so heroic souls dive deep in their search for God."

After the prayers the early morning hours passed very quietly indeed; but before eight o'clock a very large number of visitors had begun to arrive, Some went away again after being allowed to see him; others stayed on, waiting till the fast was broken. At about 10 A.M. he called for me and said: "Can you remember the words of my favourite Christian hymn?"

I said: "Yes; shall I sing it to you now?"

"Not now," he answered, "but I have in my mind that when I break my fast we might have a little ceremony, expressing religious unity. I should like the Imam Sahib to recite the opening verses of the Quran. Then I would like you to sing the Christian hymn; you know the one I mean. It begins,

> When I survey the wondrous Cross
> On which the Prince of Glory died—

and it ends,

> Love so amazing, so divine,
> Demands my soul, my life, my all.

And then, last of all, I should like Vinoba to recite from the Upanishads, and Balkrishna to sing the Vaishnava hymn describing the true Vaishnava."

When I had gone downstairs I told Krishnadas about the arrangements. He was very ill that day and I knew that it would give him great happiness to be able to keep the ceremony in spirit with us, though he could not be there in body before noon. All the leaders and friends had assembled. The ladies also were present who had loved to do him service. As the time drew near I went upstairs again, and he asked me to see to it personally that every one should be allowed to be present, including the servants of the house. Before this, quite early in the day, I had brought up the sweeper to see him, who had been serving us very faithfully, and he had spoken to him some very kindly words and had given him a smile of gratitude for the services he had rendered.

Now, at last, the midday hour had come and the fast was to be broken. The doctors were called first by themselves, and he gave them the most touching words of thanks for all their love and devotion to him. Hakim Ajmal Khan was called, who had also cheered and helped him through his fast as a doctor and friend. Maulana Mahomed Ali, his most tender and loving host, followed, and without any further order all went quietly into his room and greeted him with affection and sat down. The ladies who were present sat near the bedside. Swami Shraddhananda sat at the foot of the bed with his eyes closed in prayer. Pandit Motilal Nehru, Deshbandhu Chittaranjan Das, Maulana Abul Kalam Azad, the Ali Brothers, were all seated together near the bed with many others.

The Imam Sahib, who had been one of his closest companions in South Africa and at Sabarmati Ashram, recited the wonderful Arabic opening words of the Quran, chanting its majestic language, which tells of God the Compassionate and Merciful, the Creator and Sustainer of the universe and the Helper of mankind. It ends with the prayer for His help to be guided in the path of righteousness and not in the way of sinners. After this, as had been arranged, the Christian hymn was sung. I quote the last two verses:

> See from His head, His hands, His feet,
> Sorrow and love flow mingling down;

Did e'er such love and sorrow meet
Or thorns compose so rich a crown?

Were the whole realm of Nature mine
That were an offering far too small;
Love so amazing, so divine,
Demands my soul, my life, my all.

Then followed some very beautiful passages from the
Upanishads, which were recited by Vinoba. Three of the slokas
may be translated thus:

"Those alone can realize the Divine Light within who have
purified themselves through the constant practice of truth, self-
discipline, meditation, and continence.

By ceaseless pursuit of truth the Rishis of old attained their
goal, even the supreme Truth.

Let not my words belie my thoughts, nor my thoughts belie
my words. Let the Divine Light always shine before me. Let not
my knowledge fail me. I shall always say what is right and speak
the truth."

After the "Om, Shanti, Shanti" had been uttered with the
deepest reverence, Balkrishna began to sing. He sang the song
of the true Vaishnava. "He is the true Vaishnava who knows and
feels another's woes as his own. Ever ready to serve, he never
boasts. He bows to everyone and despises no one, keeping his
thought, word, and deed pure. Blessed is the mother of such an
one. He reverences every woman as his mother. He keeps an
equal mind and does not stain his lips with falsehood; nor does
he touch another's wealth. No bonds of attachment can hold
him. Ever in tune with Ramanama,* his body possesses in itself
all places of pilgrimage. Free from greed and deceit, passion and
anger, this is the true Vaishnava."

It was strangely beautiful to think, almost aloud, as each of
these passages was uttered, how appropriate they were; how the

---

* The name of the Divine King.

ideal had been so nearly reached, along the hard pathway of suffering, by the one who was lying there about to break his fast. Everyone felt their appropriateness and hearts were drawn together.

Before the actual breaking of the fast Mahatma Gandhi turned to his friends. He spoke to them; and as he spoke his emotion was so deep that in his bodily weakness his voice could hardly be heard except by those who were nearest of all to him. He told them how for thirty years Hindu-Muslim unity had been his chief concern, and he had not yet succeeded in achieving it. He did not know what was the will of God, but on this day he would beseech them to promise to lay down their lives if necessary for the cause. The Hindus must be able to offer their worship with perfect freedom in their temples, and the Mussalmans be able to say their prayers with perfect freedom in their mosques. If this elementary freedom of worship could not everywhere be secured, then neither Hinduism nor Islam had any meaning.

Hakim Ajmal Khan and Maulana Abul Kalam Azad renewed their solemn pledge and promise on behalf of the Mussalman community.

Then Dr. Ansari brought forward some orange-juice and Mahatma Gandhi drank it. So the fast was broken. The joy and thankfulness of those who were present cannot adequately be described. Throughout it all, as congratulations poured in upon him, he lay there unmoved, quietly resting. Soon the room was left empty. Mahatma Gandhi remained in silence, and the great strain of the breaking of the fast was over.

For the time being, owing to his vicarious suffering, a pause came in the rioting between Hindus and Mussalmans, and the relief experienced all over India was very great. It seemed at first as if the end had been obtained for which he had fasted and prayed. Indeed, it may be truly stated that from this moment onward the violence of the storm of mutual distrust and bitterness had become abated. But evils that are centuries old cannot altogether be overcome by a single act. It is not surprising, therefore, that the thunder-clouds of passion rolled back again, and after a little more than a year the rioting broke out afresh. Those in that upper room at the conclusion of the fast, who had pledged themselves to give up even life itself if the call came, have in the main kept their word. Hakim Ajmal Khan and Swami Shraddhananda, who were present in the room and took the pledge, have already, each in his own way, answered the call for sacrifice which Mahatma Gandhi made. Others who are still living have made sacrifices almost equally great. The problem of Hindu-Muslim Unity has thus been carried a long way farther towards solution by Mahatma Gandhi's heroic act of faith.

19

THE WOMEN'S MOVEMENT IN INDIA

Among all the different interests which occupy Mahatma Gandhi's attention in India, very few can be compared with his earnest support of the Indian Women's Movement. He holds absolutely the view that men and women are equal, and he has never swerved for a moment in any direction with regard to this fundamental principle of equality between the sexes. When I have been working among the villagers both in India and also in other parts of the world where Indians have settled, it has been easy for me to outline the main programme of Mahatma Gandhi with regard to reform in India by holding up my hand with its five fingers and one single wrist uniting them, and explaining the five points in his own Indian programme with its own central unity as follows: First of all there comes the removal of "untouchability." Secondly, he emphasizes the need for complete prohibition of alcohol and drugs if India is to be free and self-respecting. Thirdly, at the centre of the hand I point to the principle of equality between man and woman as both fundamental and central to Mahatma Gandhi's view of life. The two other aspects are Hindu-Muslim unity and home-spinning in the villages. The uniting factor which binds this five-point programme is the ultimate principle of Ahimsa or Non-Violence, which Mahatma Gandhi regards as the absolute necessity for any united attempt at moral and spiritual progress as a nation. This doctrine of Ahimsa represents, as it were, the wrist which holds the five fingers of the hand together.

In this chapter I propose to give some of Mahatma Gandhi's most distinctive utterances with regard to the rights of women in India. If there is a disproportion in what follows with regard to the evils which have come to India in the towns through the results of immorality, the reason for this is that Mahatma Gandhi more than anyone else in modern times has been the one heroic and chivalrous personality who, like Josephine Butler in England, has dwelt fearlessly and directly with this painful and difficult subject. It must not be thought that this social evil is more widespread in India than in other countries. Probably it is far less wide in actual extent because the main population of India, numbering 90 percent in all, is a village population where this social evil has hardly yet penetrated. The towns of India, numbering only 10 percent of the population, have, it is true, this form of immorality accentuated; but modern India through its greatest leaders is determined to deal directly with it; and the social life of India itself, if the present moral enthusiasm continues, is likely to witness a great advance in social and moral hygiene. Nevertheless, the actual condition of such great modern cities as Calcutta and Bombay is a blot on civilization in this respect, and the evil there has gone so deep that it will require the greatest courage and spiritual strength to deal with it effectively.

Recently, in books which have been written by writers from the West, the picture of Indian womanhood as it exists today has sometimes been grossly exaggerated. The fact has been overlooked that womanhood necessarily in a tropical country begins three or four years earlier than in a cooler climate. This vital human factor must always be taken into account when considering statistics concerning early marriage and child-birth in India. At the same time no one has made a sterner protest against child marriage and child widowhood than Mahatma Gandhi himself, and some of the passages which follow will give his own opinions on the subject.

At the present time one of the subjects which is most closely occupying his attention is the Purdah system. Here from the very first he has been in favour of the complete abolition of Purdah at the earliest possible moment. He has spoken about its evil effects with unsparing denunciation, and he stands out in Modern India as the champion of free and equal womanhood.

In his own Ashram he has practised in every way that which he has preached in public. Women there at Sabarmati have equal rights in every respect with men. There is no observance of any Purdah. There is no child marriage. They vote on all important matters along with the men of the Ashram. Co-education is practised from first to last in the school, and the children are brought up together as brothers and sisters. It would be difficult to find in the East a freer and a fuller life for young girls than that which can be seen and witnessed every day at Sabarmati. It needs to be added that in all that I have related concerning these things Mahatma Gandhi and the poet Tagore are absolutely one in holding the same principle of free and equal womanhood in India. The following passages may be taken as typical of Mahatma Gandhi's dealing with this central subject. He writes as follows:

> Shrimati Saraladevi of Katak writes: "Don't you admit that the treatment of women in India is as bad a disease as untouchability itself?"
>
> I am unable to subscribe that the treatment of women is a "disease as bad as untouchability." Shrimati Saraladevi has grossly exaggerated the evil. A cause can only lose by exaggeration. At the same time I have no difficulty about subscribing to the proposition that in order to fit ourselves for true Swaraj men must cultivate much greater respect than they have for woman and her purity. Mr. Andrews has struck a much truer note when he tells us in burning language that we dare not gloat over the shame of our fallen sisters.
>
> All of us men must hang our heads in shame so long as there is a single woman whom we dedicate to our passion. I would far rather see the race of man extinct than that we should become less than beasts by making the noblest of God's creation the object of our lust. But this is not a problem merely for India; it is a world problem. And if I preach against the modern artificial life of sensual enjoyment, and ask men and women to go back to the simple life epitomized in the spinning-wheel, I do so because I know that, without an intelligent return to simplicity, there is no escape from our descent to a state lower than brutality.
>
> I passionately desire the utmost freedom for our women. I detest child marriages. I shudder to see a child-widow, and shiver

with rage when a husband, just widowed, with brutal indifference contracts another marriage. I deplore the criminal indifference of parents who keep their daughters utterly ignorant and illiterate, and bring them up only for the purpose of marrying them off to some young man of means.

Notwithstanding all this grief and rage I realize the difficulty of the problem. Women must have votes and an equal legal status. But the problem does not end there; it only commences at the point where women begin to affect the political deliberations of the nation.

To illustrate what I mean, let me relate the description a valued Mussalman friend gave me of a talk he had with a noted feminist in London. He was attending a women's meeting. A lady friend was surprised to find a Mussalman at such a meeting. She inquired how he found himself there. The friend said he had two major and two minor reasons for so doing. His father died when he was an infant. He owed all he was in life to his mother. Then he was married to a woman who was a real partner in life; and he had no sons, but four daughters all minors, in whom as a father he was deeply interested. Was it any wonder that he was a feminist?

He went on to say that Mussalmans were accused of indifference to women. There never was a grosser libel uttered. The law of Islam gave equal rights to women. He thought that man for his lust had degraded woman. Instead of adoring the soul within her he had set about adoring her body, and he had succeeded so well in his design that woman today did not know that she had begun to hug her bodily adornment, which was almost a sign of her slavery. He added, with his voice almost choked: if it was not so, how could it be that the fallen sisters delighted most in the embellishment of the body? Had we (men) not crushed the very soul out of them? No, he said, regaining self-possession, he wanted not only mechanical freedom for woman; he wanted also to break down the shackles that bound her of her own will. And so he had intended to bring up his daughters to an independent calling.

I need not pursue the ennobling conversation any farther. I want my fair correspondent to ponder over the central idea of the Mussalman friend's discourse and tackle the problem. Woman must cease to consider herself the object of man's passion. The remedy is more in her hands than man's. She must refuse to adorn herself for men, including her husband, if she will be an equal partner with man. I cannot imagine Sita ever wasting a single moment on pleasing Rama by physical charms.

Of all the addresses I received in the south the most touching was one on behalf of the Devadasis—a euphemism for prostitutes. It was prepared and brought by people who belong to the clan from which these unfortunate sisters are drawn. I understood from the deputation that brought the address that reform from within was going on, but that the rate of progress was still slow. The gentleman who led the deputation told me that the public in general was apathetic to the reform. The first shock I received was at Cocanada; and I did not mince matters when I spoke to the men of that place. The second was at Barisal, where I met a large number of these unfortunate sisters. Whether they be known as Devadasis or by any other name, the problem is the same. It is a matter of bitter shame and sorrow, of deep humiliation, that a number of women have to sell their chastity for man's lust. Man, the law-giver, will have to pay a dreadful penalty for the degradation he has imposed upon the so-called weaker sex. When woman, freed from man's snares, rises to the full height and rebels against man's legislation and institutions designed by him, her rebellion, no doubt non-violent, will be none the less effective. Let the Indian man ponder over the fate of the thousands of sisters who are destined to a life of shame for his unlawful and immoral indulgence. The pity of it is that the vast majority of the men who visit these pestilential haunts are married men, and therefore commit a double sin. They sin against their wives to whom they have sworn allegiance, and they sin against the sisters whose purity they are bound to guard with as much jealousy as that of their own blood-sisters. It is an evil which cannot last for a single day if we men of India realize our own dignity.

I ask every young man, married or unmarried, to contemplate the implications of what I have written. I cannot write all I have learnt about this social disease, this moral leprosy. Let his imagination fill in the rest, and then let him recoil with horror and shame from the sin if he has himself been guilty of it. And let every pure man, wherever he is, do what he can to purify his neighbourhood.

The first occasion I had of meeting those women who earn their livelihood out of their shame was at Cocanada in the Andhra province. There it was a few moments' interview with only half a dozen of them. The second occasion was at Barisal. Over one hundred of them met by appointment. They had sent a letter in advance asking for an interview, and telling me that they had become members of the Congress and subscribed to the Tilak Swaraj Fund, but could not understand my advice not to seek office in the various Congress Committees. They wound up by saying that they wished to seek my advice as to their future welfare. The gentleman who handed me the letter did so with great hesitation, not knowing whether I would be offended or pleased with the receipt of the letter. I put him at ease by assuring him that it was my duty to serve these sisters if I could in any way.

For me the two hours I passed with these sisters is a treasured memory. They represent the shame of the men of Barisal, and the sooner Barisal gets rid of it the better for its great name. And what is true of Barisal is true, I fear, of every city. I mention Barisal, therefore, as an illustration. The credit of having thought of serving these sisters belongs to some young men of Barisal. Let me hope that Barisal will soon be able to claim the credit, too, of having eradicated the evil.

Of all the evils for which man has made himself responsible, none is so degrading, so shocking, or so brutal as his abuse of the *better* half of humanity; to me—the female sex—*not* the weaker sex, for it is the nobler of the two. It is, even today, the embodiment of sacrifice, silent suffering, humility, faith, and knowledge. A woman's intuition has often proved truer than man's arrogant assumption of superior knowledge.

Let us not delude ourselves into the belief that this gambling in vice has a place in our evolution because it is rampant, and in some cases even State-regulated, in civilized Europe. Let us not also perpetuate the vice on the strength of Indian precedents. We should cease to grow the moment we cease to discriminate between virtue and vice, and slavishly copy the past which we do not fully know. We are proud heirs to all that was noblest and best in the bygone age. We must not dishonour our heritage by multiplying past errors. In a self-respecting India is not every woman's virtue as much every man's concern as his own sister's? Swaraj means ability to regard every inhabitant of India as our own brother or sister.

And so, as a man, I hung my head in shame before these hundred sisters. Some were elderly, most were between twenty and thirty, and two or three were girls below twelve. Between them all they told me they had six girls and four boys, the eldest of whom was married to one of their own class. The girls were to be brought up to the same life as themselves, unless something else was possible. That these women should have considered their lot to be beyond repair was like a stab in the living flesh. And yet they were intelligent and modest. Their talk was dignified, their answers were clean and straight; and for the moment their determination was as firm as that of any Satyagrahi. Eleven of them promised to give up their present life and take to spinning and weaving from the following day if they received a helping hand. The others said they would take time to think, for they did not wish to deceive me.

Here is work for the citizens of Barisal; here is work for all true servants of India, men as well as women. Before these unfortunate sisters could be weaned from their degradation two conditions have to be fulfilled. We men must learn to control our passions, and these women should be found a calling that would enable them to earn an honourable living. The movement of Non-Cooperation is nothing if it does not purify us and restrain our evil passions. And there is no occupation but spinning and weaving which all can take up without overcrowding. These sisters, the vast majority of them, need not think of marriage. They agreed that they could not. They must therefore become the true *Sannyasinis** of India. Having no cares of life but of service, they can spin and weave to their hearts' content.

But what I would like you, young men around me, to do is that you should have a touch of chivalry about you. If you have that, I have a great suggestion to offer. I hope the majority of you are still unmarried. Therefore I want you to make this sacred resolve, that you are not going to marry a girl who is not a widow; you will seek out a widow-girl, and if you cannot get a widow-girl you are not going to marry at all. Make that determination, announce it to the world, announce it to your parents, if you have them, or to your sisters. I call them widow-girls by way of correction because I believe that a child ten or fifteen years old, who was no consenting party to the so-called marriage; who, having married, having never lived with the so-called husband, is suddenly declared to be a widow, is not a widow. It is an abuse of the term, abuse of language, and a sacrilege.

The word "widow" in Hinduism has a sacred odour about it. I am a worshipper of a true widow like the late Mrs. Ramabai Ranade, who knew what it was to be a widow. But a child nine years old knows nothing of what a husband should be. If it is not true that there are such child-widows in the Presidency, then my case falls to the ground. But if there are such child-widows, it becomes your sacred duty to make the determination to marry a girl-widow, if you want to rid ourselves of this curse. I am superstitious enough to believe that all such sins that a nation commits react upon it physically. I believe that all these sins of ours have accumulated together to reduce us to a state of slavery. You may get the finest Constitution that is conceivable

---

* Women ascetics.

dropping upon you from the House of Commons. It will be worthless if there are not men and women fit enough to work that Constitution. Do you suppose that we can possibly call ourselves men, worthy of ruling ourselves or others, or shaping the destiny of a nation containing thirty crores,* so long as there is one single widow who wishes to fulfil her fundamental wants, but is violently prevented from doing so? It is not religion but irreligion. I say that, saturated as I am with the spirit of Hinduism. Do not make the mistake that it is the Western spirit in me that is speaking. I claim to be full to overflowing with the spirit of India undefiled. I have assimilated many things from the West, but not this. There is no warrant for this kind of widowhood in Hinduism.

---

* One crore = 100 lakhs = 10,000,000 [i.e., 300 million people].

20

A Morning with Gandhi

During the fast at Delhi one of my own students from Santiniketan, named Ramachandran, the son of a Finance Minister in Travancore State, came and stayed with me in order to fulfil any service which might be required at such a critical period. In Santiniketan he had studied under the poet Rabindranath Tagore, who is called usually "Gurudev," meaning Revered Teacher, just as Mr. Gandhi is usually called "Bapuji," meaning Father, at Sabarmati. Some difficult questions about Art, Marriage, and the use of Machinery had been puzzling him for a long time, and he was extremely anxious to know Mahatma Gandhi's opinion about them. For, although he was personally devoted at heart to Mahatma Gandhi on account of his saintly life, he was in his own mind more drawn towards the less Puritan ideals of Santiniketan.

At first he was too modest to seek for a personal solution of his questions from Mr. Gandhi himself, but after the fast was over I pressed him one morning to do so. A graphic and accurate account of the scene and the conversation that ensued was drawn up afterwards for *Young India* by Mahadev Desai, who was present at the interview and wrote as follows:

> Among those who visited Delhi during the weeks of fasting, penance, and prayer there was a young student from Santiniketan named Ramachandran. He is one of the pupils of Mr. Andrews, and had no difficulty in persuading his teacher to permit him to stay at Delhi for some time after the fast was over. In the end Mr. Andrews took Ramachandran upstairs and said to Gandhiji, "I have not even introduced Ramachandran as yet to you. But he has been all the while with us, helping us

devotedly with true love. He wants to ask you some questions; and I shall be so glad if you could have a talk with him before he leaves tomorrow to go back to Santiniketan." Gandhiji at once gave his consent.

"How is it," asked Ramachandran, "that many intelligent and eminent men, who love and admire you, hold that you have ruled out of the scheme of national regeneration all considerations of Art?"

"I am sorry," replied Gandhiji, "that in this matter I have been generally misunderstood. Let me explain. There are two aspects, the outward and the inward. It is purely a matter of emphasis with me. The outward has no meaning to me at all except in so far as it helps the inward. All true Art is the expression of the soul. The outward forms have value only insofar as they are the expression of the inner spirit of man."

Ramachandran hesitatingly suggested, "The great artists themselves have declared that Art is the translation of the urge and unrest in the soul of the artist into words, colours, shapes."

"Yes," said Gandhiji, "Art of that nature has the greatest possible appeal for me. But I know that many call themselves artists in whose works there is absolutely no trace of the soul's upward urge and unrest."

"Have you any instance in mind?"

"Yes," said Gandhiji, "take Oscar Wilde. I can speak of him because I was in England at the time that he was being discussed and talked about."

"I have been told," put in Ramachandran, "that Oscar Wilde was one of the greatest literary artists of modern times."

"Yes, that is just my trouble. Wilde saw the highest Art only in outward forms, and therefore succeeded in beautifying immorality. All true Art must help the soul to realize its inner self. In my own case I find that I can do entirely without external forms in my soul's realization. I can claim, therefore, that there is truly sufficient Art in my life, though you might not see what you call works of Art about me. My room may have blank walls; and I may even dispense with the roof, so that I may gaze out upon the starry heavens overhead that stretch in an unending expanse of beauty. What conscious Art of man can give me the scene that opens before me when I look up to the sky above with all its shining stars? This, however, does not mean that I refuse to accept the value of human productions of Art, but only that I personally feel how inadequate these are compared with the eternal symbols of beauty in Nature."

"But the artists claim to see and to find Truth through outward beauty," said Ramachandran. "Is it possible to see and find Truth in that way?"

"I would reverse the order," Gandhiji immediately answered: "I see and find beauty through Truth. All Truths, not merely true ideas, but truthful faces, truthful pictures, truthful songs, are highly beautiful. Whenever men begin to see Beauty in Truth, then Art will arise."

"But cannot Beauty," Ramachandran asked, "be separated from Truth and Truth from Beauty?"

"I should want to know exactly what is Beauty," Gandhiji replied. "If it is what people generally understand by that word, then they are wide apart. Is a woman with fair features necessarily beautiful?"

"Yes," replied Ramachandran without thinking.

"Even," asked Bapu, continuing his question, "if she may be of an ugly character?"

Ramachandran hesitated. "But her face," he said, "in that case cannot be beautiful."

"You are begging the whole question," Gandhiji replied. "You now admit that mere outward form may not make a thing beautiful. To a true artist only that face is beautiful which, quite apart from its exterior, shines with the Truth within the soul. There is then, as I have said, no Beauty apart from Truth. On the other hand, Truth may manifest itself in forms which may not be outwardly beautiful at all. Socrates, we are told, was the most truthful man of his time, and yet his features are said to have been the ugliest in Greece. To my mind he was beautiful because all his life was a striving after Truth; and you may remember that his outward form did not prevent Phidias from appreciating the beauty of Truth in him, though as an artist he was accustomed to see Beauty in outward forms also!"

"But, Bapuji," said Ramachandran eagerly, "the most beautiful things have often been created by men whose lives were not beautiful."

"That," said Gandhiji, "only means that Truth and Untruth often co-exist; good and evil are often found together. In an artist also not seldom the right perception of things and the wrong co-exist. Truly beautiful creations only come when right perception is at work. If these moments are rare in life they are also rare in Art."

"Is there Truth, Bapuji, in things that are neither moral nor immoral in themselves? For instance, is there Truth in a sunset, or a crescent moon that shines amid the stars at night?"

"Indeed," replied Gandhiji, "these beauties are truthful inasmuch as they make me think of the Creator at the back of them. How could these be beautiful but for the Truth that is in the centre of creation? When I admire the wonder of a sunset or the beauty of the moon, my soul expands in worship of the Creator. I try to see Him and His mercies in all these creations. But even the sunsets and sunrises would be mere hindrances if they did not help me to think of Him. Anything which is a hindrance to the flight of the soul is a delusion and a snare; even like the body, which often does actually hinder you in the path of salvation."

"Are you against all machinery, Bapuji?" asked Ramachandran.

"How can I be," he answered, smiling at Ramachandran's naïve question, "when I know that even the body is a most delicate piece of machinery? The spinning-wheel itself is a machine. What I object to is the craze for machinery, not machinery as such. The craze is for what they call labour-saving machinery. Men go on 'saving labour' till thousands are without work and thrown on the open streets to die of starvation. I want to save time and labour, not for a fraction of mankind, but for all. I want the concentration of wealth, not in the hands of a few, but in the hands of all. Today machinery merely helps a few to ride on the backs of millions. The impetus behind it all is not the philanthropy to save labour but greed. It is against this constitution of things that I am fighting with all my might."

"Then, Bapuji," said Ramachandran, "you are fighting not against machinery as such, but against its abuses, which are so much in evidence today?"

"I would unhesitatingly say 'yes'; but I would add that scientific truths and discoveries should first of all cease to be the mere instruments of greed. Then labourers will not be over-worked, and machinery, instead of becoming a hindrance, will be a help. I am aiming, not at the eradication of all machinery, but its limitation."

Ramachandran said: "When logically argued out that would seem to imply that all complicated power-driven machinery should go."

"It might have to go," admitted Gandhiji, "but I must make one thing clear. The supreme consideration is man. The machine should not tend to make atrophied the limbs of men. For instance, I would make intelligent exceptions. Take the case of the Singer Sewing Machine. It is one of the few useful things ever invented, and there is a romance about the device itself. Mr. Singer saw his wife labouring over the tedious process of sewing with her own hands, and simply out of his love for her he devised the sewing machine, in order to save her from unnecessary labour. He, however, saved not only her labour, but also the labour of everyone who could purchase a sewing machine."

"But, in that case," said Ramachandran, "there would have to be a factory for making these Singer Sewing Machines, and it would have to contain power-driven machinery of ordinary type."

"Yes," said Bapu, smiling at Ramachandran's eager opposition. "But I am Socialist enough to say that such factories should be nationalized. They ought only to be working under the most attractive conditions, not for profit, but for the benefit of humanity, love taking the place of greed as the motive-power.

It is an alteration in the conditions of labour that I want. This mad rush for wealth must cease; and the labourer must be assured, not only of a living wage, but of a daily task that is not a mere drudgery. The machine will, under these conditions, be as much a help to the man working it as to the State. The present mad rush will cease, and the labourers will work (as I have said) under attractive and ideal conditions. This is but one of the exceptions I have in mind. The sewing machine had love at its back. The individual is the one supreme consideration. The saving of labour of the individual should be the object, and honest humanitarian considerations and not greed the motive-power. Thus, for instance, I would welcome any day a machine to straighten crooked spindles. Not that blacksmiths will cease to make supplies; they will continue to provide the spindles; but when the spindle gets wrong every spinner will have a machine of his own to get it straight. Therefore replace greed by love and everything will come right."

"The third question," said Ramachandran, "that I would like to ask you is whether you are against the institution of marriage."

"I shall have to answer this question at some length," said Bapu. "The aim of human life is deliverance. As a Hindu, I believe that Moksha, or deliverance, is freedom from birth, by breaking the bonds of the flesh, by becoming one with God. Now marriage is a hindrance in the attainment of this supreme object, inasmuch as it only tightens the bonds of flesh. Celibacy is a great help, inasmuch as it enables one to lead a life of full surrender to God. What is the object generally understood of marriage except a repetition of one's own kind? And why need you advocate marriage? It propagates itself. It requires no agency to promote its growth."

"But must you advocate celibacy and preach it to one and all?"

"Yes," said Gandhiji. Ramachandran looked perplexed. "Then you fear there will be an end of creation? No. The extreme logical result would be not extinction of the human species, but the transference of it to a higher plane."

"But may not an artist, or a poet, or a great genius leave a legacy of his genius to posterity through his own children?"

"Certainly not," said Bapu, with emphasis. "He will have more disciples than he can ever have children; and through those disciples all his gifts to the world will be handed down in a way that nothing else can accomplish. It will be the soul's marriage with the spirit; the progeny being the disciple, a sort of divine procreation. No! You must leave marriage to take care of itself. Repetition and not growth would be the result, for lust has come to play the most important part in marriage."

"Mr. Andrews," said Ramachandran, "does not like your emphasis on celibacy."

"Yes, I know," said Gandhiji. "That is the legacy of his Protestantism. Protestantism did many good things; but one of its few evils was that it ridiculed celibacy."

"That," rejoined Ramachandran, "was because it had to fight the abuses in which the clergy of the Middle Ages had sunk."

"But all that was not due to any inherent evil of celibacy," said Bapu. "It is celibacy that has kept Catholicism green up to the present day."

Ramachandran's next question was about the much-discussed "Spinning Franchise" which Gandhiji had enjoined, insisting that none should be a member of the National Congress who did not spin with his own hands. Ramachandran assured Gandhiji at the outset that he was a spinner, but had to confess that he, with three friends at Santiniketan, only began spinning after they had heard of the fast. He also affirmed that he believed in universal spinning. But he could not understand how the Congress should *compel* its members to spin. Persuasion and not compulsion should be the method.

"I see," said Gandhiji, "you even go farther than Charlie Andrews. He would not have the Congress to compel its members; but he would fain become a member of a voluntary spinning association. You object to any such association whatsoever?"

Ramachandran sat silent.

"Well, then," replied Gandhiji, enjoying the argument, "I ask you, has the Congress any right to say that its members shall not drink? Will that be a restriction of the freedom of the individual, too? If the Congress exercised that right of enjoining abstinence from drinking there would be no objection. Why? Because the evils of drink are obvious. Well, I say that in India today, where millions are on the brink of starvation, it is perhaps a much worse evil to import foreign cloth. Think of the starving millions of Orissa. When I went there I saw the famine-stricken. Thanks to a kind superintendent who was in charge of an industrial home, I saw also their children, bright, healthy, and merry, working away at their carpets, baskets, etc. There was no spinning because these other things were much in vogue at the time. But on their faces there was the lustre of joyful work. But when I came to the famine-stricken, what did I see? They were merely skin and bone, only waiting to die. They were then in that condition because they would under no circumstances work. Even though you had threatened to shoot them if they refused to work, I am sure they would have preferred to be shot rather than do any honest work. This aversion from work is a greater evil than drink itself. You can take some work out of a drunkard. A drunkard retains something of a heart. He has intelligence. These starved men, refusing to work, were like mere animals. Now, how can we solve the problem of getting work out of people like this? I see no way except that of universalizing spinning. Every yard of foreign cloth brought into India is one bit of bread snatched out of the mouths of these starving poor. If you could visualize, as I can, the supreme need of the hour, which is to give India's starving millions a chance to earn their bread with joy and gladness, you would not object to the Spinning Franchise."

Ramachandran still appeared doubtful, but changed the subject. "So, Bapuji," he said, resuming the first point in the conversation, "Beauty and Truth are not merely separate aspects of the same thing?"

"Truth," repeated Gandhiji, "is the first thing to be sought for, and Beauty and Goodness will then be added unto you. That is what Christ really taught in the Sermon on the Mount.

Jesus was to my mind a supreme artist because he saw and expressed Truth; and so was Muhammad. Scholars say that the Quran is the most perfect composition in all Arabic literature. Because both of them strove first for Truth, therefore the grace of expression naturally came in. Yet neither Jesus nor Muhammad wrote on Art. That is the Truth and Beauty I crave for, live for, and would die for."

Ramachandran then reverted to his difficulties as to Gandhiji's logical position with regard to machinery. "If you make an exception of the Singer Sewing Machine and your spindle," he said, "where would these exceptions end?"

Gandhiji replied: "Just where they cease to help the individual and encroach upon his individuality. The machine should not be allowed to cripple the limbs of man."

"But I was not thinking just now of the practical side, Bapuji," said Ramachandran. "Ideally would you not rule out all machinery? When you except the sewing machine, will you not have to make an exception of the motor-car?"

"No," said Bapu, "because it does not satisfy any of the primary wants of man; for it is not the primary need of man to traverse distances with the rapidity of a motor-car. The needle, on the contrary, happens to be an essential thing in life—a primary need. Ideally, however, I would rule out all machinery, even as I would reject this very body, which is not helpful to salvation, and seek the absolute liberation of the soul. From that point of view I would reject all machinery; but machines will remain because, like the body, they are inevitable. The body itself, as I told you, is the purest piece of mechanism; but if it is a hindrance to the highest flights of the soul it has to be rejected!"

"Why is the body a necessary evil?" asked Ramachandran. "There I don't understand you. But let me return to my earlier point. May not, after all, some artists be able to see Truth itself in and through Beauty, rather than Beauty in and through Truth?"

"Some may," said Gandhiji, "but here too, just as elsewhere, I must think in terms of the millions. And to the millions we cannot give that training to acquire a perception of Beauty in such a way as to see Truth in it. Show them Truth first and they will see Beauty afterwards. The famine-stricken skeletons of men and women in Orissa haunt me in my waking hours and in my dreams. Whatever can be useful to those starving millions is beautiful to my mind. Let us give today first the vital things of life, and all the graces and ornaments of life will follow."

Here the long conversation ended, and early the next morning Ramachandran started on his way back to Santiniketan, rich with Bapu's blessings, wondering how far the teaching of his own Gurudev, Rabindranath Tagore, would harmonize with that which he had just heard, and how far there was a fundamental difference between them.

This last sentence of Mahadev Desai concerning the interview introduces us to one of the most interesting contrasts in Modern India. Indeed, it is so significant of spiritual values as to have something of a world importance. What I refer to is the difference of temperament and outlook upon life between Gandhi and Tagore. Let me explain as far as I can.

Romain Rolland once in a letter, with the sudden insight of genius, stated, "Tagore is the Plato of our own times, Gandhi is the St. Paul."

With regard to Tagore the analogy is an interesting one; for there is in Tagore all the catholicity and the passionate love of ideal, spiritual beauty which the name of Plato connotes. There is much more also; and I have seen in Tagore that which his own wonderful countenance portrays, the serenity which is found in the Gospel picture of the Christ. No one has taught me more of that divine character than Rabindranath Tagore has done by his own life and example.

With regard to Mahatma Gandhi, I am not so satisfied with Rolland's analogy, although at the same time I can realize its force and meaning. For Gandhi is, indeed, the man who has gone through a great upheaval of conscience, such as we imply by the word "Conversion." He has not grown simply and naturally towards the higher reaches of humanity as Tagore seems to have done. With Gandhi the negative aspect of sin, as something which has to be rooted out by an almost violent self-discipline, is, like the shadow of the Cross, always apparent, brooding as it were over his thoughts. In this sense he is like St. Paul, who cries, "Unhappy man that I am, who shall deliver me from the body of this death?" For the human body, with its lusts and sins, is to Gandhi an evil, not a good. Only by complete severance from this human body can perfect deliverance be found. Yet he has already felt, in gleams and visions, the joy beyond all telling of that deliverance. But the word is true of him as of St. Paul, "Now we see through a glass darkly, but then face to face. Now I know in part, but then shall I know even as also I am known."

For all this pathetically strained austerity, which leads him to incredible fasts and self-denials, there is an amazing sweetness and a childlike innocence. This when seen in action makes St. Francis of Assisi the only illuminating parallel that I can think of when I have been privileged to witness it with my own eyes. For I could easily imagine Gandhi preaching to the birds, embracing the leper, wearing the coarse dress of the half-naked poor, courting a rude beating in the snow by some churlish janitor as "perfect joy." Whenever I read the *Little Flowers of St. Francis* with its medieval setting I say to myself, "What a strange thing this is! Why, I have been witnessing this very life of love in Gandhi himself and in many of his followers also." And just here I have been brought up against inassimilable features also. For there is no question that Mahatma Gandhi is one with the medieval saints in a passionate belief in celibacy as practically the only way to realize the beatific vision of God. Here more than anywhere else there seems to be a divergence from Tagore.

For there is a famous poem of Rabindranath Tagore which begins:

Deliverance is not for me in renunciation. I feel the embrace
    of freedom in a thousand bonds of delight.
No, I will never shut the doors of my senses.
The delights of sight and hearing and touch will bear Thy delight.
Yes, all my illusions will burn into illumination of joy,
And all my desires ripen into fruits of love.

In this poem Tagore appears to go poles apart from Gandhi with his abnegation of the senses to the utmost limit. Nevertheless, in another equally famous poem of Tagore concerning "deliverance," or Moksha, he seems to draw to his side again:

> Leave this chanting (Tagore cries to the ritual worshipper),
>   and singing and telling of beads!...
> Open thine eyes and see, thy God is not before thee!
> He is there, where the tiller is tilling the hard ground and
>   where the pathmaker is breaking stones. He is with thee in
>   sun and shower, and his garment is covered with dust. Put
>   off thy holy mantle, and even like him come down on the
>   dusty soil!
> Deliverance? Where is this deliverance to be found?
> Our Master Himself has joyfully taken upon Him the bonds
>   of creation: He is bound with us all for ever.

Here in this remarkable poem the two saints of Modern India— Tagore in the extreme east of India, Gandhi in the extreme west of India—seem to draw near together in their idea of Moksha, or deliverance. For Gandhi would hold as strongly as Tagore that God is to be found among the lowliest children of the soil.

> Here is Thy footstool and there rest Thy feet where live the
>   poorest and lowliest and lost.
> When I try to bow to Thee, my obeisance cannot reach down
>   to the depth where Thy feet rest among the poorest and
>   lowliest and lost.
> Pride can never approach to where Thou walkest in the clothes
>   of the humble among the poorest and lowliest and lost.
> My heart can never find its way to where Thou keepest com-
>   pany with the companionless among the poorest, the lowli-
>   est, and the lost.

Even to this day I can remember the evening, at the sunset hour of prayer, when we were seated at our devotions on the bank of the Sabarmati River at Mahatma Gandhi's Ashram, and he asked me to read some poem from Tagore. It was the last poem quoted here that

I read, and it seemed to me that in that company of Mahatma Gandhi and his chosen band of followers the presence of God was almost visibly near at hand in the cool of the day there in that Ashram where the poor were so loved and revered.

Long years afterwards I heard Mahatma Gandhi in a deeply-moving way refer to that evening worship and that reading from Rabindranath Tagore, and I realized that he had felt, as I had on that occasion, the mysterious presence of the Eternal.

21

CONCLUSION

It may be asked at the conclusion of this book what is the outlook for the future, and into what shape and form does Mahatma Gandhi expect his Passive Resistance ideals to develop. It will be noticed that the peculiar quality that he has given to the movement has been this— that instead of merely single individuals taking up a definite stand against some moral evil and offering Passive Resistance in connection with it, he has worked out a whole programme of what might be called "corporate moral resistance," whereby evil may be overcome. William James has explained in a famous essay that one of the great psychological needs of the world is to find the "moral equivalent for war." The more I have seen Mahatma Gandhi's programme of Soul-Force in action, the more I have been convinced that what he has so wonderfully effected on a comparatively small scale could be employed with a much larger programme and for the solution of far wider issues. In that case the special technique of the new movement would have to be worked out afresh in every detail. A thoroughly scientific treatment of the subject would be required in order to show both points of weakness and points of strength in its present development, thus making possible on a large scale the very same principles that he himself has used. In this sense as well as in many others his whole active life could be shown to be one great "Experiment with Truth."

In his own actions hitherto Mahatma Gandhi has been feeling his way towards this. His first attempts at Passive Resistance in South Africa were on a compartively small scale, yet they became larger in extent before he left the country. Again, in India, which had become like a new country to him owing to his long absence from it, he began his great struggles to combat injustice on a small scale. He started at first, as we have seen, in such places as Champaran, Khaira, and Viramgam. But the

260

last two movements which he initiated, called "Satyagraha" and "Non-Co-operation," were as wide in their extent as India itself. Yet it has been proved, by the foreclosure of both owing to the inrush of violence which took place, that the movements themselves were premature, and that the preparations which led up to them were incomplete. The fact is now made plain that no great movement of "corporate moral resistance" can be effectively developed, organized, and launched without exhaustive preparation. Merely to trust to a sudden wave of popular emotion is to court failure at the very outset. In the great Non-Co-operation storm which swept across India from end to end, in 1920 to 22, the very excitement that carried the movement forward was its greatest danger. The poet Rabindranath Tagore in this respect became the "Great Sentinel" on guard for the integrity of his country. He pointed out that the blind following of any personality, however devotedly noble, must in the long run lead to violence, and thus prove a failure when the cause was being based on a purely moral foundation.

When we consider, even for a moment, the vast and detailed preparations that are made for a struggle of violence such as war, and how military training occupies many years of a man's lifetime and with large numbers becomes a life-profession, it should be abundantly clear that the moral effect needed to supplant war cannot be made in an impromptu manner. "Corporate moral resistance" needs all the care and forethought of an earnestness no less whole-hearted than that which is given to world-wide military endeavour. In this respect Christ's words are still true: "The children of this world are wiser in their generation than the children of light."

Throughout the Western world there are many voluntary organizations appealing to different sides of the population—some to the women, some to the youth, some to the men. These have often displayed great enthusiasm in the cause of world peace. Europe is not lacking in the power to create and sustain such voluntary, organized effort. But what has not yet been found in the West is a moral genius of such commanding spiritual personality as to be able to unite and combine these various organized efforts into one overwhelming movement of Non-Violence which should be strong enough to sweep away on a tide of world approval the opposing forces.

A Note from the Editors
at SkyLight Paths

Gandhi's closest friend, the Reverend Charles Freer Andrews, published this personal memoir of India's "Great Soul" in 1930. Poignant words end his Conclusion to the book, a lament that in the West there had not yet been found "a moral genius of such commanding spiritual personality as to be able to unite and combine these various organized efforts [for world peace] into one overwhelming movement of Non-Violence which should be strong enough to sweep away on a tide of world approval the opposing forces." But we know better.

Charlie died the year following publication of *Mahatma Gandhi: His Life and Ideas,* and thus he did not see—at least from the vantage point of this world—the success that the Satyagraha movement achieved over the nearly two decades of Gandhi's remaining life. Charlie did not see the triumph of the Salt March, Gandhi's most public act of deliberate civil disobedience, nor did he see his old friend engaged in political negotiation with the statesmen of the world. Gandhi's fasts and protests to alleviate the suffering of the "Untouchable" poor, to bring equality to all castes in Indian society, and to revive the textile industry that had traditionally supported India's people were accomplishments of Gandhi's later years as he steadfastly continued his life's work, until it was ended by an assassin's bullets on January 25, 1948.

For those of us living in the twenty-first century, Gandhi is the founder of the world's peaceful—not passive—resistance movements, the man who led India to freedom and independence, the inspiration and role model for civil rights leaders such as the Reverend Martin

Luther King Jr. and Archbishop Desmond Tutu. His influence on the world, East and West, is without parallel. To Charlie, Gandhi was "Mohan," his best friend, a Hindu who was the Christian missionary's soul kin. And to Gandhi, Charlie was "more than a blood brother." Charlie Andrews understood that Gandhi's life was a constant search for the ever-changing nature of Truth and the power of living with Soul-Force.

APPENDIX 1

What I have tried here to express has been admirably stated by Dr. Pratt, Professor of Philosophy in Williams College, concerning his own approach to Buddhism. He says:

> It would be possible to write a learned book on Buddhism which should recite the various facts with scholarly exactness, yet leave the reader at the end wondering how intelligent and spiritual men and women of our day could really be Buddhists. I have sought to avoid this effect and have tried to enable the reader to understand a little *how it feels to be a Buddhist.* To give the feelings of an alien religion it is necessary to do more than expound its concepts and describe its history. One must catch its emotional undertone, enter sympathetically into its sentiment, feel one's way into its symbols, its cult, its art, and then seek to impart these not merely by scientific exposition but in all sorts of indirect ways.

Appendix 2

Mr. Gandhi gives his own definition of "varna" (a Sanskrit word meaning "colour") as follows:

Varna means pre-determination of the choice of man's profession. The law of varna is that a man shall follow the profession of his ancestors for earning his livelihood. Every child naturally follows the "colour" of his father, or chooses his father's profession. Varna, therefore, is in a way the law of heredity. Varna is not a thing that is superimposed on Hindus, but men who were trustees for their welfare discovered the law for them. It is not a human invention but an immutable law of nature—the statement of a tendency that is ever present and at work, like Newton's law of gravitation. Just as the law of gravitation existed even before it was discovered, so did the law of varna. It was given to the Hindus to discover that law. By their discovery and application of certain laws of nature the peoples of the West have easily increased their material possessions. Similarly, Hindus, by their discovery of this irresistible social tendency, have been able to achieve in the spiritual field what no other nation in the world has achieved.

Varna has nothing to do with Caste. Caste is an excrescence, just like untouchability, upon Hinduism. All the excrescences that are emphasized today were never part of Hinduism. But don't you find similar ugly excrescences in Christianity and Islam also?

Fight them as much as you like. Down with the monster of Caste that masquerades in the guise of varna. It is this travesty of varna that has degraded Hinduism and India. Our failure to follow the law of varna is largely responsible for both our economic and spiritual ruin. It is one cause of unemployment and impoverishment, and it is responsible for untouchability and defections from our faith.

But in quarrelling with the present monstrous form, and monstrous practices to which the original law has been reduced, do not fight the law itself.

Appendix 3

The following letter from Rabindranath Tagore to one who was intending to come out as a missionary to India endorses much that Mahatma Gandhi has also put in his own way. Tagore writes thus:

> I have read your letter with pleasure. I have only one thing to say; it is this: Do not be always trying to preach your doctrine, but give yourself in love. Your Western mind is too much obsessed with the idea of conquest and possession; your inveterate habit of proselytism is another form of it. Christ never preached himself or any dogma or doctrine; he preached love of God. The object of a Christian should be to be like Christ—never like a coolie recruiter trying to bring coolies to his master's tea garden. Preaching your doctrine is no sacrifice at all—it is indulging in a luxury far more dangerous, than all the luxuries of material living. It breeds an illusion in your mind that you are doing your duty—that you are wiser and better than your fellow-beings. But the real preaching is in being perfect, which is through meekness and love and self-dedication. If you have strong in you your pride of race, pride of sect, and pride of personal superiority, then it is no use to try to do good to others. They will reject your gift, or even if they do accept it they will not be morally benefited by it—instances of which can be seen in India every day. On the spiritual plane you cannot *do* good until you *are* good. You cannot preach the Christianity of the Christian sect until you be like Christ—and then you do not preach Christianity, but love of God, which Christ did.
>
> You have repeatedly said that your standard of living is not likely to be different from that of the "natives." But one thing I

ask you: Will you be able to make yourself one of those whom you call "natives," not merely in habits but in love? For it is utterly degrading to accept any benefit but that which is offered in the spirit of love. God is love—and all that we receive from His hands blesses us. But when a man tries to usurp God's place and assumes the rôle of a giver of gifts, and does not come as a mere purveyor of God's love, then it is all vanity.

APPENDIX 4

A delightful account of Mahatma Gandhi's relations to the European missionaries in India is found in a recent number of *Young India* as follows:

Among the new missionary friends is a Danish couple, Mr. and Mrs. Bjerrum, full of sympathy and eagerness to establish an understanding between themselves and those whom they serve. Gandhiji was at his wheel when the friends came.

"This is a new wheel," said Mr. Bjerrum, "different from the ones we saw at the Exhibition." "Yes," said Gandhiji, "it is a travelling Charkha. When you fold it, it looks like a medicine chest, and a medicine chest it is for our poor people."

After giving their pleasant impressions of the Exhibition, Mr. Bjerrum began to talk of the Indian Christian students of his College. "The dress of most of our students is Europeanized," he informed Gandhiji, not without some sorrow. "It is a great pity," said Gandhiji, "that Christianity should be mixed up with foreign dress and foreign ways of eating and drinking." "It is indeed," chimed in Mrs. Bjerrum. "But don't you think a change has already begun?" "Well," replied Gandhiji, "a change in thought is certainly coming over, but not a corresponding change in conduct," and with this he narrated some of his experiences with the friends of the Y.M.C.A. of Calcutta. "May we know," asked Mr. Bjerrum, "what form in your opinion missionary work should take if the missionaries are to stay in India?"

"Yes," said Mr. Gandhi, "they have to alter their attitude. Today they tell people there is no salvation for them except through the Bible and through Christianity. It is customary to decry other religions and to offer their own as the only one that can bring deliverance. That attitude should be radically changed. Let them appear before the people as they are, and try to rejoice in seeing Hindus become better Hindus, and Mussalmans better Mussalmans. Let them start work at the bottom, let them enter into what is best in their life and offer nothing inconsistent with it. That will make their work far more efficacious, and what they will say and offer to the people will be appreciated without suspicion and hostility. In a word, let them go to the people, not as patrons, but as one of them, not to oblige them, but to serve them and to work among them."

There can be no doubt at all that in China, Japan, and India, in quite recent years, an awakening to new national responsibilities, which is of the utmost spiritual importance, has come to the Churches in those countries.

The following passage concerning Mahatma Gandhi's recent tour in South India also reveals this new part which the Indian Christian Church is now taking in the national life:

One of the special features of the present tour is the interest, genuine if cautious, shown by the Christian Indians in the Khaddar Movement. At Tinnevelly they presented a special address, giving Gandhiji the assurance that, whilst formerly they might not have identified themselves with the national movement, now they had decided to do so. Gandhiji valued the assurance and told them:

"Acceptance of Christianity, or any other faith, should not mean denationalization. Nationalism need never be narrow or inconsistent with one's religious faith. That nationalism which is based on pure selfishness and exploitation of other nations is indeed an evil to be shunned; but I cannot conceive internationalism without a healthy, desirable national spirit."

Our hosts at Madura and Tuticorin were Christians, and one of the purest gifts for the Khaddar Movement was a beautiful gold cross presented by a Swedish missionary lady, who had worn it for twenty-five years, and gave it for a sacred cause, just because she prized it most. I may mention in this connection the gift of a beautiful cross in shell and gold by the Bishop of Tuticorin, which, though not for Khaddar, was certainly a token of the Bishop's sympathy for Gandhiji's work.

APPENDIX 5

The following passage from Mahatma Gandhi may be studied in relation to his attitude towards Christianity and Hinduism:

> I have ventured at several missionary meetings to tell English and American missionaries that if they could have refrained from "telling" India about Christ, and had merely lived the life enjoined upon them by the Sermon on the Mount, India, instead of suspecting them, would have appreciated their living in the midst of her children, and would have directly profited by their presence.
>
> Holding this view, I can "tell" American friends nothing about Hinduism. I do not believe in people "telling" others of their faith, especially with a view to conversion. Faith does not admit of "telling." It has to be lived, and then it becomes self-propagating.
>
> Nor do I consider myself fit to interpret Hinduism, except through my own life; and if I may not interpret Hinduism through my written word I may not compare it with Christianity. The only thing it is possible for me, therefore, to do is to say as briefly as I can why I am a Hindu.
>
> Believing as I do in the influence of heredity and being born in a Hindu family, I have remained a Hindu. I should reject Hinduism if I found it inconsistent with my moral sense or my spiritual growth. But on examination I have found it to be the most tolerant of all religions known to me, because it gives the Hindu the largest scope for self-expression. Not being an exclusive religion, it enables its followers not merely to respect all the other religions, but also to admire and assimilate whatever

may be good in them. Ahimsa, or Non-Violence, is common to all religions, but it has found its highest expression and application in Hinduism. In saying this I do not regard Jainism or Buddhism as separate from it, but an outgrowth. Hindus believe in the oneness not merely of all human life, but of all that lives.

The worship of the cow is the Hindu's unique contribution to the evolution of humanitarianism. It is a practical application of the belief in the oneness, and therefore the sacredness, of all life. The great doctrine of transmigration, or rebirth, is a direct consequence of that belief.

Finally, the discovery of the law of "Varnashrama" is a magnificent result of the ceaseless search for Truth.

Appendix 6

The following instructions were given by Mahatma Gandhi to the passive resisters at Vykom when he came down in person to see them and encourage them:

> This is a struggle deeply religious for the Hindus. We are endeavouring to rid Hinduism of its greatest blot. The prejudice we have to fight against is an agelong prejudice. The struggle for the opening of the roads round the temple (which we hold to be public) to the "untouchables" is but a small skirmish in the big battle.
>
> If our struggle was to end merely with the opening of the roads in Vykom, you may be sure I would not have bothered my head about it. It is true the road must be opened. It has got to be opened. But that will be the beginning of the end. The end is to get all such roads throughout Travancore opened. Not only that, but we expect that our efforts may result in amelioration of the general condition of the "untouchables" in every direction.
>
> This will require tremendous sacrifice; for our aim is not to do things by violence to our opponents. That would only be conversion by compulsion; and if we impart compulsion in matters of religion we shall be committing suicide. We have to carry on this struggle by suffering in our own persons. This is the meaning of Soul-Force. The question is whether you are capable of every suffering that may be imposed upon you in the journey towards the goal.
>
> Even while you are suffering you must have no bitterness—no trace of it—against your opponents. This is not a mechanical

act at all. On the contrary, I want you to feel like loving your opponents; and the way to do it is to give the same credit for honesty of purpose which you would claim for yourself. I know that it is a difficult task. I confess that it was a difficult task for me yesterday, whilst I was talking to those friends who insisted on their rights to exclude the "untouchables" from the temple roads. I confess there was selfishness behind their talk. How then was I to credit them with honesty of purpose? I was thinking of this thing yesterday and also this morning, and this is what I did. I asked myself: Wherein was their selfishness or self-interest? It is true that they have their ends to serve. But so have we our ends to serve. Only we consider our ends to be pure and therefore selfless. But who is to determine where self-lessness ends and selfishness begins? Selflessness may even sometimes be the purest form of selfishness.

I do not say this for the sake of argument. But that is what I really feel. I am considering their condition of mind from their point of view and not my own. Immediately we begin to think of things as our opponents think of them we shall be able to do them full justice. Three-fourths of the miseries and misunderstandings in the world will disappear if we step into the shoes of our adversaries and understand their standpoint. We shall then either agree with our adversaries quickly or else think charitably of them. In our case there is no question of our agreeing with them quickly, as our ideals are radically different. But we may be charitable to them and believe that they actually mean what they say.

They do not want to open the roads to the "untouchables." Our business is to show them that they are in the wrong, and we should do so by our suffering. I have found that mere appeal to reason does not answer where prejudices are agelong and based on supposed religious authority. Reason has to be strengthened by suffering, and suffering opens the eyes of understanding. Therefore there must be no trace of compulsion in our acts. We must not be impatient, and we must have an undying faith in the means we are adopting.

If you believe in the efficacy of Soul-Force you will rejoice in this suffering, and you will not feel the discomfort of your position as you go and stand in the burning sun from day to day. If you have faith in the cause, and in the means, and in God, the hot sun will be cool to you. You must not be tired and say, "How long?" You must never get irritated. That is only a small portion of your penance for the sin for which Hinduism is responsible.

I know that all this will sound hard and difficult for you. My presentation may be hard, but it has not been possible for me to present the thing in any other way. For it will be wrong on my part if I deceive you, or myself, into believing that this is an easy thing.

Much corruption has crept into our religion. We have become lazy as a nation. Selfishness dominates our action. There is mutual jealousy amongst the tallest of us. We are uncharitable to one another. Soul-Force is a relentless search for truth and a determination to reach truth. I can only trust you will realize the import of what you are doing. If you do, your path will be easy, because you will take delight in difficulties and will laugh in hope, even when everybody is in despair.

APPENDIX 7

The following is related by Mr. Vere Stent, editor of the *Pretoria News,* concerning Mr. Gandhi's part in the "Indian Stretcher Bearer Corps" during the Boer War:

My first meeting with Gandhi was on the road to Spion Kop, after the fateful retirement of the British troops in January 1900. The previous afternoon I saw the Indian mule-train moved up the slopes of the Kop carrying water to the distressed soldiers, who had lain powerless on the plateau. The mules carried the water in immense bags, one on each side, led by Indians at their heads. The galling rifle-fire, which heralded their arrival on the tip, did not deter the strange-looking cavalcade, which moved slowly forward; and as an Indian fell another quietly stepped forward to fill the vacant place. Afterwards the grim duty of the bearer corps, which Mr. Gandhi organized in Natal, began.

It was on such occasions the Indians proved their fortitude, and the one with the greatest fortitude of all was Gandhi. After a night's work, which had shattered men with much bigger frames, I came across Gandhi in the early morning, sitting by the roadside—eating a regulation Army biscuit. Every man in Buller's force was dull and depressed, and damnation was heartily invoked on everything. But Gandhi was stoical in his bearing, cheerful and confident in his conversation, and had a kindly eye.

He did one good. It was an informal introduction, and it led to a friendship. I saw the man and his small undisciplined corps on many a field of battle during the Natal campaign. When succour was to be rendered they were there. Their unassuming dauntlessness cost them many lives, and eventually an order was published forbidding them to go into the firing-line. Gandhi simply did his duty then, and his comment the other evening in the moment of his triumph, at the dinner to the Europeans who had supported the Indian movement, when some hundreds of his countrymen and a large number of Europeans paid him a noble tribute, was this, that he had simply done his duty.

Appendix 8

A persistent rumour went around India in 1921, towards the close of
the year, owing to some words which Mahatma Gandhi had let fall,
that if he failed in obtaining Swaraj within the year he would refuse
to take food, and thus abandon his earthly existence. He was obliged
at last to correct this rumour in the following words:

> Correspondents have written to me in pathetic language asking
> me not to commit suicide in January, should Swaraj be not
> obtained by then, and should I find myself outside the prison walls.
> I find that language only inadequately expresses my thought,
> especially when the thought itself is confused or incomplete.
>
> One great reason for the misunderstanding lies in my being
> considered almost a perfect man. Friends who know my par-
> tiality for the Gita have thrown relevant verses at me, and shown
> how my threat to commit suicide contradicts the teachings
> which I am attempting to live. All these mentors of mine seem
> to forget that I am but a seeker after Truth. I claim to be mak-
> ing a ceaseless effort to find it. But I admit that I have not yet
> found it. To find Truth completely is to realize oneself and one's
> destiny. I am painfully conscious of my imperfections, and
> therein lies all the strength I possess; because it is a rare thing
> for a man to know his own limitations.
>
> If I was a perfect man, I own I should not feel the miseries
> of my neighbours as I do. As a perfect man, I should take note of
> them, prescribe a remedy, and compel adoption by the force of
> unchallengeable Truth in me. But as yet I only see through a
> glass darkly; and therefore I have to carry conviction by slow
> and laborious processes, and then, too, not always with success.

That being so, I would be less than human if, with all my knowledge of avoidable misery pervading the land, and of the sight of mere skeletons under the very shadow of the Lord of the Universe, I did not feel with the dumb millions of India.

The hope of a steady decline in that misery sustains me. But suppose that with all my sensitiveness to sufferings, to pleasure and vain, cold and heat, and with all my endeavour to carry the healing message of the spinning-wheel to the heart, I have reached only the ear and never pierced the heart; suppose, further, that at the end of the year I find the people as sceptical as they are today about the present possibility of attainment of Swaraj by means of the peaceful revolution of the spinning-wheel; suppose, further, I find that the excitement during the past twelve months has been only an excitement without settled belief in the programme; suppose, lastly, that the message of peace has not penetrated the hearts of Englishmen, should I not doubt the virtue of my inner struggle and feel my own unworthiness for leading the movement any longer? As a true man, what should I do? Should I not kneel down in all humility before my Maker, and ask Him to take away this useless body and make me a fitter instrument of service?

Swaraj does not consist in the change of Government; that would be merely the form. The substance that I am hankering after is a real change of heart on the part of the people. I am certain that it does not require ages for Hindus to discard the error of untouchability; for Hindus and Mussalmans to shed enmity and accept heart-friendship as an eternal factor of national life; for all to adopt the spinning-wheel as the only universal means of attaining India's economic salvation; and, finally, for all to believe that India's freedom lies only through Non-Violence. Definite, intelligent, and free adoption by the nation of this programme is the attainment of the substance of Swaraj. The symbol—the transfer of power—is sure to follow, even as the seed truly laid must develop into a tree.

The reader will thus perceive that my accidental statement to friends for the first time in Poona was but a confession of my imperfections and an expression of my feeling of unworthiness for the great cause which I seem to be leading. I have enunciated no doctrine of despair. On the contrary, I have felt never so sanguine that we shall gain the substance during this year. I have stated at the same time, as a practical idealist, that I should no more feel worthy to lead a cause which I might feel myself diffident of handling. The Gita doctrine of labouring "without attachment" means a relentless pursuit of truth, a retracing of steps after discovery of unworthiness.

I have but shadowed forth my intense longing to lose myself in the Eternal, and become merely a lump of clay in the Potter's divine hands, so that my service may become more certain because uninterrupted by the baser self in me.

APPENDIX 9

The following typical letter was sent to me from Sabarmati Jail by Mahatma Gandhi in the first days of his imprisonment:

My dear Charlie,

I have just got your letter. You were quite right in not leaving your work. You should certainly go to Gurudev (i.e. Rabindranath Tagore), and be with him as long as he needs you. I would certainly like your going to the Ashram (i.e. Sabarmati) and staying there awhile, when you are free. But I would not expect you to come to see me in jail. I am as happy as a bird! My ideal of a jail life—especially that of a civil resister—is to be cut off entirely from all connection with the outside world. To be allowed a visitor is a privilege—a civil resister may neither seek nor receive a privilege. The religious value of jail discipline is enhanced by renouncing privilege. The forthcoming imprisonment will be to me more than a political advantage. If it is a sacrifice, I want it to be the purest.

With love, Yours,
Mohan.

APPENDIX 10

The following letter, slightly abbreviated, was written by Mahatma Gandhi to Hakim Ajmal Khan, Sahib, who was President of the National Congress at the time when he himself was imprisoned:

I write this to you in your capacity as Chairman of the Congress Working Committee, and therefore leader of both Hindus and Mussalmans, or, still better, of All-India.

I write to you also as one of the foremost leaders of Mussalmans; but above all I write this to you as an esteemed friend. I have had the privilege of knowing you since 1915. Our daily growing association has enabled me to prize your friendship as a treasure. A staunch Mussalman, you have shown in your own life what Hindu-Muslim unity means.

We all now realize, as we have never done before, that without that unity we cannot attain our freedom; and I make bold to say that without that unity the Mussalmans of India cannot render the Khilafat cause all the aid they wish. Divided, we must ever remain slaves. This unity, therefore, cannot be a mere policy to be discarded when it does not suit us. We can discard it only when we are tired of Swaraj. Hindu-Muslim unity must be our creed to last for all time and under all circumstances.

Nor must that unity be a menace to the minorities—the Parsees, the Christians, the Jews, or the powerful Sikhs. If we seek to crush any of them, we shall some day want to fight one another. I have been drawn so close to you, Hakim Sahib, chiefly because I know that you believe in Hindu-Muslim unity in the full sense of the term.

This unity is unattainable without our adopting Non-Violence as a firm policy. I call it a policy because it is limited to the preservation of that unity. But it follows that thirty crores of Hindus and Mussalmans, united not for a short time but for all time, can defy all the powers of the world, and should consider it a cowardly act to resort to violence in their dealings with the English administrators. We have hitherto feared them and their guns in our simplicity. The moment we realize our combined strength we shall consider it unmanly to fear them or even to think of striking them. Hence am I anxious and impatient to persuade my countrymen to feel Non-Violent, not out of weakness, but out of our strength. But you and I know that we have not yet evolved the Non-Violence of the strong. And we have not done so because Hindu-Muslim unity has not gone much beyond the stage of policy. There is still too much mutual distrust and consequent fear. I am not disappointed. The progress we have made in that direction is, indeed, phenomenal. We seem to have covered in eighteen months' time the work of a generation. But infinitely more is necessary. Neither the classes nor the masses feel instinctively that our union is as necessary as the breath of our own nostrils.

For this consummation we must rely more upon quality than quantity. Given a sufficient number of Hindus and Mussalmans with an almost fanatical faith in everlasting friendship between the Hindus and Mussalmans of India, we shall not be long before the same unity permeates the masses. A few of us must first clearly understand that we can make no headway without accepting Non-Violence in thought, word, and deed for the full realization of our political ambition. I would therefore beseech you to see that our ranks contain no workers who do not fully realize the essential truth I have endeavoured to place before you. A living faith cannot be manufactured by the rule of the majority.

To me the visible symbol of All-India unity and of the acceptance of Non-Violence is undoubtedly the spinning-wheel. Only those who believe in cultivating a Non-Violent spirit and eternal friendship between Hindus and Mussalmans will daily and religiously spin. Universal hand-spinning and the universal manufacture and use of hand-spun, hand-woven cloth will be a substantial, if not absolute, proof of real unity and Non-Violence. And it will be a recognition of a living kinship with the dumb masses. Nothing can possibly revivify India so much as the acceptance by All-India of the spinning-wheel as a daily sacrament, and the use of home-spun cloth as a privilege and a duty.

I would not waste a single worker today on destructive work when we have such an enormous amount of constructive work to do. But perhaps the most conclusive argument against devoting further time to destructive propaganda is the fact that the spirit of intolerance (which is a form of violence) has never been so rampant as now. The Moderates are estranged from us; they fear us. They say that we are establishing a worse bureaucracy than the existing one. We must remove every cause for such anxiety. We must go out of our way to win them to our side. I should not have to labour the point if it was clear to everyone, as it is to you and to me, that our pledge of Non-Violence implies utter humility and good will, even towards our bitterest opponent. This necessary spirit will be automatically realized if only India will devote her sole attention to the work of construction suggested by me.

Appendix 11

During the time that Mahatma Gandhi was lying seriously ill after his operation for appendicitis at the Sassoon Hospital, Poona, he asked me to undertake the editorship of *Young India*. The following editorial gave the contrast that was in everyone's mind at that time:

It has been Mahatma Gandhi's supreme faith that there is a nobler element in man which may be won over by love. For this reason he began his Non-Co-operation Movement, not in bitterness, but in love. For this reason he spoke with the frankness of true love to the judge who condemned him to prison. For this reason he wrote in the columns of *Young India* again and again explaining to the rulers the object which he had in view, so that there might be no possible misunderstanding. But, in spite of it all, it was nothing less than a tragedy in England to find how he had been misunderstood.

If the question is asked, What is the sum and substance of the charge which Mahatma Gandhi laid against the British Government in India? it may be summed up in a single phrase. He charged them with the oppression of the poor. In the statement which he made at his trial, his condemnation of the British Raj was this: It had oppressed the poor. The hungry, skeleton-like figures which he had seen in Orissa and elsewhere had haunted his mind till he could never forget them, by night or by day. He went so far as to offer to co-operate again, if the British rulers would join with him in a campaign to destroy the drink and drug traffic and to build up the industrial village life by the encouragement of home-spinning and home-weaving; but such simple work of lowly service seemed beyond the ken of the present rulers. They must do their work in their own patronizing way or not at all. The gorgeous magnificence of an Imperial Delhi obsessed their minds. They neglected to take note of the plain fact that all its luxury would only be an added burden to the poor. They spent fabulous sums upon it, until the treasury was empty, and then doubled the burden of the salt tax in order to prevent a deficit. The crores of rupees spent on building a new Delhi over the ruins of the old city could not be sacrificed. The one necessary of life to the many millions of half-starving people must be taxed instead.

There is a weakness due to long ages of subjection which has invaded, alas, the mind of India itself, and supports this vulgar craving for a display of pomp and power such as New Delhi affords. Mahatma Gandhi has called it a "slave-mentality." It may be seen in our own day in the gaping crowds that frequent the race-courses, whenever they are patronized by State officials in state procession. Extravagant durbars, Royal visits, imperial pag-eants, British Empire Exhibitions, all draining away the wealth of the country, have become more frequent of late in order to win back the waning attention of the common people.

But the spiritual mind of India is not captivated by things so tawdry as these. Rather it pays silent homage to this one tired sufferer in the Sassoon Hospital at Poona, who has looked into the face of death without fear. For here is a man whose sway is greater than all imperial power. His name will be remembered and sung by the village people long after New Delhi is forgotten. When all its buildings have crumbled into dust the name of Mahatma Gandhi will still be taught by mothers to their little children as one of the greatest of India's saviours.

For there is a spiritual city which he has been building up out of an imperisable fabric. Its foundations are deeply and truly laid in the Kingdom of God. No oppression of the poor has gone to create it. Love and devotion and service to the needy are its decorations. No military pomp reigns within its borders, but only the peaceful harmony of human souls. Race and colour distinctions have no place in it. Not a clash of religious controversy mars its harmony. Its empire is the heart.

Appendix 12

The following resolution was carried unanimously at the "Unity" Conference at Delhi, held during the fast. It was proposed from the chair by the Chairman and carried, while all the members of the Conference stood in recollection of Mahatma Gandhi in his fast:

> This Conference places on record its deep grief and concern at the fast which Mahatma Gandhi has undertaken.
>
> We are emphatically of opinion that the utmost freedom of conscience and religion is essential, and we condemn any desecration of places of worship, to whatsoever faith they may belong; and any persecution or punishment of any person for adopting or reverting to any faith; and, further, we condemn any attempts by compulsion to convert people to one's own faith, or to secure or enforce one's own religious observances at the cost of the rights of others.
>
> We assure Mahatma Gandhi and pledge ourselves to use our utmost endeavours to promote these principles and to condemn any deviation from them, even under provocation.

APPENDIX 13

Thoughts on the Gita

The following were written by Mahatma Gandhi from Yeravada Jail during his last imprisionment.

> If we try to understand from all possible points of view, and so continuously meditate on the Gita, we must become one with it. As for myself, I run to my Mother Gita whenever I find myself in difficulties, and up to now she has never failed to comfort me. It is possible that those who are getting comfort from the Gita may get greater help, and see something altogether new, if they come to know the way in which I understand it from day to day.
>
> The Twelfth chapter of the Gita tells of Bhaktiyoga—realization of God through Devotion.* At the time of marriage we ask the bridal couple to learn this chapter by heart and meditate upon it, as one of the five sacrifices to be performed. Apart from Devotion, Action and Knowledge are cold and dry, and may even become shackles. So with the heart full of love, let us approach this meditation on the Gita. Arjuna asks of the Lord: "Which is the better of the two, the devotee who worships the Manifest, or the one who worships the Unmanifest?" The Lord says in reply: "Those who meditate upon the Manifest in full faith, and lose themselves in Me, those faithful ones are My devotees. But those who worship

---

* In Hinduism there are three pathways of union with God. Bhakti (Devotion), Karma (Action) and Jnana (Spiritual learning). The last is sometimes translated Knowledge, but it implies much more than this English word.

the Unmanifest, and in order to do so restrain all their senses, looking upon and serving all alike, regarding none as high or low, those also realize Me."

So it cannot be affirmed that one way is superior to the other. But it may be regarded as impossible for an embodied being fully to comprehend and adore the Unmanifest. The Unmanifest is without attributes and beyond the reach of human vision. Therefore all embodied beings consciously or unconsciously are devotees of the Manifest.

"So," saith the Lord, "Let thy mind be merged in My Universal Body, which has form. Offer thy all at His feet. But if thou canst not do this, practice the restraint of passions of thy mind. By observing Yama and Niyama,* with the help of Pranayama, Asan** and other practices, bring the mind under control. If thou canst do thus, then perform all thy works with this in mind; that whatever work thou undertakest, thou dost it all for My sake. Thus thy worldly infatuations attachments will fade away, and Love will rise in thee.

"But if thou canst not do even this, then renounce the fruit of all thy actions; yearn no more after the fruit of thy work. Ever do that work which falls to thy lot. Man cannot be master over the fruit of his work. The fruit of work appears only after causes have combined to form it. Therefore be thou only the instrument. Do not regard as superior or inferior any of these four methods which I have shown unto thee. Whatever in them is suitable for thee, that make use of in the practice of devotion."

It seems that the path of hearing, meditating and comprehending may be easier than the path of *Yama, Niyama, Pranayama* and *Asan.* Easier than this may be concentration and worship. Again, easier than concentration may be renunciation of the fruit of works. The same method cannot be equally easy for everyone; some may have to turn for help to all these methods. They are certainly intermingled.

---

* Yama and Niyama represent the things to be done and the things to be avoided in order to lead a moral life.

** Pranayama means regulation of one's breathing. Certain breathing exercises are regarded as helpful in restoring health and bringing the passions under control. Asan means the mode of sitting while engaged in meditation.

In any case, the Lord says, "Thou wishest to be a devotee. Achieve that goal by whatever method thou canst. My part is simply to tell thee whom to count a true devotee. A devotee hates no one; bears no grudge against anyone; befriends all creatures; is merciful to all. To accomplish this, he eliminates all personal attachments; his self-ishness is dissolved and he becomes as nothing; for him grief and happiness are one. He forgives those who trespass against himself, as he hungers for forgiveness from the world for his own faults. He dwells in contentment; and is firm in his good resolves. He surren-ders to Me his mind, his intellect, his all. He never causes in other beings trouble or fear, himself, knowing no trouble or fear through others. My devotee is free from joy and sorrow, pleasure and pain. He has no desires, but is pure, skilful and wise. He has renounced all ambitious undertakings. He stands by his resolves, renouncing their good or bad fruit and he remaining unconcerned. Such a one knows not enemies and is beyond honour or disgrace.

"In peace and silence, contented with whatever may come his way, he lives inwardly as if alone and always remains calm, no matter what may be going on around him. One who lives in this manner, full of faith, he is My 'Beloved devotee.'"

Fearlessness is an essential for the growth of other noble qualities. How can one seek Truth or cherish Love without fearlessness? As Pritam has it, "the path of Hari (the Lord) is the path of the brave and not of cowards." Hari here means Truth, and the brave are those armed with fearlessness, not with the sword, the rifle and other carnal weapons, which are affected only by cowards.

Fearlessness connotes freedom from all external fear—fear of disease, bodily injury and death, of dispossession, of losing one's nearest and dearest, of losing reputation or giving offence, and so on. One who overcomes the fear of death does not surmount all other fears, as is commonly but erroneously supposed.

Some of us do not fear death, but flee from the minor ills of life. Some are ready to die themselves, but cannot bear their loved ones to be taken away from them. Some misers will put up with all this, will part even with their lives, but not with their property; others will do any number of black deeds in order to uphold their supposed prestige. Some will swerve from the straight and narrow path, which lies clear before them, simply because they are afraid of incurring the world's odium.

The seeker after Truth must conquer all these fears. He should be ready to sacrifice his all in the quest of Truth even as Harischandra did. The story of Harischandra may be only a parable; but every seeker will bear witness to its truth for his personal experience, and therefore that story is infinitely more precious than any historical fact whatever, and we would do well to ponder over its moral.

Perfect fearlessness can be attained only by him who has realized the Supreme, as it implies the height of freedom from delusions. But one can always progress towards this goal by determined and constant endeavour and by increasing confidence in oneself. As I have stated at the very outset, we must give up external fears.

As for the internal foes, we must ever walk in their fear. We are rightly afraid of animal passion, anger, and the like. External fears cease of their own accord, when once we have conquered these traitors within the camp. All fears revolve round the body as the centre, and would therefore disappear as soon as one got rid of the attachment to the body.

We thus find that all fear is the baseless fabric of our own vision. Fear has no place in our hearts when we have shaken off the attachment for wealth, for family, and for the body. Wealth, the family, and the body will be there, just the same; we have only to change our attitude to them. All these are not ours but God's. Nothing whatever in this world is ours. Even we ourselves are His. Why, then, should we entertain any fears?

The Upanishad, therefore, directs us "to give up attachment for things while we enjoy them." That is to say, we must be interested in them not as proprietors, but only as trustees. He, on whose behalf we hold them, will give us strength and the weapons requisite for defending them against all comers. When we thus cease to be masters and reduce ourselves to the rank of servants, humbler than the very dust under our feet, all fears will roll away like mists; we shall attain ineffable peace and see Satyanarayan (the God of Truth) face to face.

Man's delight in renunciation differentiates him from the beasts. Some demur that life thus understood becomes dull and devoid of art, and leaves no room for the householder.* But these critics fail to grasp the true meaning of renunciation, which does not mean abandoning the world and retiring into the forest, but rather the infusion of the spirit of self-sacrifice into all the activies of life.

The life of a householder may take the colour either of indulgence or renunciation. A merchant who does his work in a sacrificial spirit will have large sums of money passing through his hands every day, but his thoughts will be entirely devoted to service. He will not cheat or speculate, but will lead a simple life. He will not injure a living soul, but will lose millions rather than do any harm.

Let no one run away with the idea that this type of merchant only exists in my imagination. Fortunately for the world, it is represented in the West as well as in the East. It is true, such merchants may be counted on one's fingers, but the type ceases to be imaginary as long as even one living specimen can be found to answer to it.

If we go deeply into the matter, we shall come across men in every walk of life who lead dedicated lives. No doubt these men of sacrifice obtain their livelihood by their work. But livelihood is not their objective, it is only the by-product of their vocation. Motilal was a tailor at first and continued as a tailor afterwards. But his spirit was changed and his work was transmuted into worship. He began to think about the welfare of others, and his life became artistic in the highest sense of the term.

A life of sacrifice is a pinnacle of art, and is full of true joy which ever renews itself. A man is never surfeited with it, and the spring of interest is inexhaustible. Indulgences lead to destruction. Renunciation leads to immortality. Enjoyment has no independent existence. It depends upon our attitude towards life. One man will enjoy theatrical scenery, another the ever-new scenes which unfold themselves in the sky. Enjoyment, therefore, is a matter of individual and national education. We enjoy things which we have been taught to enjoy as children.

Again, many self-sacrificing people imagine that they are free to receive in return everything they need and many things they do not

---

* Referring to the four Ashrams or stages of the complete human life in Hinduism. The second stage is that of the householder who lives in the world, enjoys married life and has children. The third and fourth stages imply renunciation.

need, because they are rendering disinterested service. Directly this idea sways a man, he ceases to be a servant and becomes a tyrant over the people.

One who would serve will not waste a thought upon his own comforts, which he leaves to be attended to or neglected by his Master on high. He will not therefore encumber himself with everything that comes his way; he will take only what he strictly needs and leave the rest. He will be calm, free from anger, and unruffled in mind, even if he finds himself put to great difficulty. His service, like virtue, is its own reward, and he will rest content.

Again, one dare not be neglectful in service or be behindhand with it. He who thinks that one must be diligent only in one's personal business, and that unpaid public business may be done in any way and at any time, has still to learn the rudiments of renunciation. Voluntary service, where others demand the best, must take precedence over service to the self. In fact, the pure devotee consecrates himself to the service of humanity without any reservation whatever.

Acknowledgments

Special thanks for permission to reprint the photographs in this book is extended to GandhiServe—a charitable foundation aiming to promote the life and work of Mahatma Gandhi, believing firmly that Gandhi's message of truth, love, and nonviolence is more relevant than ever before. In addition to providing educational programs, GandhiServe Foundation works to safeguard and distribute documents, photographs, and films relating to Gandhi and the Indian independence movement. Its archive is the largest of its kind outside India and, along with further details about the foundation, can be viewed online at gandhiserve.org.

INDEX

About SKYLIGHT PATHS Publishing

SkyLight Paths Publishing is creating a place where people of different spiritual traditions come together for challenge and inspiration, a place where we can help each other understand the mystery that lies at the heart of our existence.

Through spirituality, our religious beliefs are increasingly becoming a part of our lives—rather than *apart* from our lives. While many of us may be more interested than ever in spiritual growth, we may be less firmly planted in traditional religion. Yet, we do want to deepen our relationship to the sacred, to learn from our own as well as from other faith traditions, and to practice in new ways.

SkyLight Paths sees both believers and seekers as a community that increasingly transcends traditional boundaries of religion and denomination—people wanting to learn from each other, *walking together, finding the way.*

We at SkyLight Paths take great care to produce beautiful books that present meaningful spiritual content in a form that reflects the art of making high quality books. Therefore, we want to acknowledge those who contributed to the production of this book.

PRODUCTION
Sara Dismukes & Tim Holtz

EDITORIAL
Amanda Dupuis, Maura D. Shaw & Emily Wichland

COVER DESIGN
Drena Fagen, New York, New York

TEXT DESIGN
Tim Holtz

PRINTING & BINDING
Versa Press, East Peoria, Illinois